DAW 02/08 £12·00

Do not W/D. On
reading list -
2014-15

MIDDLESBROUGH COLLEGE Ⓐ
LEARNING RESOURCES CENTRES
CLASS No. 792·09 Mer
ACCESSION 078690
LOCATION A

F12

Contents

Introduction

Notes on Contributors

Middlesbrough College

00078690

MIDDLESBROUGH COLLEGE
LEARNING RESOURCES CENTRES
CLASS No. ....
ACCESSION ....
LOCATION ....AL..........

MIDDLESBROUGH COLLEGE
LEARNING RESOURCE CENTRE
WITHDRAWN

Introduction

Anyone who has picked up this book in the hope they will find a quick and easy definition of the term "popular theatre" might well be advised to replace it immediately. As John Bull points out below, popular is a "very slippery term".[1] And he is in good company.Elsewhere, Raymond Williams argues that the notion of the "popular" is possibly the most "difficult term in cultural studies" and David Mayer, speaking at a conference on the same subject in 1974, came to the conclusion that he was uncertain if a definition was either possible or indeed desirable:

> because a definition must aim at limiting, at fixing boundaries, at excluding apparent irrelevancies, whereas our present experience with popular theatre emphasises the contrary.[2]

Instead of looking for definitions, the papers gathered together here (all delivered at the Popular Theatre Conference held at Liverpool John Moores University in 1994) aim to express and document the breadth and diversity of work covered by the term. What transpires is the quite staggering variety of work which either defines itself or can be defined as belonging to the field of the popular. From the notions of the popular in Elizabethan theatre, through melodrama to work in Africa and the work of practitioners such as Dario Fo, and John Godber, the sweep is broad and lively.

One conclusion can be drawn from both the conference and the papers. The traditions of popular theatre in performance are long, invigorating and expansive and current work, from the explosion of physical theatre to the growth of stand-up comedy (to name just two) would bear witness to this tradition's continued expansion and renewal. Yet, unlike the massive growth in interest in the popular in fields such as literature and media studies, the arena of drama, when it comes to analysing and documenting the popular, seems pitifully thin. These papers will hopefully be part of the inspiration to re-examine both some of the older practices of popular theatre and to start an investigation of the new. Some signs of the latter are visible here, notably Oliver Double's paper on stand up comedy, but there are still yawning gaps, particularly in any assessment of physical theatres grasp of popular traditions and fifteen years after John McGrath's ground breaking analysis of *A Good Night Out*, surely we need to begin to move on from those ideas. Clive Barker provides some beginnings here, but there would seem to much more room for development.

Two further points need mentioning in this introduction. Firstly, the papers printed here do not (nor cannot) represent the entirety of the conference. Missing are two lively sessions; one encompassing the ideas and experiences of three radically different practitioners, namely Bill Kenwright, Clive Barker and Roland Muldoon, and the other a discussion led by Bill Morrison of his own experience at the Everyman Theatre in the 1970's. Also absent is any account of the performance which informed the conference – Reject Revenge's *Crumble*, accompanied by three monologues written especially for the conference.

The final point is simply to thank those to whom thanks are due, in particular all the delegates and contributors to the conference whose lively contributions provoked debate. Thanks also go to the drama department, to Roger Webster (director of the School) and to Sue du Feu, without whose help this conference would never have been organised.

Ros Merkin
March 1996

Notes
[1] See p28
[2] "Towards a Definition of Popular Theatre" in D.Mayer & K.Richards (eds.), *Western Popular Theatre* (Methuen, 1977) p.275

Notes on Contributors

Nicholas Arnold is a lecturer at De Montfort University.

Clive Barker is best known for his book on actor training, *Theatre Games*, which has been translated into Japanese and is currently being prepared in Spanish and Hindi, and which forms the basis for the work he does in actor training. He is joint editor of *New Theatre Quarterly*, with Simon Trussler, has published numerous articles as well as writing plays for stage and television. He is also the chairman of Geese Theatre and on the board of directors for the International Workshop Festival and has recently retired from the University of Warwick where he was senior lecturer in Theatre Studies.

Peter Billingham is Programme co-ordinator for Drama at Bretton Hall University College of Leeds. He is also an award-winning playwright and is a member of the Sheffield Crucible Theatre Writers Group. His research and teaching specialism is post-war British theatre. He writes and reviews regularly for *Plays and Players*.

John Bull teaches English Literature and Drama at the University of Sheffield. He is the author of *New British Political Dramatists* and *Stage Right: Crisis and Recovery in British Contemporary Mainstream Theatre*. Amongst his other publications is an edition of the early plays of Howard Brenton, published by Sheffield Academic Press in the *Critical Stages* series, of which he is general editor. He has directed many modern plays, including two of his own, and is the Chair of the Standing Committee of University Drama Departments.

Christopher Cairns is the authorised English biographer of Dario Fo. His practical theatre work has included *Commedia dell'Arte* workshops with Carlo Boso, Adriano Iurissewich and directing student productions of plays, the most recent of which was Betti's *Delitto all'Isola delle Capre* in London. He has published widely in Italian drama, taught Italian at the Universities of Southampton and Aberystwyth (where he also taught European Drama). He is now Professor and Head of Italian at Westminster University.

Derrick Cameron was born and raised in London, and read Drama at Liverpool Polytechnic (now LJMU) and Essex University. He is the writer of *Black Sheep* (Temba Theatre Company, 1988) and *Different Decks* (Splash Theatre Company, 1990). He is currently a Research Student in Black British Theatre at Liverpool John Moores University.

Robert Cheesmond lectures at Hull University Drama Department, where he has pioneered the cross-disciplinary study of popular entertainment as an academic subject, whilst conducting research (for his Ph.D.) on English pantomime. In addition, he is engaged in an extensive programme of research in stage production, particularly in the field of scenography and is a freelance director and designer.

Richard A. Cowler is currently finishing a Ph.D on popular theatre in Merseyside at the University of Liverpool and he teaches literature, drama and theatre studies in further and higher education. He is presently Lecturer in English in the Performing Arts section of Wirral Metropolitan College.

Sarah-Jane Dickenson is a lecturer in Drama at the University of Hull. She has taught in a variety of teaching contexts and is a performed playwright. Her special areas of interest are women in performance, women playwrights, scriptwriting and drama as a learning medium.

Oliver Double is a stand-up comedian ("Delightful" – *The Guardian*) and comperes his own club in Sheffield, The Last Laugh. He wrote a Ph.D. thesis on stand-up comedy and his articles have appeared in the *New Statesman*. His book, *Stand Up!* will be published by Methuen in Autumn 1996.

Lisa Hopkins teaches English at Sheffield Hallam University. Her most recent book was *John Ford's Political Theatre* (Manchester University Press) and she is currently completing a study of representations of marriage in Shakespeare's plays for Macmillan.

Esiaba Irobi is a citizen of the Republic of Biafra and lived in exile in Nigeria from 1970 to 1989, when he was banished from the country by the military. Since 1989, when he came to England, he has been ploughing the ground for a new aesthetic, a communal aesthetic that will allow those who need theatre most, the underclass, to use the artform to tell the story of their lives. His next project is a book titled *The Politics and Aesthetics of Cross-Cultural Theatre* and he is currently a drama lecturer at Liverpool John Moores University.

David Llewellyn is head of drama at Liverpool John Moores University. He met John Godber while training at Bretton Hall and Leeds University. Since then he has worked as a playwright for Hull Truck's *Playing Away* (1988) and as an actor in Godber's television drama, *The Ritz* (1989) and *Chalkface* (1990). His production of *Bouncers* influenced the presentation of this paper.

Tom Maguire is a lecturer in Drama and Theatre Studies at Liverpool Hope University College. His research interests include popular and political theatres, Scottish theatre and post-colonial drama and theatre.

Bim Mason is Course Director of Circomedia, the Academy of Circus Arts and Physical Theatre in Bristol. Acting work includes work with Kaboodle, Bristol Old Vic and three solo shows and his extensive directing work has earned him two Edinburgh Fringe Firsts (1989 and 1995). He founded the seminal circus theatre group, Mummer and Dada and is author of *Street Theatre and Other Outdoor Performance*.

Sophie Nield teaches theatre and film at the University of Glamorgan. Her research interests include the use of theatricality in the maintenance and subversion of power systems, spatiality and aspects of film and musicology. She is assistant editor of *Theatre Annual* and the co-editor of *Knowledge, Limits and the Future: New Essays on Raymond Williams* to be published by Macmillan later this year.

Nick Owen is currently head of Community Arts at the Liverpool Institute for the Performing Arts (LIPA), having worked as Director of the Hope Street Project at Liverpool's Everyman Theatre since 1989.

As freelance director and writer he has recently worked on *Bellamy* (Unity Theatre), *Pilgrim's Progress* (Royal Liverpool Philharmonic), and *The Model Bites Back* (Tate Gallery). He previously worked as manager of Black Theatre Co-Operative, Tara Arts Group and Talawa Theatre Co. in London and in 1987 established Bramley Stop Theatre, a community theatre venture in an old textile mill in Leeds.

Tim Prentki is Programme Convenor for the MA in Community Drama for Development run jointly by King Alfred's College and the University of Southampton. The course includes field-work projects in the UK and overseas. He is also Course Director of the BA in Drama, Theatre and Television Studies at King Alfred's.

Anita Shir-Jacob teaches Modern Drama at the University of Toronto. Her doctoral thesis in an examination of the early nineteenth century aquatic theatre at Sadler's Wells under the management of Charles ·Dibdin the Younger.

Carol-Anne Upton is a lecturer in drama at the University of Hull. Special areas of research include African and Caribbean theatre in both English and French, and modern Irish drama. She is also a director and actor, and a translator of plays from French to English.

Mick Wallis teaches drama at Loughborough University. He has written on an extended practical experiment mobilising Raymond Williams' work to integrate practical and academic learning situations.

Nigel Ward read English at Corpus Christi College, Oxford, then trained as a director at Drama Studio, London. He has worked professionally as a director based in London, before becoming an assistant director for the Royal Shakespeare Company in Stratford. Currently, he is a drama lecturer at Sheffield University and is completing a doctoral thesis on the relationship between text and performance in the work of twentieth century European theatre directors.

Popular Theatre: A Contradiction in Terms?

Bim Mason

Firstly, just to say that I welcome the fact that this conference on Popular Theatre has been organised. I believe strongly that those who work in popular theatre are not valued by the Arts Establishment as much as they should be. Popular theatre is extremely important in this age and in this country and that it needs to be recognised for the valuable contribution it makes to the chaotic society we find ourselves in.

Popular Theatre has, of course, been in existence for thousands of years but as a generic term it is new, at least to me, so I want to devote some time in considering what we mean by Popular Theatre.

To take the two words separately starting with the noun – Theatre. It is a word that means different things to different people. Does it include musicals, or street theatre or Live Art events? Some would argue that it certainly does not include circus and rock concert spectacles. Some would even argue that commercial West End productions, be it *Run For Your Wife* or *The Mousetrap* are not proper theatre because they do not have serious content. We can be sure however that although it has much in common with cinema and television dramas, the key differences from them is that it is live and **unrepeatable.** Theatrical drama is enacted in the same space as the spectators and because there are different people and energies around each time it is performed it is never the same twice.

What about the adjective – Popular? It means "of the people" of course, but what people? Some would say that a group like Complicité is very popular but can we really call their style popular theatre? Amateur dramatic groups attract large followings all over the country but does that make their work popular theatre? Community plays are mounted that often involve a wide cross section of a local community but is their work popular theatre? The style of community plays is usually imposed by an outside director and does not usually come from "the people". Or does the term have working class connotations, either work that is designed for the working class such as used to be done by political theatre groups or lowest common denominator summer seasons at Skegness or Christmas panto with the stars of *Eastenders?*

The word "popular" certainly implies "general appeal" but unfortunately it is a sad and incredible statistic (according to a survey done in France a few years ago) that whilst 80% of the population go to the circus at least once in their life only 30% go to the theatre once in their life. 70% never see theatre in their lives! It has to be faced – theatre is not a popular art form any longer. It has been relegated to join the minority art forms such as opera, classical music, ballet, poetry, literature and most visual art. Popular art forms nowadays are pop music of course although this is apparently declining whilst the computer video game is mushrooming. There is also cinema & television, of course including within it by far the most sophisticated, and advanced artistic form of the late twentieth century – the two minute advertisement.

It is a tragic fact, and one that has not been widely recognised, that the arts centre circuit, which with all its limitations was nevertheless the mainstay of theatre in the provinces for the last twenty-five years, is collapsing and in the process has largely abandoned theatre altogether. One arts centre, I phoned to try to book a show told me that they couldn't even get an audience for Complicité and that the only live performance they were putting on-in future was stand-up comedy and jazz. Others arts centres have closed altogether.

For me the term Popular Theatre means more than any of these. To me it implies universal theatre – something for everyone in the same way that we are led to believe that Shakespeareís plays worked – for the groundlings stage fights, clowning, spectacle, songs, dancing, topical references, rude jokes, a good story, and for the educated elite, poetry, classical allusions, philosophy and well developed themes. It is such a shame that understanding his language and his world require such study to fully appreciate nowadays. I believe this universal theatre <u>can</u> be created in our crazy society despite all its myriad subdivisions. In my experience one can approach it much more easily away from the big cities which, because they offer such a bewildering array of choice and because of their size, encourage and enable individuals to form into more manageable sub-groups centred on shared interest.

Away from cities where individuals with a shared interest are more widely scattered there is obviously much more mixing of age, class and income brackets and the result is a much greater openness to a universal theatre and to sharing an event. For example it is virtually impossible to get any audience participation in a place like Battersea Arts Centre whereas in the country they are much more into joining in and having fun.

So does this universal theatre exist anywhere else in the world? I was impressed in southern India by the temple celebrations; there was a light show (the wonders of neon strip lighting), live music tannoyed all over the site, elephant rides for the kids, intellectual discussions, a pantheon of god statues that appealed on an emotional level (in the way that saints statues are talked to and touched in Southern European churches) and there was the incredible mystic primordial symbolism of the lingam-yoni sculpture. This may not be theatre in the usual sense but it was certainly very theatrical and very akin to some site-specific outdoor theatre work. Elsewhere in the world there is Chinese Opera, Balinese Theatre, African Storytelling, South American Carnival forms. Other people are better equipped to describe these forms but if we can include all these under the heading of Popular Theatre we can then go on to examine the attributes they share and so get closer to defining what it is.

One of the key elements in Popular Theatre is that of **direct contact.** An unsophisticated audience will quite rightly find it absolutely absurd if actors in the same room as them pretend they are somewhere else. The barrier of the invisible fourth wall will either feel like a protective barrier that a fearful performer has erected, or a snobbish superior ignoring of all the other people in the same space. In the old English Mummers Plays as each character enters they introduce themselves to the audience before addressing the other characters. Not only does the popular audience expect to be talked to, they also expect to talk back. Which leads us onto the second element of Popular Theatre, **participation.** The spectators want to feel themselves to be contributors to the live event. They may even insist on it. I remember talking to a couple of jugglers the last time I was up here in Liverpool. They were doing the kind of rough inner city kind of gigs that I used to do when I first started. I asked them how the shows worked and they said that their youth audiences were mainly indifferent of gigs that I used to do when I first started. I asked them how the shows worked and they said that their youth audiences were mainly indifferent or even hostile to amazing juggling skills until some of them were invited onto the stage and from then on things really took off.

Thirdly, **spectacle** is important. Good visual impact. This may include lighting effects (including pyrotechnics), masks, puppets, dancing, stage fights. The bigger the effect the better and if it is accompanied by music and song then all the better. This brings us to another aspect an appreciation of **craft.** Quite rightly, a popular audience won't have much time for a performer until he or she shows themselves to be capable of doing something out of the ordinary – merely acting is not enough. So skills whether they are musical, acrobatic, comic or whatever are essential. Nowadays it is technical wizardry such as sound, lasers and machinery that particularly wow a popular audience.

Strongly felt **emotions** are essential and this requires some kind of narrative, preferably with clearly defined characters that the audience can relate to. Usually these can be defined as goodies and baddies, not because the audience think that is the way life is, but because they can let their emotions get a good head of steam up. What does not appeal is a dry interplay of ideas or clever-clever innovative concepts. They like their fairly familiar format, whatever that may be.

Finally it has to be said that a good dose of **comedy, sex** and **horror** will always appeal even if the authorities in particular societies may find them to be politically incorrect.

The problem for Popular Theatre particularly in this country is its relation with the Artistic Establishment embodied in the Arts Council. Ten years ago **accessibility** was the buzz word, partly a Thatcherite approach to getting bums on seats so as to get the Arts to pay for itself. At present most fringe groups are caught between the Arts Council agenda which requires constant innovation and experimentation and the requirements of audiences who are more interested in a good night out so that groups feel they will lose audiences if they are too accessible and lose their grant if they are too innovative. It is interesting that after the war when the Arts Councilwas formed the decision was then taken not to include circus within its brief. In other countries circus is seen simply as a different and well respected arm of the performing arts rather than as a lower form. Indeed in Meyerhold's Russia the theatre workers looked up to the circus artists for their craft and audience contact. I am sure the prejudice in this country was born out of the strongly entrenched class values that still cripple us. The other cause of snobbishness towards Popular Theatre is that the Arts Establishments are well wrapped in the sophistication of the city. In the city one is able to see far more shows than in the country and the audience therefore becomes very sophisticated. Much Popular Theatre on the other hand is aimed at virgin audiences that have never seen theatre before – a true Popular Theatre artist is more concerned with pleasing them than the Michael Billingtons. One could say that the opposite extreme to Popular Theatre is when the audiences are so sophisticated they have to be selected such as was the case for Grotowski's Laboratory performances or Decroux's esoteric movement pieces.

Recently there has been a lot of criticism in the press of Popular Theatre particularly within the mime/physical theatre world. The Arts Council has quietly dropped circus altogether. The criticism is usually focused on the lack of content within the pieces but I think they fail to appreciate that with this kind of theatre the medium is the message. What do kids pick up in a clown show? They see an adult playing, someone who is unafraid of being silly and they pick up on the **freedom** of the performer. Likewise what is the message of professional street theatre? That the performers are more interested in the contact with audience and the excitement of the unique shared event than in becoming film stars. The values are promoted by the act of doing rather than as a clinical exposition within the piece. It is a cliché but the medium is the message. It is the difference between acting which after all is pretending to be something else and performing which is about being. This is why I think that Popular Theatre is so <u>important</u> in this age. It is about direct Human contact, unobscured by technology, about sharing an event, a game. Our society has lost its social cohesion with the demise of the inherited value system embodied in the monarchy, nationalism, the legal system, the trade unions and organised religion so that the creating of temporary tribes with the strangers that make up an audience can be a powerful force. Popular Theatre is also about responding to the uniqueness of each moment with all the sensitivity that requires. It is about energy/vitality/ human spirit. That is the content.

The Silent Revolution

Clive Barker

At the present time it is not profitable to give a deep analysis of where the concept of popular theatre is leading us. The last few years have seen the publication of some interesting theoretical and critical work on the field, if the practice has in certain areas run into some problems. I think particularly of Baz Kershaw's review of popular political theatre as cultural intervention, *The Politics of Performance,* the essays edited by Graham Holderness in *The Politics of Theatre and Drama* and John McGrath's revisiting of the ground covered by *A Good Night Out in The Bone Won't Break.*[1] All these authors concern themselves with re-establishing the value of past work. All have a clear sense that a moment has passed and the world has changed. As the world changes so does our thinking on popular theatre. A hard, clear look at what has passed provides a basis for action in the future and should helps us to recognise important potentiality in new and nascent beginnings. In this paper I would like to share some thoughts on the critical areas of change and to hold out hopes of future growth.

The destruction of the Berlin Wall and the destabilisation of the Soviet and other European Socialist Republics have created problems for those working in popular political theatre. Up until 1989 in the West that area of theatre was formulated on the proposition that in some way the theatre was contributing to the overthrow of the capitalist system and its replacement by some form of socialism. That is a manifestly unpopular proposition to put forward at this moment. I have argued elsewhere that there is no question of the political responsibilities and functions of the theatre being redundant but that a careful relating of form of activity to specific situation is vital for the future. John McGrath's prophetic play, written just before the events, reminds us of the need not to throw the baby out with the bath water.[2] The crisis in socialism, while heavily promoted and advanced by deficiencies and corruption within, cannot be divorced from the crisis in capitalism, which is masked by the more dramatic destructions in the East but which is equally at the heart of the process which is sadly working itself out at present.

The collapse of the dictatorships in Argentina and Chile has left the advanced theatres of those countries in something of a limbo. A theatre defined so strongly by its opposition to the regime in power, loses force and directions when that tyranny is removed. As Bouryana Zaharieva has pointed out[3], the one thing needed in the Bulgarian theatre is a concern with the present condition of Bulgaria which is precisely the thing that cannot happen because that would lead towards some form of social realism, a concept badly tainted with the previous association of socialist realism with party-directed art. The collapse of communism in Eastern Europe has created a sense of vacillation in the lives of people on a personal level. The presence of the Berlin Wall and the stability of the communist system in the USSR sustained definitions by which we marked our lives. However much we might have regretted the presence of the Wall and deplored the failure to put ideals into practice or even, on the right wing of politics, violently opposed both the Wall and the USSR, the terms in which we lived our lives were marked out and, subconsciously perhaps, were motivated by their continuing existence. I have the clear sense of the ground in personal relationships and in public conduct shifting perceptively for no clear reason other than life has changed. The tectonic plates have moved and the minutiae of our lives has are affected.

Some years ago the Cuban journal *Conjunto* signalled the demise of el Teatro Nuevo, for no clear reasons other than that the times had changed and it had run its course as a theatre movement. Three years ago in Bogota I found five of Ray Cooney's plays running simultaneously and the collapse of several politically motivated groups. Santiago Garcia and La Candelaria labour on, having acquired the status of a revered cultural monument for some or are dismissed as a dinosaur by others. If Teatro Nuevo has run its course and is now out of date or irrelevant then that position needs rethinking. I can't think that Ray Cooney is the answer – without wanting to detract from his merits as a playwright and provider of skillful and entertaining comedy. Nor does the answer lie with 28 theatres in Moscow playing Tennessee Williams in their repertories at the same time, as has been the case. I have some sympathy for Vassiliev and others caught between two unacceptable varieties of materialism trying to find the ground for some new theatre based on spiritual and/or religious values but that seems to me a return to the past.

In other parts of the world, such considerations would still be considered unnecessary. Ross Kidd's formulation of a people's theatre strengthening resistance against exploitation by the dominant still holds good.[4] But my feeling is that the abandonment of the Teatro Nuevo by Cuba is a firm sign of the times. The world is changing and concepts of popular political theatre must change with it, world-wide. There is a definite slowing down in some places of the social and political development work, pioneered by Kidd and others, whilst there appears to be a growing interest in other formulations of community theatre. The radical theatre in South Africa continues to search for a role which has influence and meaning while elsewhere, in Africa, there is a reflection of recent times in this country in attempts to establish a theoretical base for African theatre. It is too soon, or I am not sufficiently informed, to see exactly where these sought-for formulations are leading, either practically or ideologically.

There is an argument to be made that TIE in this country is under attack, not for political or educational reasons but because it has outlived its period of usefulness. Part of the attack, it must be granted, arises directly out of the reductive and regressive educational policies of the present government but the rush to defend TIE simply on the grounds of opposing government policy might mask the fact that action based upon the rationalist concepts of Enlightenment is out of sync with the times and delay the search for other more productive forms of action. One axis of this argument would rest upon asking again the question whether, or in what ways, an issue-based theatre, which exposes inequalities and poses critical questions, can be truly interventionary. Early in 1995 I took part, I can hardly say <u>saw</u> or <u>attended</u>, the fourth multi-cultural festival in Bedworth, in north Warwickshire, and experienced one of the most exciting evenings in the theatre in my lifetime. Bedworth is a small town near Nuneaton, a mining town left high and dry by the closing of the pits. The Civic Hall presents the amateurs, fourth farewell tours of 1960s pop groups grown old and occasional visits from Bernard Manning, still not persona non grata here, and Ken Dodd. The multi-cultural festival, of which I was totally in ignorance and only attended because my daughter was singing in a collective schools choir, is based upon a fortnight's programme of events in schools in the area in which children around the age of 10 are introduced to various ethnic skills, batik making, mask making and music from other parts of the world, or our own society. As part of this, the schools engaged a West African drummer to take part in a project on water. He constructed an African village scene in dance. A Punjabi dancer and drummer mounted a project on Punjabi dance. The excitement of seeing groups of 10 year-old white, English and Irish, Asian, Afro-Caribbean and Chinese kids all dancing in African and Indian dances, to a high level of skill, was inspiring. The last item on the programme was the appearance of the Leamington Spa Punjabi Dance team, which, given the name, should have been a joke. A group of large, bearded Punjabis danced with enormous energy and panache, spurred by 500 school kids at the back of the hall cheering them on. The atmosphere was close to the football match that we all aspired to arouse in the 1960s popular theatre days. On stage, a group of Punjabis, the sweat pouring off them thundering through their dances. At the back the cheering, yelling crowd of kids. In between several rows of distinctly nervous parents. Forget TIE, the kids are not the problem. The problem is the parents. The time has gone for taking plays in to schools, however skillful and well-intentioned, making a case for racial tolerance. The job is to attack the restrictions of the National Curriculum to extend the possibilities of this type of inter-cultural mixing. As I write I remember an earlier evening of excitement in Bedworth Civic Hall, the culmination of a long project financed by Warwickshire Education Authority putting the multi-cultural jazz band Grand Union into schools. A huge band filled the stage, with school kids playing alongside professional players, a seven-player trumpet section, all beautifully disciplined and professional. It's worth now going back again and extending the concept of <u>not</u> playing for school-children but playing <u>with</u> them. Also in 1995, I worked on a show with ten-year-olds, made up of scenes from *Romeo and Juliet* and *The Tempest*. No polished plays but an energetic playing with text, theatre techniques,

9

including stage fights and a Barrault-style ship wreck, and the forms and disciplines of Shakespeare's theatre. I have rarely enjoyed myself so much and we left a bunch of kids who think Shakespeare is fun.

Much of the political theatre of our past has been formulated upon the principle that if the right words are uttered the world would change, or in Brecht's case, if the right words are uttered the audience might change the world. Contingent on these premises was the search for a large enough, homogeneous audience to make it happen. That may have been the case once and may be in the future but the premise certainly won't hold up now. The whole basis of popular theatre as we have pursued it, involving the search for a mass audience, was brought seriously into question by the women's theatre movement and the gay theatre, with the restriction of audiences being considered necessary to increase effectiveness and embodying the concept of the personal being political. If the strategies of the closed theatre are now being questioned within the women's theatre movement, the time seems ripe to look again at the workings out and implications of these strategies in the wider field of popular theatre and pursuing further research into other ways of building on what has been learned in the last 20 years. The argument for the formulation of closed theatre concepts and the withdrawal from open theatre, be it women's, gay, lesbian, black or Asian theatre, arose out of historical circumstances, which have changed. I am not in any way suggesting that historical circumstances are any more liberal today, nor that those strategies are necessarily out-dated but I am suggesting that the time is ripe for a review of the strategies of closed theatres, and the reasoning behind their formulation, in their own interests and in the interests of wider theatre developments. Part of this review might go beyond the generalised groupings of the closed theatres and look at the targeting of or relating to smaller groups. The numbers of women in prison in the last two years has risen by 37%, which would seem to be either an issue about which to make political theatre or a clientele which theatre might address in terms of empowerment or self-help. The consideration of the former might suggest that the present lapse in making political theatre has been caused by a failure to identify specific issues and/or a sense of despair and impotence in the face of larger issues. Geese Theatre, of which I am privileged to be chairman of the board of directors, has been working effectively in prisons and the probation service for a number of years, employing techniques developed and frequently used in other areas of popular theatre, in the interests of aiding prisoners to rehabilitate and to prevent recidivism. The growing prison population and the savage reductions of prison budgets by the present government, which will effectively close down all education services in prisons, are forcing us to consider engaging in the wider political issues of imprisonment, extending our activities to address other areas of social distress which bear the stigma of criminality and also to deal with the victims of criminal and domestic violence. The field is almost infinite. The work is undemonstrative and the task of raising the resources is monumental but, if the will is there to answer the need, there are ways of harrying and intervening in political processes.

Any planned action will have to take into account the changing nature of British politics, in which an obsolete three-party system struggles on, where the parties no longer represent the wider constituency interests they were called into being for and where the parties themselves are riven by internal contention because they no longer, in their composition, present any coherence of philosophy or policy. Conscience appears to be totally subservient to the three-line whip and morality is easily submerged beneath pragmatic drives to win elections. It is sometime since Arden and D'Arcy warned that a political theatre could only be effective if allied to the programme of a political party and McGrath tempered this with the argument that to ally yourself to any one political party was suicidal, since you would lose the support of a broader alliance. These considerations now seem totally outmoded in the sight of the present government of this country and its opposition. Previous Labour Leaders have striven to remove socialism from the agenda. The present one seems to be trying to remove politics from the agenda. If it would be futile to argue in the country for socialism, then there is a mass of popular discontents outside which the theatre ought to be addressing, in some form or other. It is quite clear that the class structure which many of us grew up with, and on which many of the actions to create a popular political theatre were based, has long ago disappeared. There are many reasons why this should have happened, which would include deliberate policies instituted by the Thatcher governments, the diminishing role and power of the Trades Unions, the changing racial and social composition of this country. It is clear that for a long time, popular political theatre has been playing to a quite specific section of the population, of liberal persuasions, cutting across classes, or to audiences directly opposed to its ideological positions, in situations calling for extra-ordinary dialectics in the thinking behind the work. Beyond the critiques of the past, mentioned at the beginning of this paper, a new critique has to be mounted extending into theoretical possibilities for new strategies to cope with the changing nature of society. The worst thing that can happen is that we hold on to our sense of neglect and injury as the effectiveness of our past work is negated by changing circumstances. Within the popular theatre movement in this country there is a lot of beefing about the injustices of past successes unacknowledged and prestige unrecognised. However late in the careers of those artists it may be, change in society calls for change in tactics and techniques and it will not help to hold on to those of the past which established reputations.

Popular theatre arose out of a wish and a need to establish alternative positions, based on a recognition of alternative traditions in politics and theatre. It has taken many forms but beneath it has always been a sense of history and a concern with history, either through documentaries, setting out an alternative range of facts, or through dramatisation, which allows a creative intelligence to examine the nature and precepts of history. Arising from such seminal works, as Edward Thompson's *The Making of the English Working Class,* a whole critique of the processes of British history, its submerged traditions and alternative interpretations, has been undertaken and this has proved a very fertile ground from which the strongest of our alternative theatres have grown. In the light of recent political events and of keeping the baby in when the bath water has been thrown out, a further review of the whole period of the French Revolution, which has provided the thinking which defines both our political and theatrical structures, needs to be undertaken. Trevor Griffith's forthcoming, but long-delayed, play *Hope in the Year Two* may signal the start of this.

The forms of popular theatre we have helped to develop have for the most part been based on those forms which we inherited from the past and the traditional forms of working-class and oppositional culture which shaped the world and societies we grew up in. Does this still form a viable basis for popular theatre in the future? We inherited agit-prop and Brecht, we grew up on music hall, variety and radio drama, moving into the development of television. We could rely on a shared language and shared assumptions with our audiences. Does the world still allow that as a basis for constructing theatre with anything other than an ageing audience? The nature of the mass media is changing. One of the challenges that must be met comes from the development of multi-channel satellite television. The full force of Dennis Potter's dire dying warnings over the power of Rupert Murdoch can be seen in many parts of the world. To watch satellite television in Asia is to be confronted with a time-table of programming, which allows the same pap to be viewed at different hours in different countries. It also means being confronted with the bizarre choice of programmes being transmitted. Given three years to consider what of the BBC's output I would beam to Hong Kong, Thailand, Bangladesh, India and Pakistan, I would never arrive at a *Question of Sport*. More intelligence will no doubt refine and hone the conditioning techniques.

Behind the pap is the force of money made from satellite TV to buy out local access stations along the route. The process has its built-in dialectics. With the advent and growth of cable television the whole satellite market may collapse to be replaced by a system no more humanitarian but more accessible to local pressures. And in order to truly appreciate the erudition and wit of David Coleman a Bengali worker will now have to add English to his list of languages which will give access to other channels of information. A whole new world of political possibilities is opening up. John McGrath could draw on established structures of working-class culture, howbeit by retreating into Scotland, where the traditional roots go deeper and are more widespread. Perhaps we should, at the time of his retreat to Scotland, have paid more attention to his assessment that it was no longer possible to count upon a widespread working-class cultural tradition in England. I am leaving out Wales and Ireland only because of a shortage of time for illustrations. Perhaps the implications of his assessment ought to have been addressed at that time. Certainly they cannot be ignored now. Perhaps the most productive thing we might be able to do in the near future is to fight for television as a creative popular medium, as Potter and Trevor Griffiths have advocated. Certainly television drama, which has a long and honourable tradition in creating popular theatre of the highest calibre, is under threat from a number of directions. But there has not been a full realisation of the potential of local cable television and the struggle to control and use that medium has not been pursued hard enough.

In any event, whatever the future of popular theatre might be it has to take account that the growing potential audience have never lived in the world of the blessed Marx Brothers, whose comedy now seems on viewing to be so much the part of a past era, but are living in the world of *The Big Breakfast Show.* One of the significant features of popular theatre in the past was the mediating of televisual and cinematic techniques to revise our ideas of dramatic structure. This should be an on-going process not limited to fixed periods of advance. The work of Megan Terry with the Omaha Magic Theatre provides some precedents for this. Although again we should beware of ignoring the dialectics of the situation and throwing the baby out with the bath water. The growth of video culture has brought back for re-viewing the popular television of our youth. I have a ten year-old who watches *The Big Breakfast Show* yet considers Eric Morecambe to be the best example of entertainment ever to hit the screen. Are we then to take the sudden and totally unforeseen explosion of stand-up comedy as a clear indication of the poverty of existing forms of drama to articulate the forms and pressures of our times? From 1964 onwards, and particularly from 1966, a similar failure produced new attempts to stir the audience out of their torpor by direct attack. Perhaps now necessity is driving communicators towards some form of head-on confrontation in the absence of more complex structures. So far I cannot see exactly where this will lead us, although, again, one can see something of the origins, in the feminist movement and the concept of the "personal is political". It is clear though that this is not a phenomenon restricted to this country alone, nor only to those who have been brought up in a particularly Anglo-Saxon tradition.

The success of *The Real McCoy* on television and The Posse live, offer new perspectives on the world we live in building on traditional techniques. The existence of a 24 year-old, female, Asian stand-up comedienne is a contradiction in three terms, must alter our preconceptions about the nature of popular entertainment, and has to be considered as an act with profound political implications and possible effects.

Those of us in higher education will recognise that pressures of an insidious kind are taking the study of drama and theatre back into the past for no great progressive reason. The other pole is the promotion and utilisation of self-referential forms of post-modernism as the basis of practice. The past is rich with possibilities for finding the way forward and post-modernist techniques are part of the world we live in. Unless some rigour and theoretical underpinnning is introduced into the study of either or both, then the study of theatre practice, largely a lost cause in many places, will propel the study of theatre up a back-water. The potential for change that is embodied in the large numbers of students will, as I fear it is, be lost. The growth of popular theatre in this country drew heavily upon the work of student theatre groups. It is not easy to motivate in that direction again but it is suicidal not to try. If we are to cope with the world we live in and help our students come to terms with their own alternative and subversive popular forms we have to find ways to introduce them on to the syllabus. The ideas and experimental theatre of the Fringe period 1966 to 1973 and the political theatre movement of the 1973 period onwards need re-introducing into the syllabus in a critical form. In this it is necessary not to dwell on past glories but to extract a range of ideas which might be pursued in different forms to-day. The Fringe period particularly, which in the past has tended to be relegated to a dilettante subservience by the more dogmatic political theatre which followed it, needs re-examining, and rearticulating to a generation which has grown up under Thatcherism and badly needs to be introduced to the less inhibited and liberated theatre.

Dagmar Kift has recently shown how, in the Music Hall of the 1870s, the form itself was socially subversive and polarised class oppositions in the provincial society of that time. When the drama fails to articulate the social pressures, the form the theatre takes may itself be subversive. A feature of the last decade has been a steady increase in the number of small companies growing up in regional cities, rooted in those cities with, seemingly no strong motivation to follow past patterns and head for London at the earliest possible opportunity. Coventry, which I know best, began with TICTOC and has seen the rise of Snarling Beasties, Triangle and Talking Birds. The odds are stacked against these companies in competition for publicity and resources with the subsidised repertory theatres. I would not want to dismantle the structure of the subsidised theatres and acknowledgement should be made of the extent to which some of them have supported the new emerging companies. But the terms on which the reps are run and the policies pursued need very serious consideration. Many of the people charged with running them appear to have given up the struggle to engage directly with audience needs and to have resigned themselves to simply supplying what the audience will accept on simplistic terms.

The present struggles within the Belgrade Theatre, Coventry, as the populist programming has failed to prevent a large deficit, has been highlighted by a campaign in the theatre to disband the TIE team. The arguments presented for the continuing existence of the TIE team have been presented in terms of its historic status and in terms of work that was relevant many, many years ago. What has not been presented have been the attempts by people within the theatre, in conjunction with others in the local authority, through the Arts Alive project, to revitalise and develop a much stronger community and youth programme, more relevant to the needs of to-day. For well-meaning, but old-fashioned reasons the theatre may close and the building, in falling, crush much activity which is truly popular.

Some of us remember that the founding of the Belgrade TIE team in 1966 incidentally meant the closing of a strong youth theatre programme. Let's hope its death-throes don't strangle a new growth at birth. Defensive, internal politics have already prevented the return of Odin Teatret whose visit in 1994 raised theatrical temperatures in Coventry, evoked a surge of energy inside the theatre staff and brought together many people working in forms of performance activity in the city into contact where none existed before. The extension of Odin's visit, in 1996, supplemented with other groups, could have led the way to the creation of an international network of community theatre groups to match the international peace network, which Coventry already supports and co-ordinates.

The existence of such a network could have brought into the open and provided validation and support for much of the new initiatives in popular theatre for which I have coined the term, "The Silent Revolution". The grassroots work needs the presence of one major national or international project which will establish the validity of the work and will draw public attention to it. Without the major project it will always be too easy for the institutions of subsidy to withhold support or to set down conditions for support which will stunt or cripple the initiative. If the Coventry project is doomed to fall victim to the anal-retentive past then perhaps Nottingham could provide the launching pad.

Nottingham has probably the richest ethnic mix of any city in the British Isles. Like other cities, it has come into the possession of empty properties, caused by falling roles in inner-city schools. Unlike other cities, which have realised the properties as real estate for the building of super-markets, etc., Nottingham, through the County Educational Committee and its Chairman, has developed two schools as multi-purpose Arts Centres, fully equipped with studios and other resources. These centres promote non-qualificational courses in all the arts for 3,000 children a week. These centres are available for use for single ethnic arts activities or for inter-cultural arts. In co-operation with the International Workshop Festival, a Stamping Ground project has been mounted every two years, which has taken artists and groups from abroad into schools to direct activities. These artists and groups have included Lakota Sioux dancers, a Philippine Political Theatre group, Manipuri Indian artists, Koffi Koko a Nigerian dancer and drummer, David Freeman of Opera Factory and many others. The culmination of these activities is the largest festival of theatre by children in the world. The existence of all this activity has manifestly altered the role and work of the Outreach TIE group and the relationship between the Nottingham Playhouse and its community. The annual budget for all this work is huge by the normal standards of municipal support for the arts. The people working on these projects in Nottingham feel they are working in isolation and are badly in need of support by way of comparative and sympathetic initiatives in other cities. Nottingham has set new directions for placing the arts in education and for relating the professional theatre to the needs of the community. Who will follow?

Viewed from the perspective of the past it is possible to regret the crisis affecting, if not the passing away of, popular theatre. Viewed from the perspective of the future it is possible to divine a wealth of new possibilities, rich in potential, towards which attention should be paid and on which energy should be expended.

Notes

[1] Baz Kershaw, *The Politics of Performance* (Routledge, 1992); Graham Holderness (ed.), *The Politics of Theatre and Drama* (Insight, 1991); John McGrath, *The Bone Won't Break* (Methuen, 1990).

[2] John McGrath, *The Baby and the Bathwater* (unpublished).

[3] See "Ideology and After: Report from Bulgaria", *New Theatre Quarterly* VIII:29 pp.96-99

[4] See Ross Kidd, *The Popular Performing Arts: Non-Formal Education and Social Change in the Third World: A Bibliography and Review Essay* (CESO, 1982).

Popular//Mainstream Theatre

John Bull

In a brief paper, it is inevitable that a great deal of methodological and theoretical fudging will take place in any consideration of the relationship between mainstream and popular theatre. Conflicting definitions offer themselves for consideration. In one sense mainstream theatre is the popular theatre; in others it is not, for in general cultural terms theatre is not popular, either in terms of the extent of its consumption or in the constituency of its consumers. It is not my intention to revisit more than necessary old and continuing controversies of definition and delineation. However, it is worth restating at the outset that the invocation of "popular" in relation to theatre, or anything else, can never be a neutral move. Its deployment as a term is loaded with ambiguous and frequently shifting significations, and its invocation is one which takes its user into a series of ideological battle-fields. Indeed, that they are battle-fields, being actively fought over in historical and in contemporary terms, is what demonstrates, above all, the validity of the range of enquiry implied in the very use of the term.

For instance, were I to rephrase my earlier link between "popular" and theatre, and transpose it to "popular" and performance, I would already be committed to a rather different kind of enquiry – an enquiry in which both the source of the notion of "popular" would be recontextualised in terms of the potential arenas of performance, and in which the key questions of audience definition would need to be approached in a rather different way. I will be concerned with three related areas: the relationship between popular theatre and the mainstream; the relationship between popular culture and the theatre; and the particular circumstances of contemporary popular theatre. These are by no means separable areas, and my paper will attempt to sketch out some links between them.

So, in a paper that seeks to consider the relationship between popular and mainstream theatre, it would be useful to establish, or perhaps fail constructively to establish, some parameters. For a start, the two concepts of popular and mainstream theatre are exceedingly fluid – and are, indeed, frequently regarded as interchangeable. In *Stage Right*[1], I traced the history of the creation of a new serious mainstream tradition in Britain post-1979, a mainstream that has its roots in the aftermath of the first 50s "new wave", and in particular with the development, domestication and sanitisation of an absurdist tradition that is moved from a stance of overt criticism of bourgeois society to one of effective celebration, albeit frequently rather uneasily so. It is a movement that thus can be seen to have appropriated what was originally conceived as a self-consciously avant-garde model, its unique growth nurtured by the new monetarist policies of the 80s. I do not propose to dwell on this here, save to say that *Stage Right* offers, amongst other things, to define that sense of a mainstream as opposed to a popular theatre tradition.

And this leads inevitably to a problem. What exactly do we mean by talking of popular theatre today? Is it to be defined entirely in terms of box-office? – in which case we should be concentrating on, for instance, *Les Miserables* and on the various effusions of the Andrew Lloyd Webber empire; and also focusing our attention on London's West End. Or do we mean something that defines itself at a more local, regional level as popular? Do I, in the case of my own home city, Sheffield, then, take the mainhouse productions at the Crucible as a guide or the very different one-week roll-over of nationally touring productions at the Lyceum? Or do I turn away from these altogether, and look at the vast amount of amateur drama that takes place in scores of venues over the South Yorkshire region?

As it happens there is a useful link between all three and this might provide as good a starting-point as any. We are witnessing the career of the second-most popular English playwright ever in terms of the number of productions – and were it not for the fact of GCSE and A Level set book productions, he might easily by now be a more frequently produced writer than Shakespeare. The playwright is, of course, Alan Ayckbourn, and not the least important aspect of his success is that his works now successfully occupy the territory of all three kinds of location I considered above. His plays receive frequent amateur productions. Virtually all of them started life at the Stephen Joseph Theatre in Scarborough and are a constant factor in regional theatres across the country. And he is very much a national property, having first arrived at London's National Theatre in 1977 with *Bedroom Farce,* a play which became the first transfer from the National to the commercial West End Theatre, to complete the process.

In 1985 his *A Chorus of Disapproval* won the Evening Standard "Best Comedy" award. It was a play that had started life at Scarborough and was successfully revived at the Olivier before transferring to the unsubsidised Lyric as a money-spinner for the National. *A Chorus of Disapproval* is concerned with the efforts of an amateur theatre company to put on a production of John Gay's *Beggar's Opera* – a play, to further extend the link, that was easily the biggest box-office hit of the entire eighteenth century, and that, the immediate import of its direct political satire having long since faded, is indeed frequently attempted by such companies. It has a further claim to fame, in that it is effectively the first English musical. Ayckbourn's choice of this base text has many resonances, then, and in terms of its relation to popular theatre can be seen as a very different form of inter-textuality to that deployed by Stoppard, for instance, in his use of a classic high-art play, *Hamlet,* and a then classic avant-garde play, *Waiting for Godot,* as ur-texts for *Rosencrantz and Guildenstern.* In contrast, Ayckbourn's play ranges over the realms of the popular in a complicated interfacing of past and present, with a plot that parallels themes from Gay's play with the rise of Guy Jones – and the Everyman type connotations of the name are important – from social obscurity and a walk-on part, to becoming the male centre of this particular community and to playing Macheath.

Ayckbourn directed the play both at Scarborough and in London, but there is an important difference – apart from the necessary changes in staging in moving from theatre in the round to a proscenium arch. By the time it opened in London, most of the Scarborough cast – known and popular in their home base as would be the members of the amateur company depicted as producing Gay's play in their community – had disappeared. Another notion of popular is invoked; one that has national rather than local significance. And so we find the likes of Bob Peck, Michael Gambon, Imelda Staunton and

Gemma Craven being thrust into the same spotlight assumed in the play by Guy Jones.

Mainstream theatre is, of course, very adept at appropriating popular genres, and that it continues to do so is, in itself, evidence of the continuing popularity of such models as the country-house murder and the drawing-room comedy, in amateur theatre, in regional theatre, in the West End and in nationally toured productions. Tom Stoppard would loom large in such a discussion, with works from *The Real Inspector Hound* on that seek to use the forms of popular theatrical models even as they are parodied, as would writers such as Simon Gray with plays such as *Stage Fright* and *The Case of the Oily Levantine*. Or, perhaps more significantly, we could take the double appropriation made by Michael Frayn in *Noises Off*, where not only do we trace the history of a repertory production, on-stage and behind-stage from final rehearsal to late in the run, but do so from the perspective of a company intent on presenting a version of a stock popular drama – the fictitious *Nothing On* by the equally fictitious Robin Housemonger. The effect of such borrowings is to invite audiences to share with the playwright a superior critical stance; able to enjoy the echoes – thus proclaiming their knowledge of theatrical practice and history – and to savour the parody – thus proclaiming their ability to make aesthetic discriminations.

But the notion of popular here invoked is one that is endlessly self-consuming; a mainstream theatre that continually reinterrogates its own popular history will, by definition, and indeed by intent, carry with it a fair amount of audience exclusion. The suggestion in Frayn's play is that *Nothing On* is a part of past popular theatre history, recoverable only as a complicated stage-joke. The reality is that *The Mousetrap* & co. play on, and that in 1992 British Telecom withdrew their financial support for an RSC touring production of *Richard III* in order to sponsor a commercial tour of Agatha Christie's repertory stand-by of many years, *Witness for the Prosecution*.

Now, it is evident that one of the main reasons why the evocation of the "popular" is so problematic is that its very use involves a confrontation with the history of its usage and with, to put it in more ideological terms, the history of its appropriation. To talk in an anthropological way of, for instance, a medieval enactment of a mummers' play, is very different from describing a contemporary re-enactment of the same piece as a part of a summer festival of folk art in a British sea-side town. And yet, for many of the contemporary practitioners, the attempt to posit a continuity between the two will be of major importance.

I use this rather obvious example deliberately because it seems to me that one of the key planks of what I shall describe as a programme of appropriation of the popular in performance, and specifically theatrical, terms is precisely that of nostalgia. Any particular appropriation may be very well aware of the problematic nature of the enterprise, or completely unaware. The fact of, or the lack of, knowledge will certainly affect the nature of the relationship, but the general terms of reference hold good whatever the circumstances.

Although I will be concerned today largely with the relationship between popular culture and popular theatre with the mainstream, to isolate these particular models would not, in itself, provide an accurate account of the nature and significance of that relationship. In *New British Political Dramatists*[2] , I opened with a key distinction between two kinds of opposing though related traditions of overtly political theatre – that of the avant-garde and that of agit-prop. I would like to very briefly consider their positioning in relation to the popular, since this will make the very different relationship between mainstream and popular theatre more transparent.

The distinction between an avant-garde and an agit-prop stance is of importance in considering the approach to performance style, the choice of performance location and the decisions taken about targeted audience constituencies. Clearly, I do not have time to develop all these strands, but they merit fuller consideration.

Modern avant-garde theatre draws frequently from the various modes of popular culture, but it does so, consciously and almost exclusively, for its subversive potential, seeking out the destabilising rather than the conformatory aspects of the popular. For instance, in the early work of David Hare, *Knuckle* (1974) borrowed heavily from the "film noire" genre; and *Teeth `n' Smiles* (1976) from the destructive elements of late 60s rock. It offered a smashing of the components, rather than an incorporation into an effective celebration.

This alone points to a key difference in the way the popular is appropriated in mainstream theatre, as we shall see. Hare's play had a lead singer, Maggie, who was modelled on a Janis Joplin rather than a Lulu. The locationing of such incorporated material is not accidental. For both film and contemporary rock music display the most significant tensions of all the popular media historically, and in the continuing narrative of their development, between the market-led need for safe incorporation into a readily consumable product and – because of the speed with which these two economically huge areas of enterprise can change, and be changed, and because of the economic scale and geographical class range of both mediums – both the possibility of oppositional strategies and the inevitability of incorporation of that opposition. Popular music and film are able to, indeed forced to, live in a dualistic world in which the avant-garde and the mainstream co-exist in what may be constructed as single market-places; but single market-places which on closer scrutiny rapidly fragment into discrete units governed by such factors as age, gender, economic status, and so on – fragmentations and, albeit continually changing, constituency interests of potential opposition to the consumerist mainstream that have a clear significance for the programme of any modern avant-garde movement. As Hare has Arthur declare in *Teeth `n' Smiles* – " One day it's a revolution to say fuck on the bus. Next day it's the only way to get a ticket".

In more recent post-modernist avant-garde theatre, with its stress on the physicality of the theatrical event at the expense of the conventions of debate and discourse associated with a rationalistic tradition, the incorporation, and deliberate "abuse" of film conventions is of supreme importance. Consider, for example, the way in which Forced Entertainment deploy the filmic techniques of cut-up and collage in a way that works to establish their own models of cultural disintegration and fragmentation, and deliberately frustrates the conventional expectancies of a mainstream cinema focus on plot and character.

Agit-prop theatre has a rather different relationship with popular culture, seeking to define it in class terms as a point of contact with its projected audience. This can take a number of forms, of which two are crucial and distinct.

1) In the early days of modern agit-prop theatre (that is, post about 1966) it relied enormously on the appropriation of mainstream popular culture in a defamiliarised context, as a way both of offering an accessible political education and of foregrounding the essentially consumerist ethos of the borrowed material by its placement in a politicised and non-domestic context. The use of "Beat the Clock" type games shows as paradigms of the inequality of the workings of capitalism was a recurrent motif, for example; or of "Miss World" pastiches in a feminist piece. Significantly, it was to television, with its pretensions to a pan-global and cross-cultural village audience, that such agit-prop looked usually. As such, a major intent of the exercise was the desire to expose the tawdry nature of the contemporary popular culture on offer, and to offer its audience the opportunity of recognising their own implicit compliance in the consumerist conspiracy.

2) The problems with this kind of borrowing are two-fold. Firstly, its use became almost mannerist, and the predictability of its deployment emphasised the essentially patronising nature of the exercise, privileging the analysis of the performers at the expense of the assumed ignorance of the audience (an assumed ignorance that was anyway extremely problematic given the gap between the "ideal" and the actual audiences at the majority of such performances). Secondly, it failed to give popular culture any real credence as an entity in itself, choosing what were taken to be bad examples rather than good and stressing the uniformity rather than the disparity of popular forms. That is to say that it drew from popular culture in its most incorporated and least oppositional forms, those forms that were most obviously a part of the capitalist market ethos against which agit-prop theatre necessarily defined itself. The easiest way of looking at the second stage would be to consider the work of John McGrath with 7:84 (Scotland), where a conscious attempt was made to incorporate elements of Scottish popular culture that by their very nature were not a part of the mainstream or its consumerist counterpart.

I can make the point quickly by two rather different examples. The first is 7:84's best known production, *The Cheviot, the Stag and the Black, Black Oil*. In this play, McGrath used both the ceilidh form for the overall structure of the evening's entertainment -

an attempt both to appeal to an audience for whom the structure of such an event might still have cultural meaning, and a part of the programme of opposition to the detritus of an internationally marketed mass popular culture that can then be seen as, in itself, a political weapon in the destruction of a popular Scottish culture. And, in addition, McGrath drew directly and emotively from the tradition of native songs in the Gaelic language, the conscious eradication of which had been a central plank of the historical process of English colonisation, to invite the audience into a complicit notion of community which opposed those external forces. But he also used echoes of 60s "Girly Groups" for the close harmony song about the appropriation of Scottish oil by the American giants, "Texaco, Amaco" etc.

And to take a very different example. In *Oi for England,* Trevor Griffiths drew from the oppositional potential of late 70s punk music, together with, in this instance, its off-shoot, Oi music, which attracted a specifically neo-fascist youth following. He did so in order to dramatise his essentially agit-prop piece about a group of unemployed kids being wooed into supporting a fascist rally with their music. But at the end of the play, he concludes, as the white punk and his black girl friend arm themselves for the streets, having destroyed the group's instruments, with all that is symbolically involved in that act, with a rather sentimentally misplaced rendition of an Irish rebel song – again clearly standing as an opposition to the contemporary fascistic potential of Oi.

The use of the two quite distinct senses of the "popular" connect. Both McGrath and Griffiths employ a notion of popular music that pre-dates, opposes – and has arguably been destroyed by – the more contemporary notion of the popular when they seek to emphasise the need for opposition. The contemporary, in its turn, is then related to that which, it is argued, must be opposed – the take-over of Scotland by international capitalism, or the rebellious potential of the disaffected young by the extreme right.

This distinction is of vital significance when considering the appropriation of the popular by the mainstream. For, in terms of the way in which, and at the point at which it is being consumed, stress is placed not on an oppositional disruption to the status quo but on the perpetuation of organised and contained patterns of social life. That is, they deny, both by the nature of what is appropriated and by the location, the theatre, in which the appropriation is to be displayed, any meaningful link with anything like an oppositional sense of the potential of popular culture to so represent itself.

Popular is then a very slippery term, and its potential for leakage cannot be underestimated. It has connotations which allow for its appropriation as a part of an oppositional strategy but, at the other end of the spectrum, it can be seen as a central plank of the international monetarist programme, the material from which the advertisements promoting consumption are to be constructed. The history of that leakage is a central part of the cultural history of class struggle, and the attempts to define the popular are integral to the processes of incorporation and the essentially ideological concerns of such ventures.

In *Stage Right*, having identified the emergence of a new mainstream, I concluded that, just as the subsidised theatre had suffered from the effects of the new monetarism so also was that mainstream under threat – partly because of the way in which it depends on the infusion of new material from what is now an enfeebled subsidised arena. The result has been a change in the nature of what is on offer in terms of its cultural origins. A mainstream theatre that has found itself unable to draw from a subsidised theatre for its product has turned increasingly to non-subsidised sources, sources which apparently insist on a connection with the "popular". From this perspective it can be seen that the effects of economic change in the country have created new forms of popular mainstream theatre. An affluent audience still exists, content to see their capacity for conspicuous consumption displayed on stage. But the audience for professional popular theatre is now more casual, its perspectives defined no longer by an awareness of the history of that popular theatre, and thus familiar with its conventions. Its contextualisation of the popular is very different, and drawn from essentially non-theatrical mediums.

I could, and should, digress at this point to consider the importance of regionality in defining popular theatre – there is not space to do so, though I note that when I last looked at the theatre programme in Liverpool (Easter 1994), there was not a single self-produced piece to be seen; and that a city that can rightly lay claim to the active promotion of a genuinely popular home-grown tradition had been reduced to a series of receiving houses. The predominant contemporary model of theatrical production is one that stresses the exchangeability, the conformity of the product over the entire country; not only is the vast majority of individual theatre programming now linked to a pattern of nationally toured productions, but increasingly even home-produced shows are only possible if a link with other theatres, and consequent performances, has been arranged. Certainly, consideration of this situation would be merited, as would, for example, the activities of Hull Truck with John Godber in the new Spring Street base – where the economic pressures to rely increasingly on the transferability of material for national tours has seemed to a number of people to have changed its base-line sense of popular theatre. I want instead to consider two particular strands of contemporary popular theatre – the continuing development of the rock musical, and the importance of popular music as a source; and the all-important influence of television as a unifying element in the production of an homogenised theatrical culture.

It is only too apparent that musical shows of various kinds are a dominant feature of the national theatre scene. I will look briefly at just one strand of this genre – that epitomised originally by Elvis which started life in the 70s, and continued more recently by shows such as *Tutti Frutti, Only the Lonely* and *Buddy*. The last example is instructive. An uncomplicated celebration of the life and music of Buddy Holly – made easier for an audience in that it gets the unfortunate intrusion of his untimely death out of the way half-way through the second act, so that Buddy can then rejoin the cast for some more good old Rock `n' Roll. Now, with a London base and two national tours under its belt, productions across Europe and as far away as Japan, it represents an appropriation of a version of popular culture – that of late 50s American pop music – that is genuinely international in its appeal. It is a pleasantly undemanding commodity that is marketed like a Rock concert, with all the paraphernalia of T-shirts, mugs and recordings for sale in the foyer. A measure of its economic significance is that it caused a hastily reissued collection of the singer's hits to make number one in the UK album charts during its first national tour, something which never happened during Buddy Holly's lifetime.

Now, it would be possible, if somewhat dangerous, to attempt to construct an 'ideal' model of the audience for such a show – and certainly theatrical impresarios have proved their talents at the construction of such a model, as is witnessed by the commercial success of the resultant shows. The material used is popular in a way that places it in an historical context of a very particular kind. This is not a version of rock `n' roll that relates to the context of adolescent rebellion of the film *Blackboard Jungle*, in which Bill Haley was first seen performing "Rock around the Clock" in this country, nor of the ripped-up cinema seats that accompanied the first screenings of his film *Rock around the Clock*. In invoking the absent presence of teddy-boys, teenage rebellion, and the like, I am, of course, equally at risk of constructing an alternative myth of history on the back of revived memories of the kind of earlier moral panic scares that saw Brando's *The Wild One* prohibited from public screening for so many years.

But what is evident is that audiences are being offered a carefully sanitised version of a past brand of popular culture, a version for many members of the audience that will touch on aspects of their own past, indeed. Musicals are a very marketable commodity, and this particular version appears to offer an endlessly repeatable formula. Their appeal to the ticket-buyer lies not only in their predominantly escapist or nostalgic tone. They are safe in that they can deliver a product the main component of which, the songs, is already familiar to their audiences, has a living and perpetuated past history, and has already been marketed in other mediums. My ideal model of the audience might then include a high proportion of older and more affluent theatrical patrons, enjoying the experience of reliving a carefully compartmentalised version of their own relationship to that now totally unthreatening (if threatening it ever was) popular culture. But it would certainly also include a good number of much younger patrons, for whom no direct access to the original context of the music is available; equally invited to celebrate the popular in the guise of a museum exhibition of better times long past – much as audiences have been drawn back to savour the cosy late 70s recall of a sanitised version of the 50s in the stage version of *Grease* in the 90s. Consider, for instance, the likelihood of there having been a 1979 London West End production of a punk musical starring Johnny Rotten, Sid Vicious and friends.

I don't want to pursue this line of argument, although obviously there is much more that can be said. What interests me more is how this kind of appropriation of the popular should be seen as so vital to the workings of contemporary theatre. For, it has many more strands than this. As well as borrowings from the back catalogue of popular culture, mainstream theatre draws heavily on the contemporary brochure. In a survey I made of the mainhouse productions of every theatre on mainland Britain in the autumn/winter season of 1992/3, I discovered that one of the major developments was the increasing incidence of shows targeted specifically at children. As well as a number of local shows, there were six productions on national tours; everyone of them was, not surprisingly, a direct spin-off from a television programme.

And it is to television, in particular, that the contemporary theatre looks for its popular models. Just as radio stars used to be touted in the now largely defunct variety extravaganzas – which were, in themselves, watered down versions of the earlier, more subversively populist and proletarian music-hall traditions of the nineteenth century – and the seaside shows, so now George Cole, Penelope Keith, Paul Eddington, Richard Briars, etc, are advertised as offering a safe pathway from the atomised domestic hearth to the theatre in ways which suggest the safety of the enterprise, the unlikelihood of being mugged either in or out of the theatre, particularly as the theatre-going experience is increasingly defined as a part of a carefully chaperoned weekend jaunt, complete with coach trip, overnight hotel accommodation and the best seats in the house; the whole thing to be consumed in one package, like the visit to the hypermarket or the two week's charter holiday to sunnier climes.

But the mainstream does not rely on television for its pre-existent exposure of acting talent alone, it draws from it for its theatrical models as well. *An Evening with Gary Lineker*, to take an obvious example, brings together the shared experience of the domestic situation comedy and of the televised World Cup, and that it does so in the context of the further assumed shared popular experience of the package holiday in Spain only serves to emphasise the point. For, the notion of popular as defined by television is one which stresses the uniformity, the exchangeability of the product, in which any expression of an oppositional notion is there simply to be ridiculed, parodied or satirised by the other "conformist" characters in the action.

The conclusions are bleak, I think. Just as the concept of "radicalism" was dragged into the right-wing book of useful phrases through the 80s, so any notion of popular has been almost entirely hi-jacked and redefined in strictly economic terms. Of course, there are, and will be in the future, pockets of resistance, but they are conspicuous by their absence on the proliferation of weekend-breaks leaving every regional city in search of the illuminating warmth of centralised and comformatory populism offered by London and its particular version of the "good night out".

Notes

[1] John Bull, *Stage Right* (Macmillan, 1994)

[2] John Bull, *New British Political Dramatists* (Macmillan, 1984; repr. 1986, 1982)

"Who's Your Friend?"- A Popular Avant-Garde

Nicholas Arnold

Not long ago I heard Lyn Hixson, director of the Chicago-based Goat Island Performance Group, speaking about her company's work. She emphasised that, despite the experimental and, for many people, problematic nature of their work, their public was a very broad one, and had included from the beginning the janitors of the building in which they worked, who were also the company's friends. I was immediately reminded of the time when I was running an arts centre. It was not a community arts centre. Our declared aim was to experiment. But the performances were always open to the regulars from the pub next door. They had become our friends. They worked the same hours as we did, in the same environment: the man who stoked the boilers and his wife, the night security men from the nearby university. They came, watched, asked questions, declared preferences. Because there was no assumption that the work was not for them, and because they were relatively unfamiliar with the adamantine conventions of ordinary theatre, they addressed whatever work they encountered directly. Friendship had circumvented questions of taste and understanding. The audience we really disliked was the one we called "the people in black". As far as we were concerned, these art-house regulars had an agenda as narrow as any seat-holder's at the local rep, and their reception of open experimentation was uncertain and partisan.

This does, of course, raise the question of "who's your friend" – and what are your friends expectations? Shakespeare is extremely user-friendly for many of his audiences. They pay their money, go to sleep, and leave the theatre perfectly satisfied. I was once – long before the prominent role played by women in the miner's strike – appointed to direct *Close the Coalhouse Door*. As soon as I started working on the text, I developed an uneasy feeling. So I gave it to my mother, the daughter of a Durham pit-man, to read. After ten minutes reading, she raised her head and said, very precisely "this is demeaning". Clearly, whoever *Close the Coalhouse Door* was written for, it was not for clear-sighted, clear-headed female members of the mining community. But it had manifestly fulfilled its expectations for its friends.[1] The Living Theatre, once the most avant of all the gardes, attracted audiences of thousands – of friends. It also made thousands of enemies. It was always performing to a sector of society and this sector has shifted socially over the decades, so that 'Le Living' are now the darlings of the French bourgeois high-art audience, a large and powerful constituency.

The theatre avant-garde may be socially and culturally isolated, but attempts are always being made to bring it to wider audiences. Once the avant-garde is available and accessible, it is enjoyed – the visual arts have shown us this. No-one complains about the Grisedale Forest Sculpture Park.[2] Rail passengers – one of the most socially heterogeneous groups in the country – get a great kick from the running horses along the track from Birmingham to Wolverhampton.[3] Accounts of Christo's work, for example *Running Fence*, testify to the extraordinary growth of positive popular feeling among the host community as the exercise took shape.[4] There are equally striking examples within the Performing Arts. Leaving aside Madonna and her putative beginnings in Performance Art, we should consider the astonishing success and popularity of Laurie Anderson, or the enormous enthusiasm and excitement generated among schoolchildren by the work of Richard Layzell.[5]

In these examples the performance avant-garde is making friends through its work, rather than addressing itself only to a pre-existing coterie. A group such as Dogs in Honey even used quite specific devices such as the stand-up comedy format, and insisted that its work was received with more fundamental comprehension by audiences of young apprentice-welders than by art students.[6] It is tempting also to refer to the work of Welfare State, but they have made it quite clear that, under the original mantle of the avant-garde, they are specifically interested in "the revitalising of traditional popular theatre forms".[7]

I am particularly interested, in such a context, in the work of the very singular and increasingly well-known performer Bobby Baker. A short biography for those unfamiliar with her work will illustrate both its principles and its practice. Bobby originally trained as a fine artist. It seems likely that, as an unglamorous mature student, with a diffident manner but an independent outlook, she had an unsympathetic ride in an environment which was still supremely macho. While studying, she decided that food and its raw materials were her chosen areas of artistic expression. For one of her commissions she filled her bungalow with a life-size, edible family. Once the exhibition was open, the local children, coming home from school, would pop in for a visit and a bite to eat. Horrific photographs exist of the half-eaten baby in his cot. Bobby realised she was making work which was inter-active. Shortly afterwards she began to place herself within her work, as a performing feature, and began to explore the details and routines of cooking and housewifery as expressive metaphors for a range of comments about female existence.

Bobby deals in ideas and images which are mere concepts to some of her audience, while for others they are profoundly programmed elements in their lives. Her appearance begins it. She dresses in a white coat and a cap, ghosting images of the nurse, the doctor, and the white-coated expert of television adverts. This, she implies, is a woman's uniform. She seems to have a direct line to the 1950s, the era so often visited by advertising for its combination of hopes for a bright new world, with its accompanying hectoring of women back to a dirt-free, germ-free, taste-free, sweat-free, sex-free life in the kitchen. She always carries a blue J-cloth, with which she compulsively and continuously wipes things down. She thus plays on the ambiguities of the cook's life. She is addressed by demands to clean, scour and disinfect – demands which are gastronomically disastrous – and the simultaneous need to keep the kitchen running and functional, in the face of the continual clogging tide of spills, stickiness, washing-up, wet towels and dirty dishes. The cook lives the female contradictions of the hygienic model and the physical reality.

To people who use convenience foods, or cook for one or two plus dinner parties, this information is purely cerebral. For someone who has to feed four or five people daily, they are memoirs from the work-place. For me, this huge referential freight is summed up in audiences' reactions to a moment from her piece *Cookdems*. *Cookdems* premiered in 1990 and one of its first tours was of women's clubs and institutes in the Strathclyde area. Bobby did not want to appear in conventional theatre venues and also wanted to exploit the ambiguities of what she was presenting in these 'alternative-alternative' venues. I had seen the piece several times and become intrigued by what I had begun to feel were differences in reaction between different audiences and among different kinds of people in the same audience.

At one point in the performance Bobby demonstrates the making of a variety of colourful sweet sauces. She cannot keep her hands out of the pans as she works, licking her fingers and guiltily wiping away the evidence. Already our laughter has a specific quality. We are acknowledging the breaches of decorum necessary to secure a good flavour. We are acknowledging the tension between the sensuousness of food and its untouchability in the name of hygiene. We are also acknowledging a class and cultural base for this kitchen cleanliness kitsch. In France the gag would fall flat. Gastronomy is not at war with manners there.[8]

While the sauces bubble Bobby's commentary drifts into apparent non sequitur. She reminds the audience that she was trained as an artist. As she talks, she walks across to the kitchen cupboard – the kind where you keep the cleaning tools: the broom, the dust-pan and the Hoover. She opens it – and takes out a nice young man – naked except for bathing shorts. There is a great roar of laughter. It is a joyful acknowledgement of the trick which has been played, and the delightful result, but it contains other elements. Younger people, I noticed, gave the joke the response proper to a well-placed sight-gag. Middle-aged women laughed long and richly. For them, there was much more to digest than just the surprise and the apparent incongruity. The appearance of this toy-boy is central to the ideology of the performance. It is richly funny because of its significance within the complex of assumptions, taboos, clichés and prejudices which surround kitchen life.

Once hubby is off to work and the children to school, the kitchen becomes a solitary, chastely imprisoning cell: a suburban Rapunzel's tower. It is therefore, for the same reasons, the ideal place to covertly have it off. There are milkmen, postmen, dustmen, insurance men, and all the rest of the great tribe of males who mythically prowl the daytime suburbs, the recipients of the avid attentions of legions of bored housewives waiting in their kitchens. An added spice is given to these legendary unions by the fact that sexual services are being given to one male, while another set of sensual services – gastronomic and gustatory – are being simultaneously prepared for another. Supper is steaming on the stove while the wife is steaming at the milkman. All the husband has to console him is his lunch-box – a token collection of cold favours.

The kitchen is a contradictory zone. It is the suburban puritan dream. It houses a solitary, and therefore symbolically chaste woman. Ritual and convention demand that it should be kept pathologically clean. It is the arena for the constant battle against the contaminating clouds of "germs and dirt"(y thoughts and deeds). But it is also a private place, where fantasies can be (and in this case are) played out with minimal risk of detection. When we are in it, we are in the 'woman's place'. Proper, marital, night-time sex becomes improper, and shifts from the bed-room to the cook-room, from cocoa-time to coffee-time. The cook-room is a far more hopeful place for sex. The kitchen's sanitised public image is at war with its purpose, which is to produce delights to titillate and gratify the senses of smell, taste and touch, and to assuage the appetites it arouses. All this with the maximum of foraging in organic matter – peeling, cutting, slicing, stirring, pulping, kneading, jointing, trussing, simmering, blanching, sweating, seething, boiling, bathing, basting. With amazing changes of shape, colour and texture, in which things rise and firm and are well-done, rare, bloody – even blue. With an incremental sophistication of technique to ensure the retention of the juices until the proper moment, the heady enrichment of smell and taste, and the maximum impact on the tongue.

36

The sensation-numbing rubber gloves of the sanitation freak are the worst possible wear here. They must be stripped off. Cooking involves getting stuck in with your bare hands. The nice young man is well dressed for the messy acts of cooking and sex, apart from the risk of getting burned – and we all risk that. Bobby is equally well-dressed. But while He is stripped for action, She is shielded and sterilised from contaminating splashes. Their juxtaposed appearances are piquant. We speculate about the middle-aged body under the starched white overall.

Our prurience has been anticipated. Bobby continues to maintain that she is an artist and the young man her canvas. Taking a brush, she paints him with the brightly-coloured sauces. He is covered in her sweet juices. He has become a fetished sex object, a model for toy boys, all ready to be eaten up. Bobby can't resist giving him a big hug. But this transfers the sauces onto the prophylactic white coat, which is now stained with the evidence of the saucy embrace. Bobby hustles the young man away, then disappears herself, to return wearing a clean overall. The evidence of her lapse has been disposed of. The deep chords she has struck die away. She can resume her pristine kitchen persona – until the next time...

But what is striking these deep chords? Is it the material, which dares to speak about the unspeakable – 'Drawing on a Cook's Experience', as it were?[9] Or is it <u>how</u> Bobby speaks that allows her to get away with it? Physically, as is always pointed out, she is a dead ringer for Joyce Grenfell, with something of the same voice. The English are very fond of zany women – their zanyness unsexes them and removes their danger. Bobby's performance persona potentially undercuts the danger of her material. Is she accepted because of her persona, rather than her themes? Or, conversely, is it her general air of unthreatening anxiety, the disarming environment of the kitchen which she carries with her, which allows her to air matters which might be rejected in a more rhetorical and head-on approach? As a schoolboy I helped a plasterer during the holidays. One lunch-time, sitting against a sunny wall, I was extolling the previous night's TW3[10] and the satire boom. 'We don't call it satire, Nicky', shot back Fred the plasterer, 'we call it sarcasm'. If you lead a vulnerable existence, you want to be brought to terms with it gently and with humour, rather than by some untouchably omniscient outsider.

We must not fall into the trap of regarding Bobby's performance as incidental to the material. The form embraces the content. We do not assess a comedian's capacity by looking at the scripts – although we recognise when the material is weak. Here we encounter a common problem when making a critique of avant-garde performance material. The act of performing itself, as opposed to the ideological decision to perform, is often under-valued. I do not propose to go into the reasons, which are, for me, both banal and irritating. Suffice to say that many avant-garde performers approach performing with as much naïveté as one finds in rep – and with less professionalism – relying on unselfconscious natural talent to adequately deploy sophisticated artistic concepts. Only in the last two or three years has Bobby, herself a gifted natural performer, begun to be aware of the performance itself as having artistic and technical components.[11]

It is for this reason that I would like to turn abruptly to the work of a company which is made up of highly and self-consciously talented actors, and which has no aims and makes no claims to reach a popular audience. The concern of Forced Entertainment Theatre Co-Operative is with making a kind of theatre which they think appropriate to the end of the century in our culture. They generally play in art-houses. Their formal position has so far been that they do not wish to broaden the range of venues they play to include those which would conventionally be regarded as 'popular'. Yet they consciously draw their material and their approaches to performance from the popular media and its concerns: from the condition of the city – Sheffield – where they live and work. They say that what they show, and how they show it, will be familiar to 'anyone who has ever lived in a house where the television is always on'.[12] They are not being patronising, but truthful. It might be said that they are appropriating material from popular culture and experience and using it in a refined and inaccessible context. It might also be contended that the form and content of their pieces – non-linear, non-narrative, multi-layered, sometime illogical or irrational, are an actual or potential turn-off to people who, whether they are familiar with theatre or not, assume that it should involve narrative, character and dialogue.

In practice this is not the case. One of my students came from a vigorous but disrupted back-ground in working-class Leeds. She did a lot of work with Forced Entertainment and became convinced that what they did could be illuminating to a wider audience. To this end, she dragooned her relations into coming to see every possible piece of work. The reaction was always the same. After a ritual disclaimer that they did not understand 'what it was about' they would give a sensitive and perceptive reading of what they had seen.

Friendship was involved in bringing these people face-to-face with this work, but it is worth noting that the performers of Forced Entertainment spend much of their time on stage undercutting the conventional modes which operate to produce a ground-base of emotional sympathy between performers and audience. As performers they are not making friends of, or with, the audience. But their pieces as a whole clearly are: the material, which is recognised and understood, and its embodiment in the forms and activities of the performance. These are striking the deepest chords in people who are unversed in theatre practice. However, these same people clearly do not believe that this work 'belongs' to them. Can it, then, be 'popular' theatre? But this is another debate...

Notes

[1] See Alan Plater, *Close the Coalhouse Door* (Methuen, 1971), introduction.

[2] Where sculptural or found pieces are allowed to change and degenerate naturally with climate and seasons, until they disappear.

[3] Kevin Atherton, 1986. British Rail Commission.

[4] See W.Spier (trans. K.Cheesmond0, Christo, *The Running Fence* (Thames and Hudson, 1977)

[5] See R.Layzell, *Live Art in Schools* (Art Council of Great Britain (now Arts Council of England), 1993).

[6] For example, *Aliens 4*, 1992.

[7] T.Coult & B.Kershaw (eds), *Engineers of the Imagination* (Methuen. 1990) p.6.

[8] See G.Orwell, *Down and Out in Paris and London* (Secker & Warburg, 1986).

[9] Bobby's next show after *Cookems* was *Drawing on a Mother's Experience*. In it she makes a huge abstract painting on the stage floor, using the foods which she associates with her experience of motherhood.

[10] *That Was the Week That Was* to the less wrinkled.

[11] Bobby Baker, 1992

[12] Tim Etchells, director, Forced Entertainment.

The Ellusive Butterfly: An Integrated Theatre The Everyman Theatre, 1989-1993

Nick Owen

What is this about?

This paper is about buildings. And theatre buildings in particular. Slabs of concrete, brick and wood into which is piped gas, electricity and water – and out of which is produced not theatre that you would buy tickets for, but committees, consultancies, caretakers, think tanks and personality disorders.

This paper is about the contradiction of how theatre cannot be produced in theatre buildings, and in particular how the art form of popular theatre cannot happen in buildings which are dedicated to producing popular theatre.

Who produces theatre here? And for whom?

At a TMA conference in London ten years ago when everyone sat around bemoaning the annual crop of falling audiences at regional rep. theatres, the equivalent of the spotty youths in the audience (the independent theatre mob) piped up with allegations that perhaps the product wasn't accessible, had no relevance to anyone's lives, made no connection at all with its immediate neighbourhood and perhaps it wasn't surprising that audiences were in continual decline.

Some old duffer from the TMA or Equity or other member of the theatrical establishment guffawed at this and muttered, "of course, any fool can <u>empty</u> a theatre", which received much applause – the implication being of course that if any theatre management worth its salt tried following the advice of the spotty youths of the independent theatre lobby, their buildings would be emptier than they were already.

The argument ran: in order to counteract this current malaise, we have to put on <u>popular</u> theatre and bang the drum as loud as we can to tell the world about the marvellous, accessible product which is filling our auditoria.

But of course in this arena, populated by managers, funders and assorted lackeys the whole essence of what it meant to be popular was never addressed and clarified. And so at a TMA conference last year, the ritual bemoaning of declining audience sizes continued. What does popular mean?

What does popular mean?

Bums on seats is a frequent definition. But whose bums on what seats is never made clear. Do they mean the fans who run the Supporters Club and who have continued to come week after week since 1949? And do they mean that they should buy the seats in the boxes at £100 each? Or the stalls at £10 each on Fridays? Or the benches you can sit on for £1 on a Wednesday afternoon as long as its raining and you have a group booking of ten school children accompanying you?

Another definition of popular is the Burger King model. This is theatre which is easily digestible, non controversial, needs little thought or consideration, is terrified by the dread possibility that it might be difficult to understand so can be consumed in a matter of minutes. It's full of the essentials of a sound cultural diet: the bun, burger and gherkin mentality which demands a beginning, middle and end preferably in that order and preferably with extra sauce. It seems to me that as well as emptying theatres, fools can also fill them.

Popular Theatre I would argue is little to do with numbers in the audience, less to do with how many recalcitrant TV stars are in the cast, probably not much to do with a linear narrative form and fundamentally nothing at all to do with theatre buildings.

On the contrary, popular theatre has far more to do with producing and marketing original work which is drawn from people who have been excluded from the normal means of production. That is to say, women, black people, disabled people, the working class, the unemployed, the underachievers, the disappointed. Those who were failed by school, those who live down your street, those who have ordinary run of the mill lives, go to pubs, drink lager, run small hatchback cars and watch telly. The dispossessed, the confused, the unconfident. In short, everybody who constitutes the foot soldier class in this country because as we are all only too well aware it has been, still is, and will continue to be the officer class who run Britain and its venerable institutions, and the theatre is just one other institution run by officers, for officers.

Popular theatre on the other hand is not about providing the officers with their entertainment. It is about drawing from across the barriers of professional, amateur and community work (and in the process helping undermine those terms) and engaging with the audiences from whence it was formed. It is about employing a skill base not usually associated with performer training such as teaching, facilitating and narrative skills. Because it requires a new set of skills it is often looked at sceptically by those trained traditionally.

Dismissing this type of training normally takes two forms. The first asserts that "jack of all trades and masters of none" are being trained. The second, that popular theatre practitioners "teach" because they can't "do". Teachers here will know that actually to be a good teacher demands that you know how to "do", often to a higher standard than might be required of you from the run of the mill job.

Popular theatre is also about the ability of artists to place their own ego and impulses to one side and let loose the reins of control to the individuals they are working with – a potentially threatening experience if all your artistic working life has consisted of dictating terms and conditions to your collaborators or people who service your work.

But most critically, popular theatre practice hinges on practitioners abilities to identify, release and generate narrative and composition e.g. through stories, drama, music and other forms of coherent and communicable self expression. All vital components of the act of developing cultural identity and the heart of good popular theatre practice.

In short, popular theatre is an art form – not a marketing slogan, type of building or programme of events.

Because of this approach however, popular theatre is often in direct conflict with the usual influences that run our theatres – the officers. Popular theatre is not theatre for officers by officers. It is therefore a threat and when seen as that, it is not before long before the officers step in and reassert control over their usual territory.

Fact or Fiction?

If this all sounds a bit melodramatic, I'd like to demonstrate the point by discussing the case study of the Liverpool Everyman Theatre between 1989 and 1993 and in particular the relationship between what was known as the Hope Street Project and the Everyman itself.

This is a classic tale of where the practice of a particular building directly contradicts the art form it is supposed to be supporting, and the inability of buildings to embrace art forms. Dilemmas which can be traced back to the question of who produces theatre for whom in this country.

In October 1993, the Liverpool Everyman Theatre, one of the last bastions of so called alternative producing reps, went into voluntary liquidation after 29 years of producing sometimes radical, sometimes misconceived, sometimes brilliant theatre. The liquidation caused immediate hardship for 40 staff who were made redundant. But in this case, unemployment wasn't for actors but for trainees who had been engaged by the Everyman on a variety of training courses. These courses were run by a department of the theatre, the Hope Street Project, set up in 1988 by the Everyman and Liverpool City Council.

One might interpret the setting up of Hope Street as an intention to improve the lot of local young people, the quality of the artistic output of the organisation or even to re-establish its role in producing popular theatre. The motivations were however more complex than that.

At the time the Arts Council were looking for local authorities to provide funding to regional theatres on a pound for pound basis – the so called parity issue. The Theatre and City Council consequently concocted a funding package from the Urban Programme, European Social Fund and Department of Education which not only generated a hybrid of training opportunities and impressive amounts of income (supposedly to be used as parity funds) but also failed to impress the Arts Council.

They refused to recognise these funds as having anything to do with the theatre's producing activities and doggedly pursued the parity issue until the relevant Arts Council officers developed other obsessions and moved on. The Everyman found itself saddled with a pile of training courses which it didn't understand and what it saw as a cancerous like growth of the organisation. Turnover jumped from about £400,000 to £700,000 literally overnight. The Arts Council assessment of the time, which referred to Hope Street as the "blob on the side of the building", summed up this anxiety perfectly.

This initiative was taken before the appointment of a new management team of artistic director (who, it was publicly acknowledged later, was brought in to "de-Scouse the Everyman"), administrator and training director (whose brief was to link its courses into the local community). The makings of an organisational nightmare were well on their way. Over the following four years, the organisation's identity, role and direction were all questioned in the public arena and a gradual schizophrenia became increasingly evident. This culminated in the sad and embarrassing decline of the whole organisation and a public and recriminatory liquidation last year.

So What?

And yet despite this fiasco, an organisation had been created almost accidentally – which was within a hairs breadth of exploding the myths surrounding community and professional theatre practices once and for all and which were producing popular theatre practices of the kind I described earlier.

By the end of 1991, we had created an organisation in which trainees performed alongside professional practitioners, those same practitioners taught on courses which reflected mainhouse programmes and where joint initiatives (in the field of new writing for example) were generating exciting and surprising results. The supposedly mutually exclusive practices of community and professional theatre were actually feeding each other and generating work that was inconceivable at the beginning of 1988.

Integrating professional artists work with that from those of the community was producing tangible popular theatre which was stimulating, innovative and, if given the room to breath, would have produced an organisation years ahead of any other around the country.

The realities of this integration had become clear. The most obvious one being that the question of whether popular theatre is produced by professionals, amateurs, communities or residents of the local dogs home is completely irrelevant. What matters is whether it's any good. Quality was invariably at its highest when artists and members of the local community were able to control their work and at its lowest when the forces which normally set the cultural agenda (the Board) insisted on controlling the means of production.

How do you control the status quo?

This they were able to do by creating a climate in which territorial attitudes to the production, rehearsal and workshop spaces were encouraged, rates of pay were introduced with no objective assessment of the jobs being undertaken, arbitrary decisions were taken on the transfer of monies from one part of the organisation to another and division between and within staff and management deliberately promoted.

Arguably the biggest way in which they managed to maintain control of the production of the work was to have no clear consensual policy about what the role of the theatre in the city was; what its identity was, what it was trying to achieve and how it was going to do it.

It's possible that this was due to incompetence but given the range of backgrounds of key board members solicitor, architect, stock broker – and the length of time they had been involved with the Everyman (the full 29 years in some cases), I would argue that these were people who knew full well what the results of their actions would be on the morale and health of the organisation.

No, the reason for creating this climate of confusion and suspicion was to control the theatre's output and what theatre was to be produced for what audiences. The ex-Chairman admitted as much when he said in the *Guardian* in 1993:

> Some people want a theatre for social engineering, they want a theatre for the unemployed, one specialising in dealing with various cultural entities. That runs contrary to

the purpose of this theatre. We want to run exciting theatre for theatre's sake.

Quite why he was unable to see that "running exciting theatre for theatre's sake" was the precise reason his theatre had lost its audiences over the previous ten years is something which still baffles me.

But in the end the Board had managed to produce a climate in which should Hope St and its activities seem more threatening than was comfortable, they would be seen to be acting in the best interests of the whole organisation by shutting it down and consequently bringing about the collapse of the popular theatre work that was taking shape.

That opportunity came in late 1991 and was the result of a combination of various factors. The working realities of integration were still erratically being communicated to the outside world; the funders still had no clear agreed evaluation criteria of the organisation's activities; we had just started an internal restructuring period; it was the onset of a new funding year with local funders still undecided about future grants.

To cap it all, a report by a council officer to a crucial funders meeting got left off an agenda a week before Christmas. Funding for the following financial year looked shaky and before you could say Happy New Year, the attempted dismantling of Hope Street had begun: with the subsequent collapse of trust and goodwill that had been painstakingly built up across the organisation over the previous three years.

To their credit, the funders response was both to rapidly refund Hope Street's activities but the organisational damage had been done. Integration was a now a dead duck and the talk changed from how could the organisation develop as one, to how quickly could it jettison Hope Street altogether.

What can be done with a consultancy fee?
But the story took another twist. As well as refunding Hope Street, the funders also wheeled out the standard panacea, the management consultancy, to find a way out of this organisational quagmire. The consultancy, carried out by KPMG lasted six months and cost £25,000 – the equivalent of 5 actors annual

wages. Whilst there was much distrust across the organisation about what a consultancy could do, to our surprise it did at least clarify once and for all what many of us had felt for some time: that the organisation needed to fully integrate its training and production activities and identify itself as a leader in popular theatre practice. It seemed that the argument for Hope Street's role in the Everyman had been won.

Ironically the Board's response was to ignore these recommendations. This set them on a course of confrontation with the funders which, a year later, led to the collapse of the entire organisation. A company which had been developing a vision on how rep and community theatre practices can produce a high quality popular theatre was finally lost.

Enoch Powell once said that all political life ends in failure and whilst this may be true of the concept behind the Everyman of the late 1980s, its failure has led to a blossoming of both a relaunched Everyman and independent Hope Street.

Hope Street itself has taken to independence with a vigour it could never express whilst strapped into the agendas of the old Everyman. It has probably developed more networks and partnerships – particularly abroad in Germany, Spain, Turkey and Albania – than it could whilst part of the Everyman and is now set to enjoy the benefits of Merseyside's Objective 1 status.

But in reality, the problems of the old Everyman lay deeper than restructuring alone could solve. The politics of organisations which run buildings are such that they can not embrace form or artistic agendas, they can only embrace funding, political and management ones. The politics of buildings mean that the concrete, brick and wood can only ever generate committees, consultancies, caretakers and personality disorders and hardly ever art, popular or otherwise.

And by the same token, funders, whose remit it is to be supporting new work cannot actually do anything of the sort. They are as incapable of embracing artistic issues as are buildings. Their brief is necessarily about fulfiling political and economic agendas. The interests of funders and buildings therefore go hand in hand. Art forms, such as popular theatre cannot rely on them for their health and development.

To forge a contemporary popular theatre practice requires a new funding package which has vision, confidence and places its trust in the people who produce the work; namely artists and practitioners from across the professional, amateur, community, cultural, industrial and economic divides. Popular theatre will succeed when artists and practitioners alone are funded, not the buildings that pretend to support them.

Funding strategies which insist on separating community and rep theatre practices will continue to hinder the development of the very practices they claim to be supporting and the loss three years ago of that elusive butterfly – an integrated company producing contemporary popular theatre – should serve as a reminder to them all in any future development of local, regional or national theatre strategies.

It will certainly continue to haunt us all who worked through that turbulent period and who thought we had captured something original, exciting and the answer to how producing theatre could develop in the years to come.

Ar........ ....

.... College

Hall Drive

Middl.... rough

TS5 7DY

The Possibilities for a Popular Political Theatre

Tom Maguire

In this paper I want to explore the possibilities for making a popular political theatre. In this context, the term "popular" is being used in Brecht's sense to describe theatre which is:

> intelligible to the broad masses, adopting and enriching their forms of expression / assuming their standpoint, confirming and correcting it / representing the most progressive section of the people so that it can assume leadership, and therefore intelligible to other sections of the people as well/ relating to traditions and developing them / communicating to that portion of the people which strives for leadership the achievements of the section that at present rules the nation.[1]

In 1979, David Edgar summarised the impact of political theatre in Britain from 1968 to that point thus:

> while the scale of socialist work is impressive, it is obvious that its intervention in the working class struggle itself has been at best patchy and peripheral.[2]

He explained why he believed this by arguing that socialist theatre companies had not been able to find forms of theatre that were truly popular, and that there no longer existed in Britain forms which were *popular* rather than merely *populist,* stating that:

> The General Will was not the only group to realise that it was employing forms that had expired more than half a century ago. Further, the awareness grew that even those popular forms that had survived the electronic onslaught had degenerated into populism... Some groups and companies have indeed drawn successfully on other popular cultural forms, but it is interesting that they have achieved most when they have employed forms actually peripheral to the urban British working class.[3]

He continues by arguing that such socialist theatre companies were always marginalised from the real struggles of the workers because of their institutional and operational frameworks.

What I want to argue for is the continuing possibility for popular political theatres, with reference to a precise moment in recent history when the preconditions set by Edgar were met. I will centre my argument on the production of *Border Warfare,* staged in Glasgow in 1989 – ten years on from Edgar's article and ten years into Thatcherism. A co-production between Wildcat Stage Productions and John McGrath's film company, Freeway Films, this show exemplifies an interaction between theatrical work and its social, political and cultural contexts which is the key to popular political theatre.

In using Edgar's analysis as the basis of my argument, it is important to acknowledge some of its limitations. For example, Edgar treats Britain as a unified whole, eliding national and regional differences. Not only was this invalid for Scotland during the 1970s, but it was to become increasingly outdated over the period of Mrs Thatcher's term in office. From 1979, there was a growing reassessment by Scots of Scotland's relationship to Britain, particularly as a result of the growing resentment at the perceived English orientation of British institutions under Thatcherism. This resentment was fuelled by a growing dissatisfaction with the treatment of Scotland as just another English region. In the face of what was perceived as a belligerent and anti-Scots government, separate national identity and particularly cultural identity became of paramount importance in the argument that Scotland should be treated differently, and ultimately regain political autonomy.[4] Culture became the focal point for political change.

Not only were demands for change predicated on assertions of alternative images and discourses through cultural means, but since the representative democratic system thwarted political change, this impulse seemed to be displaced into cultural activity.[5] Such cultural activity, moreover, was channelled through the development of indigenous working class forms and the reorientation of the cultural infrastructure to embrace the Scottish working-class. Cairns Craig points out that:

> To the extent that much of the Scottish middle class society models itself on English values, distinctively Scottish culture has more affinity with the working class than with English culture, is more imbued with the sense of a living "folk" culture.[6]

Thus, the dominant idea of Scottishness became imbued with a class dimension and became a focal point for cultural resistance to Thatcherism. Popular culture became politicised and politicised at the centre of a movement for political change.

The politicisation of popular culture was not an instant transformation. Rather it was realised over the years after 1979. Wildcat Stage Productions was one of the groups at the forefront of this process of change. Formed initially as an off-shoot of 7:84 (Scotland) in 1978, the company developed a brand of political musical theatre that cannot be reduced to agit-prop or documentary, or be accounted for in terms of traditional dramaturgy. Importantly, this company was at its most successful in developing a constituency audience within the *urban working class* of Scotland's Central Belt. The development of the company had three main strands which are relevant to my argument today. These are: the attraction of a popular constituency audience; the development of a political theatre directly relevant to this audience; and the creation and promotion of popular forms of entertainment

Firstly, then, the company developed its audience through a combination of strategies. It began by touring its shows to community venues, such as unemployed workers' centres, community centres, and schools. Within its early years Wildcat became particularly and almost uniquely identified with this urban community circuit, particularly when it withdrew from Highland touring, and the work of 7:84 (Scotland) in such venues became more sporadic. Importantly, even as the company has grown in success, it has remained faithful to these community origins – most obviously in its retention of ticket prices at an affordable level. Alongside these community tours, the company has played residencies in theatres traditionally associated with popular entertainment, such as the Kings Theatres in Glasgow and Edinburgh, with their traditions as venues for pantomimes and popular entertainers like Stanley Baxter and Ricki Fulton. Secondly, it has mounted a volume of work – 4 shows a year – which meant that its presence within communities has been consistently felt. Thirdly, although Wildcat remains a production rather than repertory company, it has retained many of the same staff, particularly performers, for long periods, integrating changes slowly. By providing such continuity, the company is able to create a sense of familiarity between itself and its audience, a familiarity enhanced since many of these performers are to be seen acting on television or singing or performing in pubs and clubs, when not engaged in the company. Moreover, since the company's prolific and continuous output has contributed to the possibility of performers remaining to work in Scotland (able to forego the attraction of the English centre), this seems to demonstrate a solidarity with the audiences to whom the company plays.

Further proof of such solidarity is more obviously demonstrated by the kind of political theatre which the company makes. Up to *Border Warfare,* it combined directly polemical shows with productions which were more obviously entertainments, but entertainments which celebrated the culture and history of its constituency audience. So, alongside *Blooter* (on mass unemployment), *1982* (concerned with the nuclear defence policy), *Bed-Pan Alley* (on NHS cuts), *Dead Liberty* (about the miners' strike) and *Harmony Row* (about the invidious Poll Tax), the company has produced *The Complete History of Rock 'n'Roll, The Steamie* (set in a communal wash-house on New Year's Eve) and *The Celtic Story* (a history of the football club). Its polemical and campaigning shows have often linked to labour movement events and campaigns, with a number receiving trade union sponsorship, particularly from NALGO. The company's close association with the trade union movement provided the impetus for the establishment of Mayfest, Glasgow's festival of popular culture.[7]

Thus, the company was able to tap into grass-roots activism as part of its cultural struggle, such as when the tour of *Harmony Row* was linked with the activities of local and national anti-poll tax federations.

By the spacing of such campaigning shows, the company was able to build up its audiences in a way which made its forms of entertainment popular in actuality as well as in intent. In 1988-89, the success of *The Steamie* and *The Celtic Story* in particular raised the company's profile among what used to be called "non-traditional theatre-going audiences". The decision by Celtic Football Club to invest in (rather than merely sponsor) the production celebrating the Club's centenary must be seen as a recognition of a shared popular constituency.

As I have mentioned, the company developed its own brand of musical theatre: a popular entertainment form of its own. Unlike the work of 7:84 under John McGrath, Wildcat uses the idiom of rock music, which David Anderson, Wildcat's Musical Director, calls "the true folk music"; and its shows have music at their heart. It was the decision to develop this kind of "band theatre"[8] which caused the original move away from 7:84. The music, rather than accompanying or adding to a show, was to become the main part. Artistic Director, Dave MacLennan states:

> [V]ery often when Wildcat shows are reviewed they are reviewed in theatrical terms ... and the critics view the book as the bits that lie between the songs. In Wildcat shows, the songs are absolutely integral to the feel and meaning of the piece, and our songs do rather more than songs do in most musical theatre. They advance the narrative, comment on the plot, help to develop the character, carry a lot of political comment ... Very often we're criticised for the weakness of the book, when it really calls for a different kind of listening and approach. It's curious criticism when you read that the book is weak and then read paeans of praise about the songs that make up seventy or eight per cent of the show[9]

Within this theatrical idiom, the company is able to subsume different theatrical styles: documentary, agit-prop, epic, expressionism and heightened realism, for example. Since the performers and musicians are almost always the same people, they step in and out of the action to present characters and narrative. These qualities of transformability and flexibility have obvious parallels in all sorts of popular entertainment. The shows are not, however, some sort of second order form, reliant on a knowledge of other forms of entertainment for reference and meaning. They thus avoid the problems which Edgar identifies with using forms which lag behind the audience's immediate cultural reference.

So, within this increasingly politicised Scottish culture, Wildcat made its contribution by giving the processes of politicisation a very visible and public expression. The company had, over the ten years up to *Border Warfare,* created a constituency audience which was working class and drawn it to forms of entertainment which were rooted in their experience. In this context, then, the theatre is not on the periphery of political activity but embedded within it. This then meets the major preconditions set by Edgar for a popular political theatre: that the theatre is genuinely popular and close to the centre of cultural (and therefore in this case political) life.

Given that these preconditions were met, the possibility was realised of producing work which would contribute to political change qua theatre. In staging *Border Warfare,* Wildcat added further momentum to such change. The show was written, directed and co-produced by John McGrath. It was staged at the Tramway venue in February and March 1989, as well as being filmed for Channel 4 as part of the coverage of the celebration of Glasgow as European City of Culture in 1990. The venue, Tramway, had previously been the city's transport museum, but, following the removal of the museum to another site, it had remained derelict until Peter Brook had used it to stage *The Mahabharata* in 1987. The main performing area is a huge former tram shed, with a performance area of 27 x 27m, with a proscenium arch indicated at 18m in from the back wall. At the time of this production, the whole building seemed to be pitched between dereliction and incomplete renovation – creating an atmosphere around the event which marked it as outside the normal conventions of theatregoing.

Formally, the production bore the hallmarks of popular political theatre identified by McGrath in his seminal, *A Good Night Out. Popular Theatre: Audience, Class and Form.* These he describes as directness, comedy, music, emotion, variety, effect, immediacy, and localism.[10] Not only does *Border Warfare* manifest these characteristics on a massive scale, but in drawing a history of Scotland's relations with England it fulfilled a vital function for any popular theatre: a point I will go on to explain. The show is designed to illustrate, in the words of one of the characters, Lord Bon Accord, "a healthy mix of prejudice and fact / No wobbly high wire balancing act". It is a huge spectacle, combining elements of pageantry and carnival, selectively representing the history between the two countries. This relationship is presented as one of a colonial power to a subject nation, in which England has subjugated and exploited the people and resources of Scotland.

This element of pageantry and attendant spectacle has the virtues which Barthes describes as being "to abolish all motives and consequences: what matters is not what the audience thinks but what it sees".[11] This connects with McGrath's rejection of Brechtian pedagogics and his espousal of concepts of carnival as the way, forward for popular theatre.[12] So, the show does not purport to be an accurate historical account, but a summary of an attitude to history. As Alan Filewod explains in a different context:

> Properly speaking, polemical drama and pageantry are antithetical; pageantry with its emphasis on iconography, by definition precludes the reasoned argument that is implicit in the idea of polemic drama.[13]

So, the show is not creating a new interpretation of history, by which to convert the unbelieving. Instead, it has a mythological function. Myth relies on a previously shared experience or meaning system from which its own meaning is derived. In myth, for example, the historical character loses its historical context ("history evaporates"), while it is this historical context which gives a character meaning as icon. This meaning is "like an instantaneous reserve of history, a tamed richness, which it is possible to call and dismiss in a sort of rapid alternation."[14]

This use of myth was particularly potent given the political and social context of late 1980s Scotland. It was particularly potent in capturing what Tony Dickson describes as the dominant Scots attitude to Margaret Thatcher:

> The public persona of Margaret Thatcher appears to many Scots to capture all the worst elements of their caricature of the detested English: uncaring, arrogant, convinced of her own rightness ("there is no alternative"), possessed of an accent that grates on Scots ears and affluent enough to afford a retirement home costing around £500,000.[15]

The climax of the show is the entrance of a Thatcher caricature astride a huge pulpit from which John Knox had earlier spoken, lecturing the audience in a sub-Hitlerian speech about the superiority of the English and their values over the uncivilised Scots. As McGrath explained in an interview with *The Morning Star,* "In Scotland, it is a culture of resistance [to Thatcherism]. What I'm interested in is giving voice to that culture, giving it power." By analogy with the mathematical concept of a vector, one might see the importance of this more clearly. A vector is defined as a force given a particular direction. Here, a general feeling of antagonism to Thatcherism (a powerful cultural energy) is given a direction which shapes and defines it (a demand for Scottish political autonomy).

Thus, *Border Warfare* demonstrates how a popular political theatre might work: it provides a public occasion for a community to share and celebrate the myths which it presents.[16] It focuses the community's values and aspirations that the community might better apprehend the ways to implement them when the celebration is over. Such an occasion was particularly potent given the diminishing possibilities for such communal celebration of which a living popular culture is surely constituted; and in the face of the assertion by Mrs Thatcher that "there is no such thing as society." Moreover, if the community by such celebration is empowered to make the myth into a reality – then there is a very direct and obvious political outcome. [17] I hope, then, to have demonstrated that *Border Warfare* is one example of how a popular political theatre can be created, within particular historical conditions and related to a particular theatrical context. The possibility for popular political theatres did not vanish at some point in the 1970s, and the hope for new forms may be fulfilled for the current phase of history if practitioners can create or mobilise the shared myths of a constituency audience in service of political goals.

Notes

[1] Cited in John McGrath, *A Good Night Out. Popular Theatre, Audience, Class and Form* (Methuen, 1980) p. 63

[2] David Edgar, "Ten Years of Political Theatre, 1968-1978", *Theatre Quarterly* 32:viii (1979), p. 25

[3] Ibid., p. 29

[4] Such demands led to the formation of the Campaign for a Scottish Assembly, which received wide support; the issuing of *A Claim of Right for Scotland* in 1988; the establishment of the Scottish Constitutional Convention (to draft proposals for constitutional change); and the adoption by three of the major political parties of policies to provide Scotland with some form of Scottish parliament (Labour and the Liberal Democrats seeking developed powers, the Scottish National Party full independence with Europe).

[5] Scotland has for some years returned more Labour M.P.s than Conservatives. This state of affairs became perilous for the Conservative Party in the late 1980s as it was pushed into third place behind Labour and the Liberal Democrats at Westminster elections, and in 1994 when it was relegated to fourth place behind the SNP at Elections to the European Parliament. In the wake of the democratic defecit which is created between local representation and central government, as Cairns Craig wrote in his preface to the "Determinations" series of book produced by Polygon: "The 1980s proved to be one of the most productive and creative decades in Scotland this century – as though the energy had failed to be harnessed by the politicians, flowed into other channels. In literature, in thought, in history, creative and scholarly work went hand in hand to redraw the map of Scotland's past and realign the perspective of its future".

[6] Cairns Craig (ed), *The History of Scottish Literature: Vol 4: Twentieth Century* (Aberdeen University Press, 1987) p. 3. This ability to attract, effectively use, and retain trade union support contrast with the inability of political theatre movements in the rest of Britain to galvanise trade union contacts since the demise of Centre 42.

[7] It was David MacLennan, artistic director, and Ferelith Lean, company administrator, who put forward the initial proposal for a budget for a two week music and theatre festival marking May Day, to a meeting of interested parties in May 1982. Lean was to the first Mayfest organiser.

[8] Elizabeth Maclennan, *The Moon Belongs to Everyone: Making Theatre with 7:84* (Methuen, 1990) p.85

[9] Charles Hart, "Wildcat! An interview with David MacLennan", *Scottish Theatre News* 5:3 (1980) p.5

[10] McGrath (op.cit.) pp53-59. He issues the caveat that "these features of working class entertainment must be handled critically" to avoid the pitfalls of *tailsim* (p. 59). He clearly notes also that they are terminus ab quem ("the first sounds of a new language of theatre" p. 60), rather than a perscription for all time. Experience from a range of sources, however, suggest that they are adequate to account for many of the successes of popular theatre.

[11] Roland Barthes, *Mythologies* (Cape, 1972) p. 15

[12] See John McGrath, "The Theory and Practice of Political Theatre", *Theatre Quarterly* 35:ix (1979) pp. 43-54 and *The Bone Won't Break. On Theatre and Hope in Hard Times* (Methuen, 1990)

[13] Alan Filewood, *Collective Encounters: Documentary Theatre in English Canada* (University of Toronto Press, 1987) p.6

[14] Barthes (op. cit.) p. 118

[15] Tony Dickenson, "Scotland is Different, ok?" in D. McCrone et al (eds.), *The Making of Scotland, Culture and Social Change* (Edinburgh University Press, 1989) p.64

[16] While this is a potentially fascistic use of theatre, there are, however historical and strategic considerations in this and other contexts which allow it to be considered legitimate and radical move in the resistace to an alien and dominant set of values.

[17] Such a possibility of transposing the myth into a reality, is evident in the proposals for the Campaign for a Scottish Assembly for a more fully representative system, rather that a replica of the current British electoral system, given to the value ascribed to Scottish society as "democratic". *Theatre News* 5:3 (1980) p.5

A Show About Bingo
The Cabaret Community Theatre of Kirkby Response

Richard A. Cowler

Scared of sounding too derivative and not wanting to sound "old hat", I did not entitle this paper "A Good Night Out with Kirkby Response Theatre". But a "good night out" was just what it was and that phrase is a fitting place for me to start for two reasons. Firstly, because the type of theatre Response make is best understood in relation to the popular political theatre praxis described by John McGrath in his book, *A Good Night Out*.[1] Secondly, because the phrase cropped up again and again when I talked to members of the group – above all else they wanted to give their audiences a good time.

The type of "good time" offered in May 1993 by the Response show *Eyes Down*, a new play with music, devised/written by Response members, about the game-playing and social life surrounding a bingo hall, performed in working class clubs and community halls around Merseyside – is the subject of this paper.[2] So I am going to look at the choice of story, use of theatrical and dramatic space[3], patterns of communication, offering of alternatives and solutions to situations portrayed in the drama; as well as the amateur actors it was offered by, the venues it was offered in and the audience to whom it was offered.

The issues that I am dealing with here are very familiar to those who have studied, witnessed or participated in the British alternative theatre movement of the late 1960's and 70's. The debate about the nature of theatre (who it is for, where it should perform, what it should be about, what form it should take) is long-standing. Yet for Response, formed in 1987 (and for me, a toddler in the 60's and a disinterested adolescent in the 70's and early 80's) all this is fresh territory. The existence of groups like Response signals a continued but, for them, new dissatisfaction with mainstream theatre and the desire to address audiences (or communities) perceived to be excluded from mainstream "high" culture.

I came to Liverpool in 1989, attracted to it because of its reputation for dynamic theatre. What I found on the well-trodden path was a mainstream theatre in crisis – and not much else. When I went to see performances of *Eyes Down* I was offered something very different to that which I usually found in the hushed atmospheres of many of the central Liverpool theatres. The show attracted good lively audiences; at the Kirkby venues, full houses. "Spectators" sat, stood, drank, at some venues eat, smoked, talked to each other, moved about and watched the show. The actors' enthusiasm for, and skill in, entertaining the audience, the tremendous rapport between percipients[4] and the vocal reactions and enjoyment of the audience, created very lively, vibrant evenings. This mixture of drama, music and socialising was a new experience to me. The atmosphere was more like that promoted by a simple, celebratory musical. Yet it seemed that though it did not carry itself with any great bearing of seriousness, that it was serious in intent. It is my enthusiasm for the difference of this theatrical event, which seemed to me then and still does now, as much more important than the perhaps rough and ragged quality of elements of the performance. And it is that enthusiasm, a desire to celebrate that experience, that motivated the writing of this paper.

Obviously my concern here is to look at aspects of Response's work which relate to popular theatre praxis, but that cannot be looked at in isolation. Indeed, I would like to show how the dynamics that drive Response as both a popular, a political and a community theatre, not only overlap, but are mutually supportive. All can be seen as centring on "locality", on a drive towards a proximity of the cultural and quotidian.[5]

I hope then that my analysis of the performance and production of *Eyes Down,* will illustrate the way in which Response, dissatisfied with mainstream theatre and operating in the tradition of working class cabaret theatre groups, has developed an alternative performance mode based on an open access community policy, which tackles some of the problems in a search for contemporary popular theatre – problems of combining entertainment and "serious" content, of finding and appealing to working class audiences and of giving them a good night out in the financially restricted funding arena of the 1990's.

A Profile of Kirkby Response Theatre and their Community

Response is based at Kirkby Unemployed Centre in Kirkby, north-west Merseyside., Although Kirkby is now in the Borough of Knowsley, its genesis was as a satellite estate of Liverpool. Established between 1946 and 1961, Kirkby still faces the legacy of the misconceived and badly executed planning of the Liverpool City Council (LCC)

> Planned to accommodate the expansion of cities, they (the satellite estates) are now experiencing population decline and the general economic weakness of city economies. In this context, Kirkby and places like it might be seen as an unfortunate mistake.[6]

Unemployment in Kirkby is estimated to be between five and six times the national average and the borough of Knowsley is consistently found to be one of the most deprived districts in England.[7]

One of the problems with the physical environment of Kirkby is the segregation of residential, public, recreational and industrial land use, making "social and economic interaction difficult". The LCC planning seems "to have been positively designed to inhibit the creation of areas of vitality within the community, and helps to produce an effect of dulling uniformity." This problem has been exacerbated by land falling into dereliction. The consequence is an atmosphere of decay difficult to determine, but easy to sense.[8]

The intention of the LCC plan was to create a self-contained township but the phenomenal house building rate during the 1950's always raced far ahead even of the supply of basic community amenities. Despite improvements made as a result of the local administration of Kirkby, deficiencies remain. Kirkby is still, at least in terms of cultural provision by the arts authorities, a satellite of Liverpool. Knowsley Borough Council pursues the policy, in agreement with the four other metropolitan boroughs of Merseyside, to fund the Liverpool Philharmonic Orchestra, the Liverpool Playhouse and The Everyman. The Council considers these institutions, all based in Liverpool city centre, to be "a valuable investment" for the whole region and part of "a Merseyside package."[9]

Response defined its role in 1993 as "expressing the concerns of, and providing a vehicle for the talents of, the community." The idea that the group consists "of ordinary working class", performing to the "ordinary" people of their local community, about local concerns, is fundamental:

> Kirkby Response Theatre aim to take theatre out to...the type of people who would never consider going to the Everyman or the Playhouse,...to "their" community centre, "their" club, the local schools and colleges, even to the works canteen.[10]

Their idea of local culture then is in opposition to what they feel to be the exclusive nature and practice of the central Liverpool theatres. And it is rooted in perhaps their greatest social asset – their strong sense of identity created largely as a result of the clearly defined geographical area Kirkby occupies and the pretty uniform white-working-class-from-Liverpool social composition.[11]

Eyes Down was researched, devised and written over a period of just under a year, with the involvement of Response members, all of whom were working on an amateur basis. Nearly half the cast were new members of the group; for some it was the first time they had performed.[12] What key conditions then, allow Response to operate successfully as an open-access community theatre performing new, locally written plays and revues? They are threefold:

● Response's roots in Kirkby Unemployed Centre (KUC)
● Project funding and sponsorship
● Their acceptance of the limitations of community theatre.

Response's roots in Kirkby Unemployed Centre (KUC).
KUC has a good reputation both as a campaign organisation and a campaign base for the concerns of Kirkby residents.[13] It consists of a welfare rights section, an arts group, a canteen, a crèche, a meeting hall, a residential artist as well as accommodating groups such as Kirkby Response Theatre, a housing co-operative and a credit union.

As part of the labour movement KUC and its membership have a strong working class identity.

The centre provides Response with free office and rehearsal space, and a first venue for their shows. The provision of an administrative centre to Response is a crucial contribution to Response's effort to attract funding, remain accessible and ensure decision-making is collective. Most importantly, as a focal point for active members of the community and their concerns, KUC has an alternative-community centre status which enables Response to draw its membership from the local area and harness local concerns."[14]

Project funding and sponsorship.

Response received project funding for *Eyes Down* (£1,740 and £1,000 respectively) from the North West Arts Board and Knowsley Borough Council. They also attracted £1,000 in sponsorship from Buckingham Bingo, a bingo hall company. This money allowed Response to pay for the general production costs, as well as participation expenses (such as travel costs and child care), a sign language interpreter for one performance and musicians. They charged entrance fees of £2 waged and £1 unwaged.

Acceptance of the limitations of community theatre.

Response as a group have no aspirations to go professional or to try touring their successful shows on a professional basis. Their tours are short and generally within Merseyside. *Eyes Down* was performed only nine times, despite being a year in the making. They are however happy with this limitation they recognise that going professional would radically alter the nature of the company.[15] A longer tour of *Eyes Down* would have been impossible because of the family and working commitments of the participants.

Showing the Audience Themselves

For Response, *Eyes Down* was a way of celebrating a major feature of local culture with its audience. Bingo is "an important part of working class culture, especially for women."[16] The production was dedicated to reproducing the atmosphere of the bingo hall as a haven for working class women. It showed the glittery, show-biz, fantasy world of bingo, where the stresses of everyday life can be escaped, a place where women can let themselves go and have a good time.

What fed the devising/writing of *Eyes Down* was the group's knowledge and understanding of bingo halls, gathered both from personal experience and group research of local halls. And they tried to recreate the detail of those real halls in their fictional bingo hall The Bonanza; tried to give it a fictional depth, a sense of history and long-standing social atmosphere, similar to that which they found in the real thing. Many comic routines were based on such detail. The Bonanza's doorman, 'Ivor', was on continual guard against the bottle of vodka smuggled in by a punter – a practice of cheap drinking Response's audience recognised as its own.

As I have already related to you, among the Response members I canvassed, it was the entertainment value of *Eyes Down* that was the priority – giving the audience that "good night out". And this meant that the basic mode of *Eyes Down* was comedy. It was not however sublime comedy in the mould of say *Fawlty Towers* – serious issues were not excluded. As one of the actors said: "I think we use comedy very well, but in serious plays."[17]

Three main story lines, based on three female protagonists, form the dramatic core of *Eyes Down*. One of these characters, 'Joan', was based on a researched real-life story of a woman's degeneration into gambling addiction. Joan becomes addicted to tranquillisers, quarrels violently with her unloving husband and hits her children. The bingo hall is offered to her as a place where she could escape all this and cheer herself up. But after winning a little money, Joan becomes "hooked" and starts borrowing money from loan sharks to feed her addiction. The accumulated stress drives her to the edge:

> I'm a bad mother. They'd be better off if I wasn't here. I'm scared. I've got these debts. I needed to buy a school uniform for Sean ... There's so many things to pay...I got a loan off this feller, and now it's getting out a hand. "Don't let them play out on their own" he told me. He's taken my family allowance book. Why can't I manage like everybody else?...the bingo...[is] the only place I can take my mind off it now. If I could just have one big win I'd be okay...[18]

This speech is the climax of the sober side of Joan's drama. These more sober moments are constantly tempered by humour, humorous songs and fast-moving action.

I think that spectators responded enthusiastically to *Eyes Down* because it was written and performed directly and explicitly for them, by people who had direct experience of their lives. Recognition was apparent in the vocal reactions of the audience. 'Immediacy' and shared experience, tend to be highlighted as essential ingredients in this type of theatrical practice.[19] Anne Quilliam, an *Eyes Down* actor, told me about the response of spectators and how "close" the subject matter was:

> You know the bit with the women in the bingo...women in the audience – "Ah! That's me that you know...Oh yeah, I've done that, I've been there." It's surprising what comes out of the audience ... I think it makes people stop and think well, yeah, I've been through what she's gone through, I've got myself into debt."[20]

Members of Response feel that Kirkby has been the object of a great deal of media scrutiny, much of which has been damning. In this respect they feel that they are "representing" their community, both in the mimetic sense and in the sense of being spokespersons:

> it validates and voices their own experiences, which have by and large been neglected... and people have been disenfranchised on loads of levels...we are voicing that side of life that has been muted.[21]

Theatrical Space in Cabaret Venues

Response did not try to turn the venues for *Eyes Down* into theatres.[22] Instead they tried to fit their staging into the different arrangements of bar, and tables and chairs that they found.[23] This was crucial – the character of the venues was utilised rather than worked against. Indeed they were targeted as venues because a game of bingo (as part of a night's variety entertainment) would be quite common there and *Eyes Down* was intended as part of such an evening out.[24] At some of the venues the three-piece jazz band played on after the end of the show and the bar stayed open. In the second interval the spectators played a game of bingo organised by the Bonanza bingo-caller.

This acceptance of the spatial organisation of the venues was important in signalling that they "belonged" to the audience, that Response had the status of invited guests. The spectators usually gathered and got settled in, to **their** social club or local community hall, before the show started and they did not feel **obliged** to stay quiet or still during the show. On the contrary, because this was familiar territory, they were free to dominate the space or allow the performers to do so.

At two of the venues many of the spectators did not want to comply with the performance; for them the social facet of the evening was by far the priority.[25] Some "spectators" talked and moved about without regard for the show – it was, after all, their club. Others, when they were interested in the show, attempted to quieten noisy spectators.

Although Response's visits to these two venues could hardly be described as performance successes for their show, the events in their entirety had a "theatrical" quality that Response members, surprisingly, seemed to thrive on. At the Leisure Time Cabaret Club the actors battled on with the show even when, in the most adverse circumstance that night, some "spectators" queued for chicken-and-chips through the part of the venue being used for the show. Afterwards I was surprised and interested by the performers responses. They were excited by the challenge this sort of theatrical gamble sometimes gave them – one described it as like a "wrestling match".[26] Joan Manley, playing 'Joan' in *Eyes Down*, described the theatrical confrontation which occurred at the Bootle Corporation Club:

> I started saying my bit [the "I'm a bad mother" speech, quoted above] and it did, it quietened down and [then] this woman laughed...And I went – "it's not funny, it's not funny" – and I meant it wasn't funny. And then...quiet and all these men behind the bar...and they were listening...As soon as I'd stopped talking they went back to talking amongst themselves *(she laughs).*[27]

Of course these experiences represent extreme cases. At the other venues a balance was established which allowed the show to be performed without placing too much constriction on the social facet of the event. The audience would talk and move about, but not to the degree that it made the performer's task in conveying the story too difficult. Yet those extreme cases do highlight the theatrical risks a company takes in performing in this type of venue. When the spectators can give up their hold on the venue, or keep it, so the power that a company has over its audience rests on how well it entertains -that I think is truly "dangerous theatre".

In summary, the basic proxemic characteristics of the venues were informality and flexibility. Space was organised in a way which maximised contact between percipients and this created the inclusive ambience of the events. Spectators and actors were, in comparison to orthodox theatre, relatively unconfined. And when a balance was established between the social and performance elements, the spectators' and the performers', energies made a powerful combination.

Dramatic Space and Performing Style in Cabaret Venues

The whole space of the venue was identified as the 'Bonanza'. Dramatic action could be presented anywhere and spectators were encouraged to feel that they were themselves players in the bingo hall.

The main feature of the style of *Eyes Down* was "the absence of what is called style."[28] Unities of time and place were constantly violated, in quick succession and in diverse ways. Such rapid transformations around the fictional world and the crowded venue, could only be accomplished with economy of signification; set and stage properties were therefore minimal.

One example of the ingenious and varied nature of dramatic presentation in *Eyes Down* is the "Alan Hansen commentary". This portrays, and makes explicit the causes of the stale relationship between Jenny and her husband, Davy. Jenny is sat on the rear left stage, with two ordinary, upright grey chairs to signify a sitting room. She is watching TV, indicated by her glazed stare into space. Davy enters and the two of them sham a conversation – really only an exchange of domestic banalities. Jenny's eyes remain glued to the TV throughout this. We enter the scene with Davy's jealous remark about Jenny's fascination for Alan Hansen, the TV football pundit she is watching:

Davy: (*Pause*) You only ever watch this for Alan Hansen.
Jenny: (*Dreamily*) He talks a lot of sense.
Hansen: (*From the telly*) Now if we rewind the tape here
            Des[29] and play it back in slow motion I think
            you'll see the problem.

> *A rewind noise and Davy gets up out of his chair quickly and backs out of the scene. They go back through the previous dialogue in slow motion.* [So in this next bit Davy and Jenny's conversation in repeated from the top, but in slow motion with Alan Hansen's interjections from the TV]

Hansen: Here we pick it up with Davy making
            his move into his favoured position –
            the comfy chair. Watch now – she
            makes an attempt at a challenge.
Jenny: Hiya.
Davy: Alright.
Hansen: She should have been in a lot quicker.
            She seems almost afraid of physical contact.
Jenny: How was your night?
Davy: Alright. What about you?
Jenny: Alright.
Hansen: A quick one two but they're just going
            through the motions.
Davy: Yer didn't win then?
Jenny: No.
Hansen: You see Des they don't even expect to
            win any more.
Davy: Where's Ian?

Jenny: Upstairs on his computer.
Hansen: And there we've got to call into
         question the youth policy. There's a young lad
         there – could be providing them with the cohesion
         they need, but he's not even on the pitch.
Davy: Did you do that shirt for me?
Jenny: I'll do it tomorrow.
Hansen: There's no pride in the shirts any more, Des.
Jenny: Do you want something to eat?
Davy: Nah.
Hansen: He's lost the hunger he once had. I mean Dennis
         used to be a natural. They had an understanding.
         But now he hangs around the box from time to
         time, but there's no penetration. It doesn't look
         like he'll ever score again. Jenny's going to have to
         consider a plunge into the transfer market. But there's
         not much talent around Des. I believe there's been some
         speculation about the boy Frank. Although he's a bit
         flashy for me. Held be more likely to go to for one of the
         glamour sides. Are the glory days over for good? The
         pundits like nothing better than to predict the end of a
         team like this one, but maybe they'll come back to
         confound their critics.[30]

     The actor that played Hansen sat on a chair on the rear stage
right. The character of Hansen was signified by the actor's soft
Scottish voice and the football idiom, very familiar to a Merseyside
audience. The dramatic mode shifts from naturalism in its domestic
intimacy, phrasing and pace to something approaching "magical
realism", the fantastic imposition of a television commentator. This
involves an inversion of observer and observed and vice verse; a
transformation of frame, of perspective. In so doing the situation of
Jenny and Davy's relationship is given emotive force in the
replication of their dull interaction and foregrounded in humorous
terms by distanced narration. Applying the critical idiom of football
to relationships not only makes us laugh, because of the punning on
football and sexual vocabulary, but also allows a digestible, and

accessible because familiar, commentary on an important aspect of the story – Jenny's stale relationship, the possibility of an affair with Frank the bingo-caller and the problems with their computer obsessed anti-social son.

Communication Patterns in Cabaret Venues

With the intermingling of acting and audience areas in the crowded conditions of the venues, not all of the dramatic action could be seen or heard by all of the audience at one time. In the last act of *Eyes Down,* Jenny, (who has been made pregnant by the Bonanza bingo-caller) was going into labour on the rear stage right, whilst other important action was happening elsewhere. The director of *Eyes Down* noted how information was passed on from actor to spectator and then spectator to spectator:

> if people are sitting next to you ... a lot of information gets relayed back. Like the puffing and blowing when Jenny was in labour ... The nearest two people clocked that and then they do that *(he mimes turning round and nudging with elbow and pointing with a nod of the head to direct attention)* ... it was a tide...and the whole audience were encompassed. It was being filtered back.[31]

Freed from the conventions demanding inertness and near silence, spectators could take a greater part in the dynamics of the event; communication patterns could go far beyond the usual oblique communication from actor to spectator. These more unusual patterns were facilitated by the "sense of identity" which gave rise to a natural rapport between percipients. John Lipson, the *Eyes Down* director, described the role of one of the actors, Kellee Davies, at a venue in Halewood:

> ...[she] had right next to her three women who were obviously bingos [bingo players] who were constantly talking and she was milking that and telling them to – "sh! what's happening over there" – directing people where ... and when to look and people were coming to her and asking – "where is it now? Oh! Over there!" – using her as a way of accessing the play – "what have I

just missed then" – it wasn't directly part of the play, but Kellee was going – "well he thinks she's got AIDS and she doesn't think that" – like an action replay if you like...[32]

Davies was communicating indirectly, through the drama, and directly; so that the story was ostended and narrated simultaneously.

"Untrained" Audiences

The venues used by Response had a distinctive working class identity and clientele – like the R.A.O.B. "Buffs" Club in Kirkby.[33] Having played to the audiences in these venues the group seemed to be addicted to the spontaneous response they gave (even if it was, at times, negative). They felt that their working class audiences were untainted by "orthodox theatre training", had a highly developed taste in drama and entertainment and were extremely discriminating:

> People have come to expect polite audiences who sit in The [Liverpool] Playhouse and even if they're bored they don't say nothin' and they just go home and they don't say nothin' and everyone can live in this little dream world of theatre where it's all nice and polite...but like dead kinda thing...that's not real theatre as it was years ago or as it should be.[34]

How can this apparent paradox of "untrained" or "non-theatre" audiences actually making sophisticated spectators be explained? What level of demand did the variety of styles used in *Eyes Down* make upon spectators? In order to answer this question I will return to the "Alan Hansen commentary" which, as I have already suggested, exemplifies a skillful combination of dramatic modes but also provokes sophisticated performance dimensions for the actor/character. The Alan Hansen actor was also playing two other roles and was part of the chorus. Lipson remarked on the "quick gear changes of understanding"[35] required to consider an actor as: Dennis – Joan's violent husband, Alan Hansen – the caring football commentator, Ivor – the doorman, Ivor who breaks into a two line gag addressed directly to the audience, as an actor talking directly to spectators on the periphery of the action and then, as part of the chorus of "If I Won the National", singing the experiences of a woman. This is enjoyed, in John McGrath's words, "[not] because the ... audience is naively accepting"[36], on the contrary, the audience is able to read this lack of consistency because of its very sophistication.

Paul Cosgrove, an *Eyes Down* actor, commented on what he and many of the other actors felt were attributes peculiar to their audiences – the spectator's visceral understanding and spontaneous, unfiltered reaction. Again it is the strong feeling of shared experience between actors and audience:

> The violence,...the tranquillisers the bingo, everything within that was totally appreciated and understood, without saying hey let's analyse this play. They actually knew who the stories were about, where they come from and why it was being done.[37]

Having experienced this type of audience many of the Response members, although not all, were very dismissive of "theatre-trained" audiences. At the performance of *Eyes Down* in the Shaftesbury Hotel in the centre of Liverpool many Response actors felt that the audience was inferior, their reactions muted by middle class, liberal thinking. "Political Correctness" was frequently cited as an example of this. Only a few found performing outside home territory more challenging. For the majority city centre spectators were more inclined to be "analytical" and not to "let themselves go."[38] They were part of a world characterised as "cliquey", inward looking, elitist, "arty" whose product was "acting for other actors".

The Critical Relationship: Is Bingo a Bonanza?

Eyes Down, as I have already said, aimed both to celebrate the social and recreational nature of bingo and to present serious social issues relating to it. Bingo was not therefore unquestioningly accepted as part of Kirkby working class culture; its social function was scrutinised. The 'Bonanza Bingo Hall' was placed in its ideological frame as a combination of useful social space and a potentially harmful populist commercial venture. The realism at which *Eyes Down* aimed then was a critical realism.

The game of bingo is shown to be at best a pleasing diversion, and at worst a damaging narcotic and a surrender to fatalism. Women that become obsessed with bingo are shown to be misdirecting their energies. Joan is attracted to bingo for the wrong reasons – because of her sense of inadequacy, her feelings of failure as a mother and wife. She looks to the bingo hall not as entertainment and a safe place to socialise with other women, but as a way out of her financial problems and her unhappiness; as a way to become a better wife and mother.

Although the last act of *Eyes Down* centres on a £10,000 bingo game and the destinies of the three protagonists are seemingly tied to it; the dramatic action stops abruptly before the game ends and the audience never discover who wins. The play denies the game of bingo as a resolution of the protagonists' predicaments. Instead, closures are offered in the frame of the characters' quotidian life. Joan is shown seeking help from a credit union and a tranquilliser support group. The inference is that the real world of everyday life can never be entirely escaped; it has always to be returned to.

Offering closures to the dilemmas of the protagonists and possible solutions to their problems was a significant part of *Eyes Down*.[39] For John McGrath this is the first difference between working class popular theatre and orthodox theatre. He calls it "directness"[40] - people speaking their minds.

As we saw in the Alan Hansen section of *Eyes Down*, Response also try to foreground how and why things happen. By foregrounding crisis moments and making clear why they happened as they did, it offers the possibility of an alternative flow of events. The elements of celebration and realism are combined with a vision of "the world as changeable", an acknowledgement that alternatives are possible. Joan Manley, an *Eyes Down* performer, wanted to show that her character, 'Joan', had choices:

> That there are different ways to go instead of perhaps looking at Joan as the down-trodden woman, let's look at her... and say look here are the points that could have changed Joan's life.

The representation of life given then, is not just reflective, it has a reflexive action. *Eyes Down* also constitutes what "could" be: "It's not ... the raised fist still fighting... It's got to go beyond that." [41]

The Receptive Attitude of the Audience

Response obviously hoped that *Eyes Down* would have some kind of residual effect on its audiences. And I have suggested above some of the techniques *Eyes Down* used to that end. Further to that, I would like to offer some suggestions about a crucial factor affecting the potential efficacy – the receptive attitude of the audience. The nature of the venues provides some clues.

Establishing a good relationship with the audience in a non-theatrical venue is vital – conventional "theatre-audience behaviour" cannot be relied on. This can be facilitated by the visiting companies acceptance of the lay-out of the venue, as detailed above, which puts into play a type of venue powersharing between actors and spectators. The audience has "ownership" of the venue, so it controls the greater part of the theatrical dimension of the event. What is performed and how, is controlled by the theatre group. A settlement between the two groups, an agreement for co-operation, allows for the creation of a "trust relationship" – crucial if a group adopts a critical attitude to its audience or, as with *Eyes Down,* gives them information (about credit unions for example) without making it confrontational or patronising.[42]

The nature of audience's engagement with the drama is also qualified by the nature of the venues. If emotions are engaged, but involvement is continually disrupted by the cabaret theatrical features described above, in what way does the audience respond? John Fay, the *Eyes Down* script-writer, gave an insight:

> There are times when you're just ... well into what is happening
> ... you just forget ... but continually your undies get stuck up
> your crack or something and it'll bring you back to reality and
> I think that's always the case and that's a good thing. You don't
> need artificial devices ... particularly when you're performing in
> venues where the people are getting up constantly to go to the
> bar or to have a piss.[43]

In the dynamic informality of the cabaret venues, spectators are in a state of constant flux. Richard Schechner's description of the audience's involvement in environmental, theatre shares many characteristics with the *Eyes Down* performances:

> The audience...must look to itself, as well as to the performers ... This less sharply delineated division of roles, actions and spaces leads not to deeper involvement, not to a feeling of being swept away by the action – the bottomless empathy enhanced by darkness, distance, solitude-in-a-crowd, and regressive, cushioned comfort of a proscenium theatre – but to a kind of in-and-out experience; a sometimes dizzily rapid alternation of empathy and distance.[44]

Amateur Acting

This alternation of empathy and distance is enhanced by the amateur status of the *Eyes Down* actors and that amateur status is itself, a key element in Response's drive for efficacious theatre – both for spectators and for actors. Response's open-access policy means that having amateur actors with different levels of skill and experience is a given, but not one which has to be considered a limitation. Again, it is the proximity of cultural and quotidian life, a "familiarity factor", which is important – both for the efficacy, and also for the aesthetics of the event.

As the *Eyes Down* audience is never immersed in the fictional world, nor are the performers immersed "in character" – this would not have been congruous with the rapid transformations of role and entertainment mode. Consequently the shared experience of the performers and spectators, as people, was emphasised:

> It does make it a better theatrical experience for me if I can see the people beyond the characters ... You can go and watch a play and none of them [the actors] are recognisable as people ... they're just like these things saying lines that somebody else has written, getting deep into the character and all that, but it's all a little soulless ... I like to see the person... I don't think... actor[s] should submerge themselves completely ... when you see Ann

> [Quilliam, an *Eyes Down* actor] on stage, not particularly Ann
> but [as an example] ... to me she brings with her certain things,
> like she is a mother of two or three kids, who is in kinda middle
> age and you might see her in the town here shopping or
> something and that adds something for me rather than detracts.[45]

This is not to deny the importance of skill, but to recognise that the amateur community actor, locally known, is imbued with a strength of personality and an experience of life which can be a positive asset – she can add weight to the drama and make the audience more receptive to it:

> We've got people [actors] like people in the audience...members
> of their own family, friends, their work mates, voicing their
> experience, which makes you feel empowered... it makes you
> feel – "well I can do that as well" – There's no distance between
> me and this form of expression...And very often it encourages
> people to get involved...[to] express themselves.[46]

In purely aesthetic terms, amateur acting can also maximise the intrinsic pleasure based on the dual perception of and tension between, the real and fictional worlds, the character and actor, coexistent, standing side by side on stage.[47]

Although the participatory working methods of Response gave the *Eyes Down* performances many aesthetic advantages, it would be wrong to over-emphasise their importance. The "community" accent of Response directs the group towards being purposely process, not product, centred. There will always be therefore, tension between the requirements of their free participatory ethos as an amateur community theatre and their desire to give their local community quality entertainment. That both these desires exist in equal strength gives Response, I think, a remarkable quality. *Eyes Down,* so powerful because of the close relationship between cultural and quotidian life manifest in it, is also about that relationship. It is about the relationship between bingo halls and their working class clientele; and finally about the relationship between the working class of Kirkby and theatre.

Update, May 1995

In November/December 1994 Response presented a show about undertakers called A *Grave Mistake: A Dead Funny Play*. It followed the same development process as *Eyes Down,* had a cast of approximately 25 (nine of which were new members) and was performed in clubs and halls around Merseyside.

In 1995 the future of Response is in doubt. One member described it as being in a "permanently cocooned state.[48] Response has always been funded on a project by project basis. It was always reliant therefore on volunteer administrators to keep the company together between shows, to attract funding, sponsorship, etc. After eight years those volunteers are, understandably, unwilling to shoulder that responsibility. The company does not expect to receive revenue funding to support the employment of an administrator.

Notes

[1] This is the practice of, genuinely popular, (in the colloquial sense of the word), radicalised entertainment for working class audiences which has remained in opposition to, and radically different from, the character of mainstream theatre. It is what might be called "cabaret theatre" and it aims to offer both entertainment and challenging political perspectives. The characteristics of cabaret theatre are: the cabaret spatial design of the venues (several small stage areas with spectators arranged around tables instead of in ordered rows); the drinking, eating, smoking and socialising; the intimate atmosphere; the variety of performance arts utlised (acting, music, dance, stand-up comedy) and the narrative/storyline that utilises (and sometimes unifies, but not always) the variety elements. See John McGrath, *A Good Night Out* (Methuen, 1981) and Christine Hardy, "Keen Edge in Sheffield: Towards a Popular Political Theatre and Cabaret", *New Theatre Quarterly*, IX: 35.

[2] My study is based on three performances of *Eyes Down* that I saw and interviews and time spent with members of Response during May and June 1993.

[3] I am using an expanded version of Keir Elam's distinction between drama, the mode of stage fiction, and theatre, the performer-audience transaction. See Keir Elam, *The Semiotics of Theatre and Drama* (Methuen, 1980). By the "dramatic sphere", I mean the fictional realm of the play. By the "theatrical sphere", I mean the real, concrete world with which the dramatic co-exists.

The theatrical sphere contains the actors and spectators, the communication between them, what they bring from the quotidian world to the presentation/reception of the drama, the organisation of the event and everything about the venue and the vicinity. See also John McGrath (op.cit.) p.5

[4] "Percipients" means "all those present at a performance". See John O'Toole, *The Process of Drama: Negotiating Art and Meaning* (Routledge, 1992)

[5] John McGrath (op.cit.) p.58 lists "localism" as a marker of working class, as opposed to middle class, taste. Localism covers both subject matter, that which is anchored in a specific area (as opposed to what he terms bourgeois cosmopolitanism) and the "sense of identity" between audience and performers. I found cultural/quotidian proximity to be a nexus in the production and performance of *Eyes Down*. It was manifested in their ethos of participation by local people in acting directing, devising, writing and producing, in the nature of the chosen venues, the nature of amateur acting, the sense of identity between percipients at events, the subject matter and how it is presented. The nexus springs from the commitment to a "purposeful" or efficacious theatre, addressed to local concerns.

[6] Centre for Environmental Studies, *Kirkby Joint Study* (MS, Kirkby Public Library, 1982) p.12

[7] Government figures for unemployment in Kirkby in May 1993 were 30.2%. KUC estimated the real figure to be between 30-40%. A 1991 *Census Atlas of England* (SAUS Publications, University of Bristol, 1993)) found Knowsley to be the most deprived district in England.

[8] *Kirkby Joint Study* (op.cit.) p.72 & p.67

[9] Alison Jones, Knowsley Borough Council Arts Officer, interview, 21 July 1993

[10] Kirkby Response Theatre Annual Report (1993) back cover; programme notes, *Stop the War I Wanna Cop Off* (a Response adaptation of *Lysistrata*, performed June 1990-July 1990), Kirkby Response Theatre Archive, Kirkby Unemployed Centre; publicity leaflet (n.d.), Kirkby Response Theatre Archive.

[11] Kirkby is the size of a small town covering an area bordered to the north and east by greenbelt land, to the south by the East Lancashire Road and to the west by the M57 motorway. It has a population of approximately 50,000. Those re-housed in Kirkby by the LCC were primarily working class families with children from inner city slum areas such as Everton and Kirkdale. Ironically the, the LCC policy which broke-up many of the old working class communities post-war also served to create (contrary to intentions) a new

Xsingle-class community. *The Kirkby Joint Study* confirms Kirkby as "overwhelmingly working class" (p.14).

[12] Some members of Response consider theatre as a full-time career, for others it is a pastime. Some members worked full-time on the show. The only *Eyes Down* participants to be paid however were the band and the scriptwriter. Participants were:

Writer: John Fay. Director: John Lipson. Poster Design: Jim Scott. Lights: Nicky Patterson, Ian Laffrey. Music composition: Tony Barton. Lyrics: John Fay. Band: Mr Beat. Set design and props: Paula Rooney.

Performers: Cathy Bell, Sandra Bullock, Paul Cosgrove, Mark Cuddy, Carol Cullington, Kellee Davies, Jo Fitzsimmons, Geraldine Judge, Tina Kelly, Paula Loughlin, Angela McQueen, Christine McNamee, Joan Manley, Billy Naylor, Suzanne Palmer, Ann Quilliam, Howard Reeve, Jill Ridgeway, Dot Rotheram, Phil Savage.

Response have produced twenty-six shows since their foundation in 1987. All but two were newly written.

[13] KUC was founded following the 1981 March for Jobs as a response to the need for a trade-union type organisation for the unemployed. Its overtly non-sectarian "popular front" policy means that it is used by people of diverse political affiliations, although all could roughly be said to come under a progressive banner.

[14] Response developed from a KUC based writer's group. It is significant that Response originated in an initiative located inside the community and not as a result of an "arts intervention" by the arts authorities.

[15] The position of company administrator (needed for organisation and to attract funding and sponsorship) seemed to be the only one that needed to be filled professionally. Generally a volunteer takes on that role but because unpaid, such work is ad hoc.

[16] Geraldine Judge, interview, 22 June 1993. According to the 1982 household survey in the Kirkby Joint Study, 22% of Kirkby residents went to the bingo hall at least once in the month previous to the survey. The bingo hall registered as the fourth most popular place to visit after relatives, public houses/clubs and friends.

[17] Paul Cosgrove, interview, 25 June 1993

[18] *Eyes Down*, p.94

[19] See both John McGrath (op.cit.) p.57 and Christine Hardy (op.cit.) p.239

[20] Anne Quilliam, interview, 23 June 1993

[21] John Lipson, interview, 25 June 1993

[22] The venues were as follows:

1 May Kirkby Unemployed Centre, Westhead Ave, Kirkby
8 May Hale Village Hall, High Street, Hale
9 May Leisure Time Cabaret Club, Orrell Lane, Orrell
13 May R.A.O.B. Club (the "Buffs"), Gaywod Ave,
Southdene, Kirkby
14 May The Great Float Social Club, Seacombe, Wallesey
17 May St Peter's and St Paul's Social Club,
Towerhill, Kirkby
20 May Shaftesbury Hotel, Mount Pleasant, Liverpool
21 May Arncliffe Social Club, Arncliffe Road, Halewood
22 May Bootle Corporation Social Club, Stanley Road

[23] Actors used three platforms for stages – a slightly larger main stage, with two smaller platforms t the left and right at the rear of the room. They also frequently moved amongst the spectators.

[24] It lasted over three hours in performance, beginning at 7.30 or 8.00 p.m.

[25] The Leisure Time Cabaret Club, in Orrell and the Bootle Corporation Club in Bootle.

[26] Paul Cosgrove, interview, 23 June 1993

[27] Joan Manley, interview, 23 June 1993

[28] Peter Brook, *The Empty Space* (Penguin, 1972) p.74

[29] Des Lynam, BBC sports programme presenter. Alan Hansen is, of course, the ex-captain of Liverpool Football Club, Scottish international player and football pundit.

[30] *Eyes Down*, pp.21-23

[31] John Lipson, interview, 25 June 1993

[32] Ibid.

[33] R.A.O.B. stands for the Royal Order of Antediluvian Buffaloes. Commonly known as the "Buffs", it was described to me by a member as the "poor man's masons".

[34] John Fay, interview, June 1993

[35] John Lipson, interview, 25 June 1993

[36] See John McGrath's (op.cit.) discussion of this, pp.28-29

[37] Paul Cosgrove, interview, 25 June 1993

[38] John Fay, interview, June 1993

[39] The *Eyes Down* programme gave the addresses and telephone numbers of the Association of British Credit Unions and a tranquilliser addiction advice group. KUC itself accomodates a credit union.

[40] John McGrath (op.cit.) p.54

[41] Joan Manley, interview, 23 June 1993

[42] See John McGrath (op.cit.) p.99 and Baz Kershaw, "Poaching in Thatcherland: A Case of Radical Community Theatre", *New Theatre Quarterly* IX:34 ,p.131

[43] John Fay, interview, June 1993

[44] Richard Schechner, *Environmental Theatre* (Hawthorn Books, 1973) p.18

[45] John Fay, interview, June 1993

[46] John Lipson, interview, 25 June 1993

[47] Bert States, "The Dog on the Stage: Theatre as Phenomenon", quoted in John Birch, *The Language of Drama* (Macmillan, 1991) p.39, gives an exemplification of this phenomenon – the show stealing appearance of a real-life dog on stage. The warmth with which an audience receives a dog on stage is drawn from their pleasure at witnessing actions which are clearly not those of the fictional world (the dog is not an actor) yet are imbued with dramatic significance because it is "on stage" (it acquires actor status). See in contrast P.P. Howe (ed.), "Whether Actors Ought to Sit in Boxes?", *The Complete Works of William Hazlitt* (J.M.Dent, 1931) pp.272-279

[48] John Lipson, 24 May 1995

"Better a Bad Night in Toxteth": Black British Popular Theatre

Derrick Cameron

In the 1988 anthology of essays on Black Arts and Culture, *Storms of the Heart*, Jatinder Verma, the Artistic Director of Tara Arts theatre company, asked the question: "What is Black about Black Theatre? In other words, does the fact of Black performers on the stage, or of Black content, constitute the totality of Black theatre?".[1] If we rephrase the question by looking at specific types of theatrical production, is Black theatre defined by all-Black productions of "classic" plays set in a Black historical context? Or is it better defined more in terms of original and contemporary work, presented in a style that could be recognised and described as "Black"? And which of these – or even other approaches could truly described as "popular"? The one that makes a greater connection with its audience, or the one that generates the greater box-office takings?

As I hope to show in this paper, these issues are not new to Black British theatre: if anything, they reflect both the continual tensions as regards the identity of Black theatre in Britain, and also the struggle of Black theatre to gain recognition, acceptance, and financial and critical support in relation to the white community. In addition, I would like to explore the parallels between the search for a Black British theatre that is popular with its intended audience, and the work of John McGrath who, as a former director of the Scottish and English 7:84 theatre companies, has attempted to create and develop a distinct kind of popular theatre. If we refer – if only initially – to McGrath's 1981 book, *A Good Night Out*, as a guide, model and text of theatrical criticism, we can consider the examples and possibilities of a distinctly Black British Popular theatre.

Though McGrath only makes passing references to racism in his book, in doing so he does acknowledge that a theatrical experience for a Black audience member can be different from a white one. As he states in his opening chapter, "Behind the Clichés of Contemporary Theatre":

> ...this story we watch can have a meaning: a very specific meaning. What if we are black, say, and we go to see some splendidly effective, but completely racist theatre show?[2]

The question is stated, however, chiefly as part of a wider opening argument regarding the political nature of which stories are told in what way to which particular audience in a theatre. Indeed, the subtitle of *A Good Night Out – Popular Theatre: Audience, Class and Form* – indicates McGrath's own theoretical and political standpoint – that of a revolutionary socialist who believes in the class-based nature of economic, political, and – in the case of theatre – cultural struggle. Thus for McGrath the elements that make up what he calls "the theatre event" (the play, the cast, the size and location of the venue, the bar prices, the cost of the tickets, etc.) are, or can be, signifiers of class bias or class content, usually that of the bourgeois middle classes that constitute the traditional theatre-going audience.

According to McGrath, this occurs even when the form or content of the work appears to possess some radical, that is apparently authentic, working-class content. In his critical reconstruction of the Royal Court in 1956 – enshrined in theatrical and academic legend as the New Era of the Angry Young Man – McGrath argues that:

> What Osborne and his clever director Tony Richardson had achieved was a method of translating some areas of non-middle class life into a form of entertainment that could be sold to the middle classes.[3]

Or as Smith and Jones once deftly summarised it in a sketch: "Where's the fucking French windows?"

More importantly than the idea of anyone-for-bloody-tennis plays, McGrath also argues that the apparently "new" audience for these works were "absorbing as many of the values of the middle class as possible, and contributing one or two new ones of their own to the reformation of middle class behaviour that was necessary if the middle class were to survive."[4] Thus the hegemony of middle class dramatic form, content, style, performance, and theatre-going rituals perpetuated itself, to the exclusion of any other approach.

By contrast, McGrath identifies both a working-class audience and theatre that has been ignored and/or patronised by critics and writers alike:

> I do believe that there is a working-class audience for theatre in Britain which makes demands, and which has values, which are different from those enshrined in our idealised middle-class audience. That these values are no less ëvalid' – whatever that means – no less rich in potential for a thriving theatre-culture, no thinner in ëtraditions' and subtleties than the current dominant theatre-culture, and that these values and demands contain within them the seeds of a new basis for making theatre that could in many ways be more appropriate to the last quarter of the twentieth century than the stuff that presently goes on at the National Theatre, or at the Aldwych.[5]

If we refer to McGrath's initial connections with the Everyman Theatre in Liverpool we can find more concrete examples of this contrast. He compares visiting the theatre in 1968-9, and witnessing "a highly pretentious piece of avant-garde whimsy, the hero of which was a pair of Siamese twins dressed in green and purple satin" – and from which he left early – with seeing a play about local Labour MP Bessie Braddock a year later in autumn 1969. This McGrath regarded as "a bit more to the point, and at least something to do with Liverpool". More crucially, the style of the Braddock show was influenced by the work of Joan Littlewood and Theatre Workshop. McGrath's subsequent involvement with the Everyman as a writer resulted in as body of work that succeeded in attracting a large local working-class following to the Everyman, as opposed to those who, according to McGrath, "had the Playhouse in the centre of town with the West End, and occasional Royal Court plays to go and see." [6]

McGrath combines the actual practice of the plays in production with a number of theoretical and practical models: a working men's club in Chorlton-cum-Hardy, Manchester; traditional pantomime; rock concerts; the historical antecedents of agit-prop groups like the Russian Blue Blouses; and the work of Brecht, Piscator and Theatre Workshop. Using these influences, McGrath cites nine key differences between what he sees as "the demands and tastes of bourgeois and working class audiences."[7] To run through them quickly, they are:

1. **directness**, in that a working class audience prefers clarity of opinion to inference and ambiguity;
2. the use of **comedy**, which is no barrier to seriousness of purpose;
3. the use and presence of music (especially folk or pop.)
4. **emotion**, or an audience's openness to honest and direct emotional expression on stage;
5. **variety** of material and style;
6. effect, or the moment-to-moment impact of a show;
7. the **immediacy** of the material in relation to an audience's lives;
8. the **localism** of the dramatic material; and lastly
9. **localism**, as defined by McGrath as a sense of identification with the performer and, presumably, vice versa.

Consequently, McGrath's work at the Everyman, and with the two 7:84 companies, all attempt to feature or utilise many or all of these elements in his development of a distinct and autonomous working-class theatre.

All of what I've described so far is a somewhat necessary prelude to the rest of this paper, as meanwhile, at roughly the same time in the early 1970s, the first real beginnings of Black British theatre were occurring in London. For this paper I will focus on two contrasting companies whose work has been documented, if only briefly: the Dark and Light Theatre of Brixton, and a local community group from London, the Fasimbas. But before I do that, I wish briefly to draw attention to one key area of apparent difference between McGrath's working class theatre and Black British theatre, namely that of integrated, or non-traditional casting. Though the subject could provide for a paper of its own, the basic issue at stake in integrated casting – that of an end to discrimination within the acting profession – cannot be over-emphasised. The demand that Black performers should be able to play whatever parts in a drama alongside their white colleagues in any theatrical production is a vital part of the history of Black theatre in Britain, and is a counterpart to the struggles against racial discrimination in society at large. It must be noted, however, that the practice of integrated casting has become as much a means of demanding access to the "classics" of English and European drama as it is a means of ensuring equal opportunities. For some directors and performers, this is a necessary process if Black people are to achieve their due and rightful position within British theatre: as the Black actress Dona Croll stated in relation to playing Cleopatra, "I can warble Shakespeare as well as Juliet Stevenson."[8] For others, it merely represents an abandonment of Black audiences and identity in the pursuit of some form of acceptance by a potentially unappreciative white audience. As Kwesi Owusu argues:

> the demand for more integrated casting of Black actors and actresses, through the Actors' Union, Equity and the Campaign for Equal Opportunities in the Arts, is more appropriate to the 1940s and 50s than to the 1980s. So too is the constant, understandable urge to "prove" oneself by playing the major roles of the European classical theatre. Such demands and desires are not, strictly speaking, part of the dynamics of a Black theatre. they are part of the old beaten track of Black people seeking to operate within white British theatre.[9]

There is perhaps in Owusu's last point an echo of McGrath's argument as regards the number of working class actors and directors who were absorbed into the mainstream theatre and its value system, though inevitably a Black performer's racial identity is ineradicable and ineluctable compared to, say, a working class non-metropolitan accent. Nonetheless the issue of integrated casting does connect to notions of what constitutes Black British popular theatre. Similarly, the work of the Dark and Light theatre and of the Fasimbas in the early 70s highlights a similar tension between divergent theatrical approaches.

In the 1976 Commission for Racial Equality report, The Arts Britain Ignores, Naseem Khan wrote:

The idea of the Dark and Light was first floated by the ebullient Jamaican actor, Frank Cousins, at a press conference in 1970. By the following year a building had been found, with the help of Lambeth Borough Council. Longfield Hall, situated on the fringes of Brixton, was a large outdated council hall. In that year (with Arts Council support of £1,000), the first production was mounted – Athol Fugard's The Blood Knot, a play about the tensions between two brothers (one black, the other passing as white) in South Africa. The audience – apart from official well-wishers and friends – was predictably small: not surprising for a new venture. However, it never appreciably rose for all the theatre's three and a half years of life.

Khan goes on to search for possible reasons for the company's failure. Surprisingly, she downplays the politics, policies and preconditions surrounding the company's funding. Instead, she focuses on what in a musical context would be called A & R – Audience and Repertoire. She writes:

> The answer lies not in who did (or didn't) so what. It lies more in definition. Frank Cousins was being asked to do what he was never by nature equipped to do – to discover a form of theatre for non-theatre going community audiences and to popularise it locally. It was rather like asking a hare to enter a high-jump race. To be fair to the funders, however, Cousins did also voluntarily enrol himself in the race.

If the previous quote partially explains the nature of the audience at the time, it does not explain who that audience was or what it did or did not respond to. Taking the latter point first, since any audience needs a repertoire of some sort to respond to, Khan argues that Cousins crucial mistake was to believe he could draw a non-theatre-going urban Black audience with material such as The Blood Knot: in other words, with a repertoire and approach drawn from the world of "proper" or professional theatre, Whilst the aim is laudable, not least in its attempt to provide substantial roles for professional Black actors, Khan's comments make it clear that the approach was both alien and alienating to its intended audience. As Khan notes:

Black members of audiences frequently disliked plays. "Raas" (a sentimental picture of a so-called archetypal West Indian family, by a white American academic) was booed off the stage in Birmingham, an audience reaction with which one can sympathise.[12]

By way of contrast, Khan mentions two occasions where the Dark and Light did attract a capacity audience. Significantly, they were both pantomimes based on the West Indian Anansi folk tales, the first of which – which set the figure of Anansi the Spiderman in Brixton – Khan describes as ìthe most original thing Dark and Light ever did".[13]

Given that pantomime was one of the models or influences McGrath cites for a popular working class theatre, we can begin to see both the reasons for the Dark and Light's failure with its target audience, as well as the overlap between class and race in the preferred forms and kinds of theatrical experience of that same audience. The codes and conventions of the traditional (that is, middle class) theatre event did not apply in this instance because the audiences clearly weren't inculcated with them. Equally, the contrast between the reception of a play set in and about South Africa and a play set in and about Brixton is telling as regards the immediacy of the material that the audiences enjoyed responding to – the same immediacy and localism that McGrath claims as an element of working class theatre.

The way this theoretical overlap works out in practice is best demonstrated by Khan's description of her attendance at a Sunday night performance by the Fasimbas, a Lewisham social action group, in 1971:

I have rarely been present at a more exciting occasion. The audience was very mixed age-wise – parents and aunties were there in force – and at first a bit restive during an exposition of the facts of slavery. But then the group got into the meat of the show – a series of witty, affectionate, factually-based sketches: back in the Caribbean being conned with visions of golden streeted England, goggle-eyed on arrival in London, being conned with visions of an exploited minister in a Pentecostal

Church (shrieks at this from the audience, eyes streaming, thighs slapped -'Oh Lord' – till the cast could barely continue). Then a family scene showing parents much disturbed by their children's political involvement. The youngsters explain why it is a necessary commitment. The parents listened. Not only the parents on stage, but the whole audience listened attentively to the arguments. Maybe with some it was the first time that they had heard their consternation expressed and dealt with respectfully. You could have heard a pin drop.

The play itself was roughly acted; direction was unsophisticated. But it made for a stunning evening that could not fail to have impressed everyone there. The contrast between that and the Dark and Light productions could not have been more marked.

The reasons are not hard to find. The Fasimbas were all known in their community. They had a following ranging from political confreres to parents, relatives and family friends. They were also very aware of the issues of the black working class situation, involved as they were in Saturday Schools truancy programmes and other forms of community action. But they had also had the vision to present them in a form that was accessible, vivid and immensely funny, without dodging the issue at all, The Fasimbas knew what they wanted, who their audience was, and how to speak to it. The Dark and Light – for all its undoubted labour never worked that one out.[14]

I think it is useful to quote the extract at length because it both describes and summarises a clearly successful attempt at a Black British Popular theatre. Many of the elements McGrath cites are contained in Khan's description, as well as a political/revolutionary dimension that was common to McGrath's work with 7:84. The one element not cited by Khan is the use of music, which is surprising, given the long, diverse, and extremely rich tradition of Black music, whether it is Reggae, Rap or Jungle. Nonetheless, Khan's description of the evening makes it clear that the Fasimbas had – accidentally or deliberately – found a way of making theatre that connected directly to its audience, however "raw" the material, though "rawness" may only be discernible by slicker, more professional standards and values.

Given that the examples of the Dark and Light and the Fasimbas are both over twenty years old, it is of course necessary to look at what has happened since. Without wishing to enter into a lengthy or detailed history of the intervening years, I would argue that the tension between the approaches of the Dark and Light and the Fasimbas has neither disappeared nor been resolved, despite the many advances that black performers, directors and writers have made since. If anything, these advances have not only resulted in a greater pool of Black talent, but it has also resulted in a greater presence of that talent within mainstream theatre. We can see Josette Simon in Arthur Miller's *After the Fall*, or an all-black cast in *Antony and Cleopatra* at the Everyman, or a new Black writer's latest play at the Royal Court. There is a sense that the mainstream is final accepting and embracing Black people – maybe.

I say maybe because Arthur Miller is, after all, a white American playwright, Shakespeare a long-dead white playwright and epitome of certain ideas of "Englishness", and the Royal Court a key venue for new – and predominantly white – playwriting. To what extent do any of these examples connect with a mass Black audience? Or reflect Black experience? Here in Liverpool, I have seen August Wilson's play *Fences* at the Playhouse and Talawa's *Antony and Cleopatra* at the Everyman. Both shows were well attended, but not by a predominantly Black audience. Similarly, two Temba shows at the Unity have been less well attended, even by Black audiences. Is this a failure of marketing, or have we failed to learn the lessons from the Dark and Light Theatre? Is the only difference between then and now the growth and development of a Black audience who have become inculcated with the middle class conventions of the theatre event as McGrath's contemporaries did in the 1950s? An interview given by Temba's Artistic Director Alby James in 1992 seems to bear me out:

> Temba was created in 1972. It was considered an alternative
> company. its audience was often termed "black". In reality
> Temba's audience was white, liberal, middle-class

predominately universitycentred. As the years went by, some black community centres became established on the regional touring circuit. Temba visited those places. The audiences who came there were, on the whole, black, middle-class, with some black and African students coming as well.[15]

It would seem that the bells and smells of High Culture still surround the form content and theatre-going experience of seeing *Fences*, *Antony and Cleopatra* or a Temba touring show. Indeed Temba's long-term aim of moving into the mainstream via productions of plays such as *Romeo and Juliet* and *Ghosts* was only restricted by the funding policies of the Arts Council, who eventually cut off their grant. In other words, a generation of trained and skilled theatre professionals, allied to policies of integrated casting and some measure of socio-economic progress, has resulted in making some Black theatre acceptable to the mainstream/middle class/white theatre-goers, whilst also giving the war-horses of Western drama a funky new beat to dance to. At worst it could be called a form of theatrical "crossover" that abandons its original audience.

Yet it is this theatre, and those black writers who are working in or towards the mainstream, that has received the bulk of critical attention via reviews and articles, just as McGrath argues that middle class theatre presents itself as the theatre. The difficulty is that Black audiences are not necessarily taking any notice, just as the Dark and Light's audience stayed away from its shows, apart from the pantomimes. Similarly, there is a separate strand of popular Black theatre that exists, often well away from even the London fringe, and like McGrath's working class theatre it draws on similar elements to entertain and address its constituency directly. Possibly the best known recent example of this approach is the work of The Posse, a group of Black actors formed in 1992. Fascinatingly, the style of their work closely echoes that of the Fasimbas: a variety of sketches featuring recognisable aspects of Black life. Having seen their show *Armed and Dangerous* at the Everyman, I could even echo Naseem Khan's enthusiastic response to the atmosphere of such an occasion: the sense of a packed, knowledgeable, vociferous Black audience enthusiastically responding to material that related to their lives in a way that Shakespeare could only ever address obliquely, if at all. The Posse have also performed a Christmas show – *Pinchy Kobi and the Seven Duppies* – with distinct echoes of *A Christmas Carol*, and there is also a parallel all-female comedy team called The Bibi Crew, working in a similar style from a Black woman's perspective. Both companies are proving extremely popular and exciting in a way that cannot simply be explained by getting the benefit of good reviews in the mainstream press.

The work of The Posse and The Bibi Crew are just two examples of a Black British theatre that is less reliant on proving its artistic credentials to the mainstream than on making a commitment to entertaining the community it comes from. In some ways this work represents a recognition that the mainstream seems capable of only accommodating Black theatre so far and no further, in a similar fashion to society as a whole. As The Posse's slogan put it: "There's no justice – just us". Yet the emergence of The Posse has to be seen, as I have tried to demonstrate, as a recognition of the overlap in popular theatre between class and race – more Stratford E15 than Stratford-upon-Avon. Having witnessed the poor attendance at some Temba shows in Liverpool, it does not surprise me that the Unity has gone "off-site" in order to reach a Black audience. McGrath himself described such a situation in 1975:

> The point really is that the National Theatre and the Aldwych have got the facilities for very exciting work, with the workshops and everything else. But it's that "everything else" that would make me run ... I'd rather have a bad night at Bootle. You get more from it if somebody's going to come up at the end and say, do you know what's happening in Bootle? You see they're being amalgamated with Southport, and Southport is a big Tory stronghold, so the people of Bootle are being ripped off...[16]

McGrath's point would equally hold true for Toxteth. So too, perhaps, does the kind of popular working-class theatre he developed at the Everyman and with 7:84. In some ways the journey from the Fasimbas to The Posse may seem a circular one, but I feel it rather marks the parting of the ways. To paraphrase Sandy Craig in the book *Dreams and Deconstructions* on the one hand we have Black plays that form part of a middle class play-going experience, and on the other a Black theatre that is aimed at and appeals to a working class Black constituency.[17] A bad night in Toxteth may be disappointing, but it may prove far more informative than watching Lenny Henry playing Hamlet at the Playhouse.

Notes

[1] Kwesi Owusu, *Storms of the Heart: An Anthology of Black Arts and Culture* (Camden Press, 1988) p.193

[2] John McGrath, *A Good Night Out: Popular Theatre, Audience, Class and Form* (Methuen, 1981) p.2

[3] Ibid. p.10

[4] Ibid. p.12

[5] Ibid. p.4

[6] Ibid. p.50

[7] Ibid. p.54

[8] Kate Miller, "No Colours Barred", *The Stage* (9th May 1991)

[9] Kwesi Owusu, *The Struggle For Black Arts in Britain: What Can we Consider Better Than Freedom* (Comedia, 1986) p.93

[10] Naseem Kahn, *The Arts Britain Ignores: The Arts of the Ethnic Minorities in Britain* (Commission for Racial Equality, 1976) pp. 112-113

[11] Ibid. p.113

[12] Ibid. p.114

[13] Ibid. p.113

[14] Ibid. p.114

[15] Sandy Carpenter "Black and British Temba Forges the Mainstream: An Interview With Alby James", *Drama Review* 34:1 (Spring 1990) pp 28-35

[16] Catherine Itzin, *Stages in the Revolution: Political Theatre in Britain Since 1968* (Methuen, 1980) p.125

[17] Sandy Craig, *Dreams and Deconstructions: Alternative Theatre in Britain* (Amber Lane Press, 1980) pp. 30-31

Popular Theatre and Participation in the Work of John Godber

David Llewellyn

It is difficult to conceive a model of contemporary popular theatre that excludes the work of John Godber. His output as a playwright, artistic director and actor with the Hull Truck Theatre company exemplifies a search for a popular live theatre. Godber ranks alongside Willy Russell as the most performed contemporary British playwright. His work has proved popular from the village hall to the West End. The content of his plays are full of the stuff of popular culture and the narrative styles are likewise influenced by popular form.

Ironically, his credentials as a popular playwright have been strengthened by the fact that his work has been either been shunned or ignored by the critical establishment. On the one hand, there are the apologists of the "great tradition" who regard his work as "low culture" and therefore unworthy of academic scrutiny and on the other the "textualists of popular culture" who remain suspicious of the work's moral credentials. Melvin Bragg's recognition of his work in an *Arena* documentary went some way towards redressing the balance in favour of a playwright who for the past decade has been responsible for some of the most innovative successful work in the field of popular drama.

When it comes to definition there is a certain irony implicit in the terminology invented or appropriated by our critical academic culture. The process of analysis, reflection and thesis, which aims towards new insight and understanding, often conceals more than it reveals. It seems to me there are two schools of obfuscation: The first, the Anglo-American, invents jargon to conduct its "cerebrations"; a language that can be only understood by the initiate.The second, the Anglo-European, takes the vernacular, in this instance the word "popular" and redefines it to describe theatre forms that are in terms of popular appeal often anything but. In this case the irony is compounded as the popular theatre in question intends to ideally engage a wider constituency of the population than the minority middle class audience that regularly attend live theatre.

This ideal, to produce accessible theatre has consistently informed John Godber's work with Hull Truck and likewise this attempt to explore the idea of a Popular Theatre. The following analysis aims to identify and unravel an aesthetic, illustrated by his work that engages an audience in a distinct popular participatory experience of theatre.

Taking a cue from Grotowski, I am satisfied by his conclusion that theatre exists at the moment an actor performs before an audience and describes what happens during that interaction. Therefore, the idea of a Popular Theatre implies a specialized interaction that distinguishes it from the currency of the serious theatre of high culture and its traditional audience.

It is beyond the scope of this paper to detail the playwright's complete works. Though I intend to reference a range of his plays, my particular focus will be on *Bouncers*. The evolution of the stage play into a television drama, *The Ritz* (1989), was a natural development of a work that had evidenced such popular appeal. However, the dichotomy of its reception highlights the cultural conflict that informs a significant debate in this field.[1]

I am aware of the pratfalls of an argument that asserts John Godber's work and his play *Bouncers* as a singular paradigm of Popular Theatre, forms of which, both historical and contemporary are legion. Scholars have identified a popular theatre culture as having a legacy in the West longer than the high cultural form that marks its genesis with the literary theatre of Hellenic Greece. In Africa, the Orient and amongst the indigenous cultures of the Americas, forms of popular participatory drama and ritual have been identified as existing for centuries. In this country an impressive range of popular theatre form has been evident. The Melodrama, the Music Hall and their contemporary doubles the Musical and the Pantomime continue to dominate the mainstream.

In the established playhouses, however, the viability of participatory community drama is, on occasion, tried out. The Liverpool Playhouse, under the commercially minded management of Bill Kenwright, has recently staged successfully *Fall from Grace*

(1995), a work whose roots lie in the history of Liverpool's Irish. The process of its creation, under the artistic direction of local playwright and director, Andrew Sherlock, engaged the community and in performance provided an experience that was both participatory and popular, the audience ultimately joining with the cast in a traditional Irish dance.

The radical theatre and theory of Brecht advocates a popular ideal and informed the best of British political theatre in the seventies and eighties. Many of these texts engage forms of popular entertainment to make the theatrical experience "a good night out" for an audience who no longer finds one in the literary theatre of high culture.

The community plays of Ann Jellicoe, the celebratory forms of Welfare State International, the recent influence of Boal's revolutionary poetic and it's applications can all claim a popular mission; as can thousands of amateur theatres across the land in which theatre is experienced in a profoundly popular way. When the Alhampton Village Players of Somerset present Wilde's *Importance of Being Earnest* the production values and the aesthetics are largely irrelevant to the theatrical experience in the village hall. In this context the currency of exchange between stage and audience is revalued by the relationship of the players to the spectators, the quality of craftsmanship and the cultural status of the text being subsumed by the event having a symbolic function that unites and celebrates a village community.

Mass participation distinguishes popular cultural activity from high art. In the theatre this is demonstrated in the enduring vitality of the pantomime and in occasional works, such as Richard O'Brien's *Rocky Horror Show* (1970) in which the audience "takes part" in the event. The idea of an audience that "takes part" in the act of theatre is central to my analysis. The popular playwright then is one whose scripts and production rhetoric not only recognize popular culture but more significantly engage the audience in an event. My contention is that John Godber's theatre, in particular, *Bouncers,* does just that.

The background and motives behind John Godber's work are illuminating in this context. The son of a miner from the village of

Minsthorpe in West Yorkshire he was brought up and educated in a working class community. Unlike many working class writers like Alan Bennett or Dennis Potter, John Godber is not a product of the state grammar school and of Oxford University. His education at Minsthorpe Comprehensive School was marked by the formative experience of visiting the local teacher training college, Bretton Hall, in a school party to watch a student festival that was featuring a selection of Harold Pinter's early plays.

The impact of that night and the inspiration of the school's drama teacher led him to want a career in drama. When he expressed a desire to study drama at college he was ridiculed by many members of his community. In a recent interview I had with him he told me that people in his village couldn't understand his ambition. He quoted me a line from one of his friends of the time that seemed to sum up the antipathy, "The theatre, it's boring, it's not a place for us and not a place for a man". He resolved at that time to make a theatre that would appeal to his local community; a theatre full of humour that would stage material which was relevant and recognisable to the daily lives and concerns of his community and class. He wanted to put on plays that were loaded with the popular culture of the people that he knew, respected and cared for.

Bretton Hall provided the environment for Godber's creativity to flourish in an educational context that encouraged experimentation and production. It was here that he explored the theatrical means that were later to become the trademarks of his work. His natural gifts of storytelling, his ear for the poetic rhythms of dialogue, his sense of humour and bitter sweet perception of the human condition found a facilitating form in the actor centred style of physical theatre that was introduced to him at college. *Bouncers*, which was originally written as a performance vehicle for two players, had it's earliest incarnation whilst he was still studying at Bretton(1976).

The play, which is now a four hander, is "about working class Britons at play".The connection between popular cultural behavior and style are immediately evident in the opening movement. Four actors, dressed in the costume of night club doormen, introduce the idea to the audience that they are going to tell a story of contemporary urban night life.The style is borrowed from the popular form of rap:

We four will try and illustrate
The sort of thing that happens late
At night in every town
When the pubs are shut
And the beers been downed

I said Hip Hop
A Hippy A Hippy
A Hip Hip Hop and don't you stop

However, this prologue is not the true beginning of the play. Godber's stage directions indicate that the audience is prepared for an *event* rather than an artwork that will appear from behind plush curtains:

> As the audience enters, the music plays, the lights flash and the bouncers establish the mood of the evening; walking up and down the aisles, generally surveying people, ushering them to their seats, passing the occasional threatening comment, etc.

This interaction with an audience immediately establishes a sense of *participation*. The fourth wall is ignored the whole auditorium is the playing space and the spectators are participants in an event. This sense of participation is taken onto another level by the style of the play which requires the actors to portray over thirty different characters in a variety of locations without changes of costume and only the minimum of prop signifiers – four red handbags are usually the only accessories necessary. The audience has not merely to suspend disbelief, while their imaginations are furnished with realistic sets, they are required to creatively participate in the construction of the fictional world in which the play takes place. I maintain that this is far more significant to the popular aesthetic that Godber achieves in his work than the quotient of popular culture that infuses the content of this or other works.

However, the play is located firmly in the context of contemporary popular culture. The author's note in the published version encourages would be producers to "keep it alive for today" by updating the references and the musical framework. In this way, Godber recognizes the need and the theatrical efficacy of confronting and referencing contemporary culture.

After the first transition from the Bouncers Rap into a radio broadcast the audience discovers the second transition to be a radio playing in a ladies hairdressers where the four male performers are playing the girls getting a hairdo in the local salon. The scene is full of topical popular references. The published version's references to the Radio One disc jockeys; Steve Wright, Bruno Brooks and Gary Davies as the author suggests need to be updated to connect with the lived experience of the audience. The rapid speed of scene change and character transition is in accordance with a cinematic tradition. Again from the authors note:

> Directors of the play should never think of Chekhov; rather, they should think of cartoons and cinematic techniques.

This fast cutting style is accessible to the experience of an audience whose aesthetic sensibilities have been framed by television and film.

The significant difference, however, from the conventions of the screen is where the strength of Godber's popular theatre writing lies. There is the essential theatricality to *Bouncers* and Godber's vision that makes it popular and participatory. Unlike cinema and television the audience is drawn into a creative act in which the mimetic signifiers on stage act as a catalyst to the imagination to design the scene. In this instance the mime of the hairdo is often taken in production to absurd extremes suggesting a ten foot beehive rearing precariously from 'Maureens'/Lucky Eric's head while Suzy's hair goes up in flames under the hairdryer. Godber's theatre, like the imagination, inhabits both the real and the fantastic and the production rhetoric is as significant in sealing a mutual interaction with the audience as is the structure and the language of the playtext.

The narrative style Godber employs blends stand up comic routines with epic interventions that always remain aware of, and above all speak directly to, its audience. Lucky Eric's speeches cut across the comic tone of the lads and lasses night out and the bouncers banter like a chill wind. He offers no answer to the nightmare world of contemporary human degradation he describes but his humanity and realism redresses the grotesque comic world that surrounds him:

> *(A spotlight picks out Lucky Eric. He speaks directly to the audience).*
> Lucky Eric: We have these "Miss Wet T Shirt" and "Miss in String" evenings. Eighteen year old beauties displaying their orbs through string vest or firm outlines on wet cotton, naked some of them, save their skimpy knickers. All of them somebody's daughter – mothers some of them. And the glossy Polaroids on the doors outside show more hideous antic. Breasts in beer glasses. Breasts smeared in shaving foam. Breasts oiled and on show. And Michael Dee, the D.J. kisses and sucks as if they were his own. Slimy bastard. I see the girls selling themselves for five minutes of fame. I can see the staid state of exploitation. I can even smell the peaches of their underarm roll-on. The working class with no option left, exposing its weakness. I feel very sad ... I feel very protective. I might pack it all in. I might pack it all in, fuck off and go and listen to Frank Sinatra.

The ambivalence of this monologue both in terms of the character of Eric and its tonal shifts confronts the audience with the serious side of Godber's social critique, what he calls the "warning". The uncompromising honesty of the speech that integrates a disturbing sensual obsession, a desire to protect and a hopeless disillusion in the state of his class hints at the drama of social criticism rather than the celebratory comic form normally associated with popular theatre. In effect all of Eric's speeches work like interludes counterpointing and providing relief to the action packed popular comedy that is *Bouncers*.

The last illustration from *Bouncers* that I want to draw on to support my point of view concerns an anecdote told by the playwright of an audience member who complained about a scene in the play set at the men's urinals in which "the lads" take a break to relieve their beer stretched bladders. Three actors establish the urinal facing the audience miming their excretions while the fourth narrates the fetid state of the male toilets late on in the evening.

The action concludes with a sharp piece of observation: The lads secretly eyeing up each other's relative penis sizes. The movement climaxes in comic envy and horror at the huge construction indicated by the actor playing Ralph. The incident was described by a shocked audience member as "the most disgusting exhibition he had ever witnessed on an English stage". The temptation to claim Artaudian transubstantiation is almost irresistible. For him at least the symbol had indeed become reality. His imagination was clearly working overtime on the realization of Ralph's appendage. However, the degree to which the style acts as a catalyst to the creative participation of an audience, is evident.

In *Bouncers* the level of physical participation by the audience is limited. However, *Up and Under* (1984), a play set in the world of amateur rugby league, was written with the playwright's express purpose of attracting a local community audience to the Spring Street Theatre and succeeds in effecting a level of physical participation congruent with the popular experience of spectating at a match.

As in *Bouncers* the subject matter of the play and narrative form are deliberately chosen to reflect the popular culture of the audience. In *Up and Under* the context of amateur rugby league is integral to the popular culture of the locality near Hull. The plot references, and is structurally influenced by Silvester Stalone's *Rocky* films. The content and the form are familiar to his intended audience but the crucial feature of the play in production and the reason why the theatrical experience is popular is that it climaxes in an event in which the audience participate spontaneously identifying themselves as the a crowd of supporters cheering their side while six men and a woman enact both teams on a green carpet in a theatre.

Godber's plays have no great message spelt out in them. He expresses none of the vaulting ambition of Boal's revolutionary aesthetics. At one level he tells stories that are both funny and sad and sometimes unashamedly sentimental. The recent long run of *April in Paris* (1992) on tour and in the West End is recent evidence of the efficacy of this form. This two hander is acted on a small white square against a minimal backdrop. The square becomes the living room, the boat and the streets of Paris in the minds of its audience. Thus, the actor centred theatre style that Godber employs in his most innovative work facilitates a popular experience of theatre. The content and the narrative style give access to the popular experience of theatre but the production rhetoric of an actor centred physical theatre allows the audience room for their imaginations to work towards an experience of theatre as popular event in which they are true participants.

Notes

[1] The high culture/low culture debate was exemplified by events surrounding the planned second series of *The Ritz*. Pebble Mill received more letters of appreciation from the public than were received for the acclaimed *Boys from the Blackstuff*. The viewing figures were excellent. However, in the light of severe criticism from the executive levels of the corporation (Richard Attenborough & Richard Eyre) who "loathed" the work, the second series was axed.

Popular Theatre: The Case for Redevelopment

Tim Prentki

Some of the recent pronouncements of the Government reveal an intention to extend its ideological activity more vigorously into areas of social policy additional to its current obsession with crime. Some of us might be inclined to the view that the Government has done more than enough since 1979 to damage the social fabric without wreaking further havoc on the welfare state in order to demonstrate to an increasingly sceptical Party that there is still more work for the New Right before the Tories have finished building Mahagonny in England's green and pleasant land. This process mainly consists of the search to find new things to privatise and privatisation is itself predicated on the notion that a market value can be established for all transactions, not just those formerly assigned to the sector of economics, and further, that a profit can be gleaned from these transactions. It follows that in such an ideology culture is conceived not as a dialectical relationship between different groups within society making meanings and communicating them to each other, but as a commodity which can be marketed by an individual or institution for sale to as many other individuals as possible. This notion accounts for the process by which history is perverted into Heritage, theatre into classics for tourists or 'A' level consumption and art a series of commodities passing through an auction room.

In the field of culture there is a profound contradiction, though it is one which the ideologues of the Right have generally hidden effectively. The elevation of the "free market" to sacred status, the reinstatement of the moneylenders to the Temple, has created a society driven by the ethics of competition and the demands of individual choice based on payment. This is the ideology of *laissez faire,* the Victorian value so beloved of this regime. However, for this ideology to be inscribed effectively on the consciousness of its victims, a sustained campaign is required through all those channels of discourse by which people adopt the values of the dominant group. Whereas a democratic government may attempt to exert some controls on the economic sphere while adopting a hands-off approach to that of culture, the righteous Right buttresses its free market by seeking control of those institutions concerned with the making of meanings, such as schools, universities, broadcast agencies and theatres. Hence the rapid moves made by successive Thatcher Governments to put their own people into institutions like the BBC and the Arts Council.

It must therefore be evident that such institutions are unlikely to sponsor the kind of work which attempts to enlist its audience's support for counterhegemonic practices. The hands-off approach to subsidy which characterised the 1960s and 1970s and gave rise to radical practices in alternative theatre and occasionally in the BBC, disguised the dependent relationship of these producers of counter-hegemonic meanings to their apparently benign masters. Lacking any access to the means of independent sustainability the likes of 7:84 Theatre Company and the Wednesday Play could vanish almost without trace. The same fate befell so many of the radical cultural activities that were born of the *largesse* and excess of that period. If a genuinely popular theatre is to be created which does not subscribe to the dictates of the dominant, it will have to be set up on a different basis.

By popular I understand work that is generated by and performed to ordinary people, recognising their social reality and created out of the conviction that this reality is in a constant process of change. The challenge of popular theatre is to enable those who make it and those who watch it, in terms of status the same people, to become the agents not the victims of that change. The need for counter-hegemonic practices in the field of popular theatre is more urgent today than for many a year. The successive assaults on those institutions concerned with the maintenance of quality of life have resulted in the decline of standards of living to the point where a fifth of the nation's children are living in poverty. The centralised power of government and its unelected quangos is daily diminishing its ability and inclination to relate to those areas of our society in which it is unable to detect an electoral interest. Subsidised theatre, even supposing it could be afforded, does not offer a set of meanings that relate to the lives of the culturally alienated majority. Broadcast media are concerned to deliver customers to advertisers, directly in the independent companies and indirectly via the ratings war in the BBC. As people cease to be in a position to perform their consumerist role, they will cease to be of interest to the advertisers and hence the programme controllers. The widening gap between rich and poor in English society leaves an increasing number of people on the wrong side of the divide, gazing with passivity and indifference on the commodity culture of the bourgeoisie until the pressure of deprivation gives vent to the violence and rage of Gethin Price in Trevor Griffiths' *Comedians.* The paradox of Griffiths' play is that he can only present Price's position as uninvited guest at the banquet of high culture within the structure of the traditional middle-class theatre, limited by the wrong conventions, playing to the wrong audience.

There is a substantial tradition of British political theatre which has foundered on the contradiction between form and content. Many of the plays in this tradition have misleadingly been labelled "popular"; more a reflection on the origins of their authors such as Arden and Bond than on their production processes. Within this tradition performances have usually missed their required audiences; where they have not, the audience has still been reduced to passivity whether approving or hostile. A tradition which lacks the means of releasing the productivity of its subjects will leave them either believing in the immutability of society or else expecting an external agency such as the Author or the Revolution to do the changing for them.

Yet there are at least fragments of a tradition available to those intending to engage in popular theatre today. These fragments are sufficient to point a way towards a properly theorised practice, a *praxis,* of popular theatre. At the end of the 1920s and the beginning of the 1930s when there was a real, imminent prospect of Germany participating in the socialist revolution, Brecht developed his *Lehrstücke* as a means of abolishing the distinction between performers and audience and presenting situations for debate that could arise in the post-revolutionary period. These were short pieces intended for production with amateur actors such as workers' choirs and communist youth groups. They were grounded in Brecht's interpretation of classical Marxism under the guiding principle that reality is in a constant state of change and that at that historical moment the proletariat was the motor for that change. He later described this work as his "major pedagogy" and the later so-called "great plays" as "compromise forms", forced on him firstly by exile from his means of production and later by historical circumstances such as the revival of capitalism and the decline of communism into grotesque parody represented by the Stalinist state.

The two key principles of a world capable of being changed by human actions and a theatre which abandoned the classical distinction between performers and spectators were adopted by Augusto Boal who was working on his Forum Theatre at a time in the 1960s when Brecht's theories and practice were being disseminated world-wide. Boal took up Brecht's notion and radically recontextualised it for and with the ordinary people with whom he worked. The prospect of revolution was indeed remote for the people of the *barrios* of Sao Paulo but they were at least able to stage rehearsals for revolutions at the local level.

The pedagogical theories which underpinned Boal's practice and which are now regularly rubbished by the New Right were developed from the practice and writings of Paulo Freire in the context of development projects in the Third World as a means towards promoting self-help in areas such as literacy and health. These were contexts where there was no welfare provision and no means for communities to represent themselves to the power structure, other than means of their own making. Today it is fashionable to talk of Britain as a Third World country, a description which obscures Britain's historic role as colonial exploiter and neo-colonial extortioner of debt repayments. Nevertheless, contemporary British society does bear some resemblance to aspects of Third World countries, notably the policies of the Government which increase the earning potential of the already rich, while lowering the earnings of the poor or denying them work entirely. Oxfam recently announced that it is investigating the possibility of starting up operations in Britain. There is no shortage of under-development. It may therefore be felt to be an appropriate time to reclaim the lost pedagogics of the 1960s as a means of rebuilding a theoretical framework out of which relevant popular theatre practices can be formed. The last twenty years have witnessed an assault of growing ferocity on the whole notion of communities forged independently of the prevailing power structures, whether these be communities of interest such as trade unions or geographically defined communities, from mining villages threatened with extinction to inner cities threatened with redevelopment. Robbed of their former identities the inhabitants of these communities have lost their voice and, lapsing into silence, have either been forgotten or have allowed others to speak on their behalf.

These kinds of situation have been addressed by communities using theatre as a tool for their self-development in parts of Africa, Asia and South America for more than a decade. Typically the communities in question are already the victims of development initiatives from external agencies sponsored by the World Bank. Such initiatives have either told these communities what they need for their own development (that is, in order to provide cash crops as cheap exports to North America and Europe) or have taken the words of the village and tribal elders at face value and ignored or overlooked the needs of the urban poor and the rural peasant, particularly women. It is a basic premise of theatre, for development that the content for dramatic representation is provided by ordinary people whether or not they have the confidence to make the representations themselves. The catalyst for provoking such representations is likely to be an outside presence but the theatre or development worker operates as a facilitator not as a director. At a workshop I attended in Northern Nigeria there were two external agencies combining to initiate a week-long development workshop in two different village communities. W.I.N. (Women in Nigeria) had a programme for highlighting issues in women's health and they had approached the N.P.T.A. (Nigerian Popular Theatre Alliance) with a view to using theatre in this process. The crucial phase in the process was the research period during which the facilitators engaged in interviews, attended meetings and joined in chores in order to get an insight into the dominant concerns of the community. It was essential to set up informal and private moments in the research because most of the women were not accustomed to speaking out in public and indeed were prevented from doing so by patriarchal pressure. In one instance this pressure was too great to permit the women to represent themselves in their dramatised story and the facilitators took on their roles. In the other a group of women re-enacted a story which exposed the oppression of the men of the village. At a crucial moment in one rehearsal all the facilitators and village men were asked to step outside the meeting hut where the rehearsal was taking place, so that the women could debate the situation which the dramatisation had made clear to them. When we returned, the women announced that they had set up a women's co-operative and sent round a bowl for contributions. On the last day of the workshop the whole piece was performed before the chief and the elders to their considerable embarrassment and with promises of changes. The theatre facilitators also made sure that the existing performance skills within the villages such as drumming, singing and story-telling were fully used in the organisation of the event.

Some of the key features of this theatre for development process were that the piece of theatre had been made by ordinary people; the content of the piece was developed out of topical issues of concern to the community; participant appraisal had ensured that grass-roots feelings and needs were expressed and the piece of drama created had a role in a larger process of improving the quality of life of the community. Its efficacy could only be gauged at a later date when the sustainability of changes would be checked by the initiating facilitators. One of the strengths of the process was that theatre needs no resources other than the human body and does not depend on literacy for participation. The function of the facilitators is to provide the opportunities for a different perspective to be given to daily life. In the Brechtian sense they make the familiar strange in order that it may be better comprehended and that it may be most effectively changed. As in all societies, the barriers to change are the products of false consciousness or vested interests in the *status quo.*

The kinds of theatre-for-development practices which have continued to operate in a range of Third World contexts, perhaps made easier in situations where the oppressed and the oppressors are clearly demarcated, need to be applied to popular theatre in Britain today. Whilst some of the material problems are not yet as acute as in other parts of the world, the issues of identity and community are sometimes even more intractable. Many communities in Britain have today become suitable cases for self-development but it is futile to look for assistance to a central government whose ideology is directly contrary to the needs of those communities. Such assistance when it is offered by enlightened local government or arts associations inevitably involves high-profile 'experts' directing the members of the community in one-off projects as a recreational escape rather than a sustained confrontation with a changeable reality.

Instead of the director, there is need of a facilitator, trained in the skills of listening and establishing dialogue. Theatre workers have the vital experience of *praxis* built up from working in specific contexts and susceptible to constant re-evaluation to guide them. The notion of dialogue is central to the relationship between the community and the facilitator. Furthermore, theatre practices are in a unique position to take advantage of a range of expressive capacities which may owe nothing to skills and competencies associated with writing. In keeping with a popular form, its roots and sources are located within oral traditions. These kinds of drama processes can initiate a significant shift in the community's perception of the theatre as a place which sells expertly constructed cultural artefacts to those sections of the community which have financial and cultural access to their products, to theatre as a place (literal or figurative) where hitherto neglected or marginalised sections of the community can investigate ways of expressing the meanings of their social existence through processes of cultural negotiation either amongst themselves or between themselves and outside agencies to whom they wish to represent themselves.

None of these notions are new. Dusting off the shelves of the despised 60s will put us back in contact with the theoretical framework and case-studies which offer a way forward through this anti-welfare age. They are not models, only fragments of a tradition which must be constantly reassessed against the new context. Brecht retreated from his most radical practice into a version of bourgeois theatre; Boal was unable to transpose the radical potential of his South American work to the European context; McGrath developed a new audience for political theatre, but it was an audience which did not have to commit itself to action. These fragments towards a dialogical practice must now take account of some recent work in cultural studies, particularly in the area of post-colonial criticism. Many of the ideas surrounding notions of identity, ethnicity and gender which are explored in the writings of such as Fanon, Giroux, Ngugi, Said and Spivak can be usefully imported into the contexts of domestic popular theatre. The absence of any rigorous theoretical base has rightly been observed as one of the causes of the relative ease with which the radical practices of the 60s and 70s have been subsequently disembodied and discredited.

Efforts to establish an effective theoretical base for popular theatre practices today are greatly hampered by the way in which the New Right has acquired the terminology and discourses of development as a way of suffocating its counter hegemonic potential. Empowerment on the lips of Tory ministers, "democracy" intoned by U.S. ambassadors in Third World countries or "student-centred" on the breath of vice-chancellors of new universities are about as meaningful concepts as "consensus" as articulated by Attila the Hun or 'conciliation' in the mouth of Ian Paisley. Coining new terms is not the answer since they will only be appropriated as quickly as they come into circulation. Rather the existing jargon of development must be reinvested in meaning through those critical practices for which Brecht applied the concept of *verfremdung*. Thus the full implications of ideas such as empowerment and sustainability may be analysed in the context of a practice whose stated aim is to give voice with a view to using that voice as a motor for social change.

Where the practices of the 60s cannot be replicated is in their belief in large scale institutional change. The political trend today is away from influence through traditional political bodies towards influence through pressure groups campaigning for change around a specific issue, often related to culture, personal freedom or the environment. It is to the work of these groups, both at home and abroad, that popular theatre practices need to address themselves. Here are communities of interest trying to represent themselves effectively in their interventions into the dominant discourse. There is, as yet, little evidence that practitioners of popular theatre are coming forward in significant numbers to facilitate this process. It is my belief that the primary function of theatre is to enhance the quality of life for all who engage in its processes. Today in Britain the quality of so many lives is deteriorating but dramatic and theatrical practices are failing to confront this deterioration effectively. If practitioners are waiting for help from the traditional sources of support such as government, local authorities, arts councils or general elections, they will wait in vain and many more lives will be diminished. In the words of Herr Brecht: "Taught only by reality can/ Reality be changed." Is it not better that we lose our voices by shouting loudly and long than that we surrender them without a squeak to the culture of silence?

McDonald Drama[1]
And the Future of British Popular Theatre

Esiaba Irobi

There are several ways to look at the phenomenal response of the British populace and theatre industry to 'musicals' in recent times. The first approach, as some high-brow theatre critics have done, is to dismiss musicals as shallow offerings; the frippery, escapist, sugar-coated distractions of a chocolate culture. The second approach, usually by serious-minded middle-class scholars, has been to study musicals, condescendingly, as a sub-art; an apolitical, unprofound genre that skims the surface of life, implicitly inferior to the sublime literary classics presented at the West End and other subsidised theatres in the country.[2] The third and most fruitful approach is the cross-cultural which, being intrinsically international and comparative, attempts to isolate the aesthetic similarities between musicals and the ritual structure of the indigenous theatres of non-European cultures and can therefore give musicals a suitable non-derogatory redefinition as a viable theatre genre in the West. Such an approach should be able to articulate, from a sociological and artistic perspective, why the British and indeed, international, audience for musicals cuts across age, class, gender, culture and even race. And perhaps, even more crucial for the state of the art today, a penetrating cross-cultural gaze may, and should, identify the huge potential of the musical form, especially its non-verbal aesthetics, as a politically-subversive artistic weapon in the discontented yet creative hands of the proliferating underclass and culturally-disenfranchised populace in Britain.

In his book, *Understanding Popular Culture*, John Fiske has argued that in a society where there is no authentic 'folk' culture (he possibly means communal, vernacular or indigenous culture handed down from generation to generation) to provide an alternative, popular culture is necessarily the art of making do with what is available.[3] He goes on to say that the economic system, which determines mass production and mass consumption, reproduces itself ideologically in its commodities: "A commodity is ideology made material."[4] More revealingly, Fiske points out that a mass culture produces a quiescent, passive mass of people, an agglomeration of atomised individuals separated from their position in the social structure, detached from and unaware of class consciousness, of their various social and cultural allegiances, and thus totally disempowered and helpless.[5]

On the other hand, in her book, Apidan Theatre and Modern Drama, Kacke Gotrick, a Swedish scholar, argues that "the African concept of entertainment is more complex than the Western."[6] Using the example of an indigenous Yoruba community drama (The Apidan), she illustrates most vividly how the theatre in a non-industrialised part of the world, goes beyond diversion, commercial considerations, class interest, and instead reaffirms, in a regenerative sense, a people's concept of community, history, politics, spirituality and the creative flexibilities of their indigenous aesthetics in their continual attempt to tell the story of their lives, theatrically, by themselves.

This essay is, thus, an attempt to build a bridge between Fiske's picture of a dispossessed populace who have been conned out of their vernacular forms of expression by the industrial revolution (with its attendant urbanisation, uprootment, social mobility, class system, capitalism) and Gotrick's analysis of a once-artistically-empowered-people who are watching, due to Western influence, the gradual erasure of the cementing function of the theatre in their spiritual and material lives. The essay will focus on the interface between economics, politics and aesthetics and will highlight the perspectives from which the European musical theatre form can re-examine the communal and mutative ethos of indigenous African theatre aesthetics in a bid to revalidate itself as a potential political and indeed threatening if not dangerous artform in Britain.

In order to clarify the crucial differences between the European and indigenous African conception of the theatre event and theatre experience, I will pitch the phenomenal success of Andrew Lloyd Webber's *Cats* against Omabe, a less well-known but surprisingly similar drama of the Nsukka-Igbo people of Nigeria. By looking at the elements of iconography, myth, functionality, popularity, authorship, audience participation and duration of performance, this essay will draw attention, from a cross-cultural perspective, to the following vexed issues of contemporary theatre practice:

How does "ritual structure" i.e. individual or communal authorship of a theatrical piece determine "performance dynamics" and how does this, in turn, affect "audience participation?" At what point does a work of theatrical art metamorphose from the merely "exhibitionist" to the "cultic" as Walter Benjamin points out in his book, Illuminations? What does the term efficacy mean in drama and how does music contribute to the achievement of this state in theatre? Do the qualities of musicals that societies produce and consume reflect in some way the quality of their lives in contemporary times? Why are musicals so popular these days? Could it be that they strike at the primitive i.e. "primal" core of the Western `civilised' mind? Are musicals in their colourful imagery, suffusion of songs, symbolism and other non-verbal structures, modern replicas of visceral ancient dramatic forms which have existed in non-industrialised African and Asian societies since the beginning of time? Can the non-verbal aesthetics of British musicals be expanded or reified so as to provoke, politically, a more pragmatic, gut-level reaction to the contradictions in British society? In short, can musicals be refashioned in such a way that they can accommodate more serious if not subversive political pre-occupations and responsibilities? And, finally, who will bell the cat?

An Encounter with *Cats*

I watched Andrew Lloyd Webber's musical, *Cats*, on the 12th of November, 1994, at the Empire Theatre, Liverpool. It was a cold, wintry evening. I marched bravely to the venue hoping that the much-touted musical experience would be an aesthetically-engaging and spiritually-uplifting experience. Having read "The Wasteland", "The Hollow Men" and *The Possum Book of Cats* and knowing how profoundly spiritual T.S.Eliot can be even when he is satirically sculpting caricatures of mischievous English characters under the smokescreen of feline metaphors, I even envisioned some depth, an exploration of the human anima, some sort of Jungian dimension to Webber's interpretation of *The Possum Book of Cats*. Dreaming the more, I even foresaw some sort of participatory element woven into the feline phenomenon. That evening I desperately wanted something that would move the bowels of my spirit . However, at the end of the *Cats* performance, I discovered that the only thing that had moved was my constipated bowel because of the cheap ice cream I had eaten.

Despite this misgiving which was obviously prompted by my own cultural expectation of the essence and efficacy of a theatrical performance, I did not, however, fail to notice and appreciate the aesthetic richness of the production in the areas of costume, scenery, dance, lighting, mime and song. The technical competence and sleekness with which the performance was executed also struck me as impressive. Most overwhelming was the impact of the music on the audience, especially the teenagers who hummed excitedly to most of the lilting tunes even after the show. As we left the theatre, I noticed, however, that little pockets of argument were exploding here and there. A well-fed school teacher was asking her equally not-so-slim husband, in a beautiful upper-middle-class accent but ungentle tone, a relay of questions:

"So, what's the plot of *Cats*, then?"
"The plot of *Cats* is cats," her husband replied curtly.
"Does that mean that *Cats* has no plot?"
"Must every performance have a linear plot?"
"How then do you know what a show is all about if it has no plot?"
"If you watch it 3 times you'll notice what remotely resembles a plot."
"It inspires hallucinations, then, does it?"
"I don't know. Go and ask Andrew Lloyd Webber."
"Do you have Webber's phone number?"
"Please, where are the car keys? And where was it we parked our car?"

The dialogue above is revealing. It offers us an important insight into the uses of audience research. The husband has, either out of native intuition or innocence, articulated the crucial thematic, structural and performative correlative between *Cats*, a European musical, and the non-linear story-telling theatre structure of Omabe and indeed many indigenous African ritual dramas. His statement that "the plot of *Cats* is cats" reinforces Neelands and Goode's argument that theatre uses both verbal and non-verbal sign systems in the construction of a performance text. However, they remark that the dominant theatre tradition in the West is built on the achievements of Euro-American playwrights and tends to emphasise words and their meaning (the signs of language). In other cultures of the world the theatre tradition is often founded on earlier modes of performance and popular entertainment; in a heritage of performance texts rather than literary texts. These performances tend to be non-linear and to work with highly symbolic physical and visual signs rather than with the spoken word. So, instead of demanding that an audience should understand a play, by literally following the actors words, as in the Western realist or naturalist tradition, these (often non-industrialised) cultures employ a metalinguistic approach which encourages a subliminal/visceral decoding of the contradictions, tensions, multilayered resonances created by the non-verbal signs/symbols within 'the story' being communicated.[7]

Omabe, whose non-linear plot is made up of culturally-determined spatial, auditory, olfactory, and visual metalanguages, (the leopard being central to this iconic vocabulary used to symbolise abstract ideas, themes, or living myths) is a good example of this formal necessity. Just as well, the power of *Cats*, despite its intellectual and ideological limitations, and what accounts for its popular appeal can be argued to be its visual grammar, the imagistic beauty of the human yet animal presences on stage, the extra-sensory impact of its cumulative musicality and the tantalisingly cubist structure of what could have been an easily predictable linear plot. As T.S. Eliot would put it, "a heap of broken images!"

In performance, the cats, in Webber's musical, as characters, leap out of the prismatic backdrop of the poems via the non-verbal signs of costume, make up, dance, songs, music, movement and lighting to communicate the composite meaning of their presence physically and dynamically on stage. So the experience becomes synaesthetic, sensuous even, creating a fragmentary narrative held together by the metaphor of "felinity" on which all the elements above hang.

These same observations about visual and structural dynamics can also be made about Omabe as a performance. But it is here that the similarities between *Cats* and Omabe end. For whereas *Cats* sacrifices its hermeneutic meaning to the audience or fails to employ the metaphor or symbolism of cats as an interpretative superstructure to analyse or explore the human, economic, social, political and spiritual condition of the audience, Omabe, whose own central icon is the leopard engages its audience at a cultic level. Instead of pandering to the exhibitionistic expectations of the audience (and possibly financial interests of the creators) of *Cats*, the Nsukka-Igbo people who created Omabe use the annual or bi-annual performance of this festival drama to reify their sense of themselves as a community. The iconography of the leopard, Omabe, and the myth it encapsulates, therefore, becomes the pivotal metanarrative for the fundamental functions of the drama: Bonding, identity, celebration of the political entity of the community, renewal of human ties and rewiring the threads of broken relationships among the people in the course of the past year through the sharing of food and other festive activities.

Iconography
    Thus, Omabe, the ritual drama of the Nsukka-Igbo of Nigeria, belongs to a category of indigenous theatre of images and uses masks, costumes, movement, music and dance to symbolise the abstract metaphysical concept of communal renewal/regeneration as conceived by the Nsukka-Igbo people of Nigeria. Both the visual motif of the leopard and the metanarrative of "tearing out the future with its fangs" is authored by the entire Nsukka community. The dream of faith embodied and physicalised through the leopards' i.e. the actors' uncompromising but artistic duel with the future, as a form of stylised theatrical performance, has been handed down from generation to generation. But Omabe is more than a dramatic outing. It is part of a whole nexus of ceremonies and beliefs that govern and give meaning to the lives of its creators. It is a process of regulating their existence. Thus, the process of theatre-making, for the Nsukka community is part of a composite artistic process for the social, educational, religious and political engineering of the people. For this community, theatrical experience is not a diversion or mere entertainment. It is an encounter, a confrontation with the cosmic, geographical, political, social and economic forces that influence and shape their lives.

Myth

More revealing, perhaps, as the analysis of the functionality of the drama below illustrates, the myth of Omabe and its employment as a performative metanarrative highlights the crucial difference between a Western (contemporary) use or understanding of the word "myth" and the indigenous African conception of the same word. For while admitting that African myth possesses the traditional form of a narrative, this narrative is not just a simple story, a relation of past events, but a system and mode of knowledge which can become, and indeed usually does become the structure of a plot. As Maximilien Laroche has observed, myth in an oral culture, before being a narrative fixed by writing, is the spoken word, the facial expression, the gesture which defines the event within the individual heart. It unites the sacred and the historic, expresses a world order, is situated within a religious framework, and possesses a situational character i.e. it is a socio-economic product, an ideological superstructure inseparable from its social structure. It ties together the everyday, the ephemeral, to the atemporal, the metaphysical. Myth then, is not simply narrative, something static or fixed, but action.[8]

Functionality

The central action in Omabe drama involves the extremely colourful and choreographed descent of the spirit of the dead ancestors from behind the Omabe hills, their abode and resting place. The spirits, who represent different lineages in Nsukka, are magnificently costumed as leopards and appear in hundreds. Sometimes, the exposed parts of their bodies are rubbed with honey so that they bristle in the sun as if wet. There are however a few ugly, disruptive animal characters such the civet cat and the hyena but these are out shone by the beauty and grace of the leopards who display their feline distinction through the Omabe gait and dance in response to Omabe music. There are young and old Omabe, the age ranges differ since, in Nsukka-Igbo world view, the spirit world mirrors the human world. But what is breathtaking is the massive appearance of hundreds of Omabe, in fluid formations, on the brow of the hill in the setting sun amidst gunshots, songs, chants and ululations from the crowd below. The visual beauty of this spectacle has been described by Enekwe as "poetry in motion." These ethereal presences in glinting appliqué material are coming to commune and stay with the living, who flank the hillside in thousands, for one whole year during which they (the Omabe) will replenish the population, economic wealth and agricultural harvest of the community. After eleven months, in another communal festival drama, the dead will depart. Thus, their movement from the hills to the market place, the public and occult centre of the community, is highly symbolic since the Nsukka Igbo are actually ritualising an abstract concept, a myth, an idealised future, through theatre and performance. On arrival at the market the Omabe actors impersonating the leopard employ mime, gestures, dance and feline movements to "tear out the fruits and flesh, the harvest of the future" to the spectators who, themselves, have been acting and dancing and making music in the absence of the real actors, the Omabe. The performance is interactive, multi-focal and uses expansive space. After it, the Omabe retire to the cult house, after paying homage to the Goddess of the market. Individual Omabe masquerades however continue to perform and receive lavish gifts of money. At about seven p.m., the community then return home for eating and drinking with friends and relatives.

However there is much more to the festival drama than I have just described. The drama in itself signals the temporal divisions in the ecological, hence occupational, world of the Nsukka-Igbo. It is the marker or watershed between the season of dryness and the season of plenty or feasting. The outing is usually preceded by a period of peace in the community during which enmity and disagreements are reconciled. Commensality or the sharing of food among friends and relatives plays a very important role in the festival. Prior to the drama, young male children are initiated into the Omabe cult, an exercise which is a form of census within the community and also an induction into the civic responsibilities of the younger generation and the political hierarchy of their society. Most of these educational values are however encoded in the artistic forms and iconographies preserved and administered by the older members of the Omabe cult. On Eke (the name of a market day of the week) nights, the same masquerades, muffling their voices, expose the injustices perpetrated on the poor and the weak by the powerful and rich through out the past year. Thus, we begin to see how participation in every aspect of the festival drama and its accompanying social activities for the rest of the year is a reflection of the organic and communal nature of the theatre- making process among the Nsukka-Igbo of Nigeria. Since the super-objective of the festival drama is to allow the populace to experience the myth of its origin and well-being, through communal performance, it is important to observe that by participating, every member of the community leases out his or her individuality to the political status quo. The festival myth, as we can see, serves the ideology of the moment and is used for social restructuring. The drama also has psychotherapeutic value in the sense that the myth of the return of the Omabe ancestors serves as a way of dealing with the phenomenon of death and its accompanying traumas.

Popularity

The entire Nsukka community take part. The metanarrative of Omabe which is encapsulated in the symbol of the leopard is known by everybody because it was fashioned by the community and perpetrated year after year as a festive instrument of bonding. This is why members of the Nsukka community who live in other parts of Nigeria return home to take part in the festival drama. The drama belongs to them. It is part of their identity as an Igbo people. It also sets them apart, thereby emphasising their uniqueness. The artistic index of that uniqueness is the Omabe drama which they have created, and produce, design, advertise, act out all by themselves. The myth beneath however is a secret or unknown until explained just as is the interconnectedness between myth, ritual, art, theatre, performance, social, spiritual and political life. That the festival drama can be postponed during periods of economic hardship highlights the financial demands of the theatre on the community. It is this proprietary and participatory element that, in my thinking, accounts for the popularity of Omabe among the Nsukka-Igbo in Nigeria. *Cats*, on the other hand, is popular for many reasons. First, there is the animal element in it; the sentimentality about cats. In atomistic societies where the love of animals substitutes human love and companionship, due to accidents of history and geography, this is understandable. Then, the massive advertising and the music, the costumes, the songs, the dance which redeem the work from the tedium of verbiage often found in naturalistic drama. It is also a work we can watch without any form of intellectual distraction. Its appeal is emotional and visual. It works. But the whole experience is packaged by someone else who is not interested in our lives and does not see his art as something we could use as a form of social, spiritual or political intervention. We have no hand in the matter.

Authorship and Participation

The dialogue between husband and wife which I quoted earlier reflects the detached attitude of an audience to theatrical experience in a society where drama (and the thematic preoccupation of the theatrical piece) is authored by a single individual or a group of professionals essentially for commercial, diversionary purposes. Audience participation, spatially and physically, is virtually non-existent. In the case of *Cats*, what resembles participation occurs only when the cats run into the stalls to touch the knees of the seated audience and, in the process, knock down ice cream cones off children's hands or when beams of light are projected on the spectators so that they can know its time to clap to the tune of "Mr Mistoffelees." This kind of organised spontaneity, one would argue, is symptomatic of alienation (what the theatre by its very essence and function is against.) It also echoes Fiske's argument about a quiescent, disembodied populace. Omabe, on the other hand, is a collective creation. Dancers, choreographers, musicians are drawn from various segments of the community to celebrate and reinforce the Nsukka - Igbo people's worldview and perception of themselves as they perform themselves. It is this collective involvement, we can argue, which gives the performance its mythic and epic structure; a synthesis of all the artforms; sculpture, music, drum language, dance, mythic language, poetry, costume, body painting, incantations etc. whose cumulative impact on the senses open up the subconscious and make ritual efficacy or transformation possible. The collective ethos also demands that there must be space within the plot of the performance for the community or non-Omabe cult-members to experience or participate, even if peripherally in the myth that regulates their lives. The link between authorship and participation is therefore clear. When a people feel a sense of ownership and belonging to the theatrical process, the end product will inevitably reflect their aspirations and frustrations. The performance will, thus, embody and validate their experiences and cement their sense of community.

Duration of the Performance

What makes all this possible is the duration of the performance. Whereas Cats lasts nearly three hours, the Omabe drama lasts a whole day and continues as individual performances for months. This elastic time frame is made possible because the festival suspends chronological time and ushers in primordial time within which creativity flourishes and communication with the revered ancestors is possible. The suspension of labour, the holiday factor, facilitates liminality which helps in pitching the minds of the people out from a secular to a sacred state. The festive time thus becomes a time that is no time, a time of marvels. This internal calendar is often unknown to foreigners who think the drama is a sporadic one-off event whereas it is the beginning of an eleven month-period of the perpetuation of a living myth when the dead, through dramatic make belief, can stay with the living .

The Future of British Popular Theatre

One of the assumptions of the creators of British musicals is that they know what the people want and can prove it by the box office accounts. Cats, the longest running musical in British theatre history, which has grossed £15.7 million within ten years, is a useful example of this misconception. The magic formula for this economic miracle is due to a kind of artistic ingenuity quite different from what I have described above about the cultic and spiritual pre-occupations of Omabe:

> The secret of Andrew (Lloyd Webber)...is that he picks subjects that would make great theatre...like T.S. Eliot's Old Possum's Book of Practical Cats. He has a nose for what plays on stage...He knows how to write a tune which sticks to you and whether you like it or not, grabs you and holds on to you. It holds on to a lot of people. Another secret is he knows when to bring that tune back, how to milk his material for maximum

musical and theatrical effect, and he creates great superstructures on which to hang these songs.[9] (my emphasis)

It is the tendency described above which places musicals within the category of commodity drama or McDonald drama. McDonald drama, like its fast food corollary, is produced for mass consumption. It is also formulaic and predictable. It uses the same ingredients despite the differences in agriculture, place and time. The McDonald recipe for sandwiches hardly changes from bread, cheese, burger: fish, ham, chicken, beef, and the fried meal is always potatoes (even in countries that produce the more nutritious yam, cocoyam or other indigenous tubers). Operating by the same logic inherent in a culture of consumption, Andrew Lloyd Webber recycles the same sugary lyrics, provocative and flamboyant costumes, tawdry plots, eclectic choreography, songs, music (often with a pelvic thud to flex the muscles of the heart and groin) in order to package a performance which hardly changes it message or alters its dynamics or aesthetics wherever it is performed. It is this formulaic aesthetic that has enabled Webber to produce , with amazing rapidity, like McDonald recipes, a diet of hits whose inner structures are essentially the same: *Jesus Christ Superstar, Evita, Aspects of Love, Cats,* etc. The financial success from these works have also made it possible for enthusiasts of popular culture to presume that musicals are the popular theatre of the future. In fact, when the National Theatre of Britain asked, a British Prime Minister, Margaret Thatcher, great advocate of monetarism, in 1990, for subsidies and funding that will enable them produce the classics of dramatic literature, she said to them: "Why don't you do musicals like Andrew Lloyd Webber?" [10]

But is this really what British people want? Do the younger generation of British theatre-goers want something more than attractive distractions as theatrical experience? The thematic preoccupations of the dissertations of many final year drama students of Liverpool John Moores University (1995) are very revealing. They all border on the healing power of theatre through participation and interaction. The students are deeply interested in ritual, myth, psychodrama, dramatherapy, process drama, raves, and any alternative types of theatre that involve an expression of the self by the performative self (not the passive self) using artistic approaches suitable to the self. Carmella Gallea, describes the healing effect of a physical theatre workshop she had participated in as "an uplifting experience. I left after four hours feeling like I had had a personal counselling session.... Theatre can be therapeutic and ...we need a theatre which goes beyond both physical and literary theatre."[11] Amy Ball, in her excellent dissertation on the interface between political and physical theatre, argues that "British theatre is currently witnessing an explosion of forms, of different modes of expression: Physical and visual theatre...and moving in a direction... in which the body is the focal point through which oppressions are expressed."[12] The body, she argues, is the purest vessel and the most universal for this form of exorcism. Amy Creech goes further to highlight how theatre can heal both a performer and a community. Focusing first on the performer, Annie Sprinkler, Creech analyses how this ex-prostitute used her play, *100 Blow Jobs*, to confront and come to terms with the sexual and psychic abuse she suffered while engaged in the trade. Repeated performances, punctuated by crying and rounded off with a ceremony, eased the pain until Sprinkler could do the play without any guilt feelings or sense of humiliation. Creech extends this healing function of theatre to include whole communities within which problems of the particular community are dealt with in the theatre. Incisively she observes that "what is being healed is the dissolution of community, which needs to be repaired through celebration."[13] Creech then wrote a powerful ritual for coming to terms with the death of her mother. *Titled Dancing With Medusa*; a blueprint for a ritual she describes the music, dance, chants, spatials, time, duration, number and type of people needed for the ritual to be truly efficacious.

From the above evidence, we can argue that the likely way forward for British popular theatre will be a return to a kind of theatre that allows people maximum participation in both the process of its making and performance. This participatory ethos is crucial because among all human beings the desire to watch a performance is as strong as the desire to participate. As the students' dissertations have demonstrated, what the British populace should consider is how to appropriate the best of the visual, auditory and physical aspects of McDonald drama and weave these elements into their own individual and communal forms of theatre whose structures must be expansive enough to accommodate the peoples' growing disenchantment with the political system, the monarchy, the class system which predicates itself on wealth, snobbery and persecution.[14] The Criminal Justice Bill which denies British people (unlike in Sweden) access to public space for communal celebration as well as criminalises citizens who gather for ritual, carnival, festival or art-making must be challenged. This piece of legislation, which appears to me to be an evidence of unnecessary persecution in a society that presents itself as a leading member part of the free world, needs to be fought by the very instrument which it fears most: Communal theatre. This form of anti-establishment theatre, in which every single element including the theme, will be authored and executed by the people (without the aid of animateurs) in their rural and urban communities will be functional, like the Omabe, in practice and performance. Its celebratory structure will make for spaces where British people can truly participate as well as confront their human condition and the contradictions within their society. It is through this process of reclamation that popular theatre in Britain can go beyond the dominance of McDonald drama, forge a way for the future and, for the sake of posterity, become a symbol of the beauty of resistance.

Notes

[1] John Bull, *Stage Right:Crisis and Recovery in British Contemporary Mainstream Theatre* (Macmillan,1994), p.18

[2] Ibid, p.19

[3] John Fiske, *Understanding Popular Culture* (Routledge, 1992), p.15

[4] Ibid. p.14

[5] Ibid, p. 20. John Fiske also argues that excorporation is the process by which the subordinate make their own culture out of the resources and commodities provided by the dominant system, and this process, he argues, is central to popular culture, for in an industrial society the only resources from which the subordinate can make their own subcultures are those provided for them by the system that subordinates them. Popular culture is therefore part of power relations; it always bears traces of the constant struggle between...power and various forms of resistance to it and evasions of it. Popular culture, in an industrialised society , can then be defined as a continual self-defining process characterised by the creativity of the weak in

using the resources provided by a disempowering system while refusing finally to submit to that power. This is the line of argument I have tried to negotiate using a cross-cultural paradigm.

[6] See Kacke Gotrick, *Apidan Theatre and Modern Drama* (Almqvist &Wiskell Int., 1984), pp.124-133

[7] Jonothan Neelands and John Goode, "Playing in the Margins of Meaning:The Ritual Aesthetic in Community Performance", *Nadie Journal* 19:1, 1995, pp 39-57.

[8] Maximilien Laroche, "The Myth of the Zombi", in *Exile and Tradition* (Heinemann, 1974), p 45.

[9] Stephen Citron, *The Musical from Inside Out* (Hodder & Stoughton, 1991), p.82

[10] Margaret Thatcher, *Culture in the Eighties*, on Channel 4, 1992

[11] Carmella Gallea, "Physical Theatre and the Avant-Garde", unpublished dissertation, Drama dept, Liverpool John Moores University, 1995.

[12] Amy Ball, "Does Political Theatre Still Exist in the 1990s", unpublished dissertation, Drama dept, Liverpool John Moores University, 1995.

[13] Amy Creech, "Dancing With Medusa,: A Blueprint for a Ritual", Independent Study Unit Project, Drama Dept, Liverpool John Mooores University, 1995.

[14] Through out the essay I have tried to illustrate why it is dangerous to be dismissive about musicals. Musicals are competent forms of cultural confidence tricks which promise a reward that is hardly ever delivered while emptying the pockets of the passive viewers. It is therefore necessary to see why they work so powerfully at a subliminal level and exploit the aesthetic elements that make this fickle efficacy possible. By using these uplifting elements in a subversive or confrontational way, both in the process and performance, to undermine the ruling class and the deflectionary artistic values they impose on the British populace, the British theatre will, I believe, enter into a new combative phase of using art as a form of communal determination and the interrogation of a moribund and complacent status quo. This form of risky intervention, I believe is more useful than plucking songs from musicals and singing them in the bath to keep depression at bay and suicide in the basement.

Alternative Comedy: From Radicalism to Commercialism

Oliver Double

"Alternative comedy" is a controversial and unfashionable term, and it is often used very loosely, so I will start with a precise definition. Alternative comedy is a specific circuit, made up of a specific set of clubs, and an alternative comedian is somebody who works in, or began his or her career in, this specific set of clubs.

Alternative comedy is the third of three major traditions of stand-up comedy in Britain. The first is the variety tradition, within which the form of stand-up comedy evolved from the intersong patter of the Victorian music hall. Among the great variety comics are George Robey, Billy Bennett, Max Miller, Tommy Trinder, Frankie Howerd, Beryl Reid, Tommy Cooper and Morecambe and Wise. The second major tradition was Working Men's Club comedy, which developed a flavour of its own by the 1950s, and became the main forum for live stand-up after the death of variety in about 1960. The great club comics include Bobby Thompson, Les Dawson, Bernard Manning, Charlie Williams, and Marti Caine.

Alternative comedy sprang into life in 1979, as a result of two important events: the opening of the Comedy Store, and the formation of Alternative Cabaret. Both of these events provided a focus for a group of refugees from the alternative theatre circuit, who had become disillusioned whilst working for groups like 7:84 and Belt and Braces. They believed that political theatre tended to patronise its audience, and saw stand-up comedy as a way of being more direct, more honest and more popular.

The importance of the opening of the Comedy Store has been somewhat overplayed in existing histories of alternative comedy.1 Certainly, it was important in drawing media attention to the new comedy movement, but Peter Rosengard's suggestion that he set the venue up with the specific intention of starting a new non-sexist, non-racist comedy movement is clearly untrue. In fact, the Comedy Store was set up as a venue in which comics of any description could get up and perform without payment, and the early shows were completely shambolic. The early alternative comedians worked alongside hopeful amateurs, minor club comics, and even big names like Les Dawson and Lennie Bennett. As a result, the material was far from being ideologically pure, and it was only after months of what Tony Allen has described as a "civil war" between these old hacks and the alternative comedians that the Comedy Store became a *bona fide* alternative comedy venue.[2]

In fact, the formation of Alternative Cabaret was far more important, firstly because it was set up specifically as a forum for a new kind of comedy; and secondly because in touring round pubs and colleges in London and beyond, it laid the foundations for the alternative comedy circuit as it exists today. The key figures in that first wave of alternative comedians were Alexei Sayle, Keith Allen, Jim Barclay, Tony Allen, Andy de la Tour and Pauline Melville.

Alternative comedy was a direct challenge to the two traditions of stand-up that had preceded it. Alexei Sayle's attitude to variety comedy was revealing:

> Actually, people are always going on about, um, about the British Music Hall and, um, how and why it died out. I'll tell you why it died out, 'cos it was <u>shite</u>!!! Have you ever seen a bigger load of old shite than the Royal Command Variety Performance, you know, all them fucking old acts going, 'Ey oop, mind mee marrows!'[3]

There were a number of aspects of variety and club comedy which were violently opposed by the new comics. Firstly, they abused the stylistic conservatism of their predecessors. Both of the previous traditions tended to demand adherence to rigid comic conventions, producing comedy which was often predictable. Variety and club comedy both tend to rely heavily on stock subjects: mothers-in-law, domineering wives, old maids and commercial travellers in the case of variety; and homosexuals, West Indians, Pakistanis and the Irish in club comedy.

Neither tradition prized originality. Variety comedians tended to resort to the same joke books for material, books like Lewis and Fay

Copeland's *Ten Thousand Jokes, Toasts and Stories* published in 1939.[4] Similarly, club comics can buy standardised joke-sheets costing a few pounds each, which are sold via small-ads in the back of *The Stage*.[5] Moreover, stealing material from other comics is an accepted practice in Working Men's Clubs, and the extent of this was highlighted by a recent incident. When Jack Dee kicked up a fuss about one of his jokes turning up in the mouth of club comic Mike McCabe on the recent revival of *The Comedians*, McCabe's response was, "You can't have a monopoly on jokes. Once they have been told, they spread. If a comedian wants to keep a gag to himself, then he shouldn't tell it".[6]

Alternative comedy laid into the predictability of the comedy which this kind of attitude had produced. Tony Allen used to start his act with a list of the clichés of club comedy:

Anyway, there was this drunk, homosexual Pakistani squatter who takes my mother-in-law to an Irish restaurant and he says to the West Indian waiter, "Waiter, there's a racial stereotype in my soup," and the waiter says, "What d'you expect for 40p-a Caucasian stockbroker?"[7]

20th Century Coyote (Rik Mayall and Ade Edmondson) deconstructed the simple riddle joke by taking an overly literal-minded approach to it.[8] Ben Elton's attack on stale joke structures was more straightforward:

I tell lies. That's my job, only bit of truth is: I tell lies, we're like politicians, stand-up comedians tell lies, it's our job. I mean, imagine what it'd be like if stand-up comics started telling the truth, what a true joke would be like: "A bloke goes into a pub. . . orders a pint . . . drinks it. . . fucks off again," brilliant eh? I mean it wouldn't work, would it, he's gotta have a crocodile up his arse or something. Turn it into a joke.[9]

A second aspect of existing comedy which was torn apart by the early alternative comics was the notion of a cosy and friendly rapport between comedian and audience, a notion typified by the existence of the catchphrase. Catchphrases were an important part of variety and to a lesser extent club comedy, and they were important in injecting a note of reassuring familiarity into a comic's act. Alexei Sayle's angle on the subject was:

> You've got to have a catchphrase as well, you know, like umm, "Nick nick" or "Shut that door" or "Sieg Heil".[10]

He also claimed to have invented a catchphrase of his own..

> 'Ere, it's good catchphrase that, innit, eh: "Shit piss want fuck cunt," eh innit? Better than me last one, which was, "Don't tell Mr Mugabe!" Don't know what the fuck that one was about, I tell you.[11]

Many of the new comics replaced the traditional friendly rapport with confrontation and vitriolic abuse. Alexei Sayle often called his audiences "bastards", "fuckers" and "fuckfaces". Keith Allen went further, and even resorted to physical violence on occasion, threatening hecklers with broken fruit juice bottles, throwing darts at the audience, or turning a fire extinguisher on a reviewer from the *Evening Standard*.[12]

A third major break with tradition was alternative comedy's attitude towards obscenity. Variety comedy was subject to various forms of censorship, and the response of the variety comic to this restriction was a heavy reliance on jokes which covertly referred to sexual or lavatorial matters. Club comedy is not so restricted, but club comics have to exercise some restraint in their use of obscenity. One minor club comic, Wee Georgie Wheezer, has outlined his own cautious approach:

> You sort of feel your way as you go along. You say "piss" once, which mostly you'll get a good laugh. . . if they take that, they'll take "shit" with it. . . if they don't take "piss" then you know they're not going to take "shit" so you've got to try and cut that down a bit.[13]

Alternative comedy spat in the face of such pussyfootedness. Obscene language and an undisguised, uninhibited and often graphic approach to sex and defecation became not only possible, but also expected.

Bearing Wee Georgie Wheezer's attitude in mind, witness this Alexei Sayle routine:

> All right, skanking, wanking and ranking, all right. Do what, bollocks, knock it on the head, all right, eh? Shit piss wank fuck cunt all right bollocks knock it on the head do what wanker all right you fucking cunt eh shit piss wank fuck cunt bollocks knock it on the head all right eh? Shit piss fucking cunt wank shit piss wank fuck cunt bollocks wanker fucking cunt all right shit piss wank fuck cunt bollocks do what as it 'appens fucking cunt. Eh, you fucking wanker? Eh, shit piss wank fuck cunt bollocks leave it out do what as it 'appens shit piss wank all right give it a portion be lucky be brief. Fucking wanker, eh bollocks, how you doing fucking cunt all right shit piss wank all right, eh? Do what bollocks, leave it out all right ship piss fucking cunt all right? Fucking wanker shit piss wank fuck cunt bollocks leave it out all right do what knock it on the head fuck cunt wank all right bollocks shit piss wank fuck cunt bollocks leave it out give it a portion be lucky be brief fucking cunt all right you wanker shit piss wank fuck cunt bollocks. . . 'ere, I don't have to remember any of this you know, 'cos it's all written on the inside of me hat![14]

The final and most important difference between alternative comics and their predecessors was their political stance. Both variety and club comedy tended to avoid overt political allegiance, but both tended towards the political Right. Variety comedy usually exhibited a kind of cosy conservatism, which reaffirmed traditional family values by ridiculing deviation from them. Club comedy was more extreme, making often savage attacks on minority groups like homosexuals, the Irish, West Indians, and particularly Pakistanis, whilst exhibiting a rabid anti-immigration stance.

In the face of this, alternative comedy's violent Leftward lurch was quite extraordinary. Alternative Cabaret was founded on a non-sexist non-racist manifesto, and in contrast with their predecessors, the new comics were completely open about their political stance. They gave themselves political labels, for example, Alexei Sayle referred to himself as a "Marxist comedian", Tony Allen called himself an "anarchist comedian", and Jim Barclay was, in his own words, a "wacky and zany Marxist-Leninist comedian." Later, there was Jenny Lecoat, the self-professed "feminist comedian", and Simon Fanshawe, the "radical gay comedian". This is a far cry from, say, Bernard Manning, who in spite of expressing admiration for Enoch Powell, and even Adolf Hitler, would scarcely describe himself as a "wacky and zany racist-fascist comedian."

The tendency to satirise cliched joke-structures sometimes had a political dimension. For example, one of Ben Elton's early routines was an assassination attempt on the kind of sexist *double entendres* which kept variety comics in business:

I saw this sitcom, working title: "Can You Show Me the Way to Oldham?" That was the first laugh, "Oldham" sounds a bit like "hold 'em" doesn't it, very funny, well done BBC, well worth sixty five quid a year license money I don't think. I watched 'em all, Benny Hill, laugh? I nearly did, fantastic. And in this sitcom, there was Gloria, behind the bar, she's a big woman, bring in the camera, steam up the lens, everybody loves it, big tits, best gag in the world, that's the one for the British punter. In comes Tom, he's an amicable northern stereotype, he says, "By 'eck, you don't get many of those to the pound," he gets a laaauuugh!! Nice one Tom, 'cos she's got big tits, oh ho ho ho ho! He says, "By 'eck, I wish I were her doctor," yes Tom, second laugh, same pair of tits, I couldn't believe it, it's happening in front of me. He says, "By 'eck, no wonder they built the extension," go on Tom, you're winning, he says, "By 'eck, that's the loveliest pair of. . . eyes I ever saw!" Oh amazing Tom, we thought he was going to say "tits" didn't we, fantastic.[15]

Alternative comedy and the Thatcher government both came into being in the same year, 1979, and the class conflict which followed the Conservative election victory was reflected in the material of the new comics. For example, Andy de la Tour addressed the new poverty which accompanied the economic recession of the early 1980s:

I'll tell you what it's nice also to be away from in London is there's a lot of trendy bastards in London. . . a few up here and all, aren't there? You know what they do? They come and look, and see what's going on in the real world, and they just turn it into a fashion, you know, you've got all this poverty right now, so in London they've got this whole poverty 1930s revival fashion thing, you know what I mean, yeah, you get a recurrence of rickets in the North of England, and in London they turn it into a dance craze. They've got their own clubs, you know, poverty clubs, Monday Night's 'Diphtheria Night' yeah. . . videos of people being means tested, it's terrific, you know.[16]

Alexei Sayle's attitude to class conflict was simpler and more abusive:

I'll tell you another fucking myth, right. It's like education, you know life if, er. . . when you went, when you went to school about twenty years ago, they told you if you came out with two CSE's you're gonna be head of British Steel, you know? That's a load of bollocks, innit, eh? If you look at the statistics, right, like 82% of top British management have been to a public school and Oxbridge, 83% of the BBC have been to a public school and Oxbridge, 94% of the KGB have been to a public school and Oxbridge. All you get from a public school, right, is, is one, you get a top job, the other thing, the only other thing you get from a public school is an interest in perverse sexual practices. That's why British management's so ineffective, as soon as they get in the fucking boardroom, they're all shutting each other's dicks in the door! "Go on, give another slam, Sir Michael!" Whack! "Go on, let's play the panzer commander and the milkmaid! Eeuh eeuh!". . . bastards![17]

Inevitably, the fashionable middle class London Left culture which thrived in opposition to Thatcher made up a large part of the early audience for alternative comedy, but this subculture was also the subject of satirical attack. For a while, the Hampstead Lefty became a stock comic figure. For example, Pauline Melville's Edie character was a parody of a well-meaning liberal, desperate to fit into the Left culture but constantly making *faux pas*:

I'm expelled from everywhere, you know, I was expelled from
a commune once. I'd only been there two minutes. Two
minutes! They said, "You're on the cooking rota tonight," so I
went off to the shops and I saw this book that said *Mussolini for
Beginners*. So I thought, "Oh, well I'll get that. That'll be nice
for supper. [18]

The immediate impact of alternative comedy was to smash
the existing rules and assumptions which had restricted stand-up. For
a while, anything became possible. Comics like Keith Allen and
Alexei Sayle could be genuinely surreal, and some of the comics that
followed were even more bizarre. Kevin McAleer for example, now
a big star in Ireland, presented a comic slide show which defies
description. Even the most fundamental rules of comedy were
broken, with comics like Keith Allen sometimes deliberately
refusing to be funny, for example, by telling the audience his father
had just died and going into great detail about the funeral
arrangements.[19] Later, Norman Lovett built an entire act on
deliberate unfunniness, pausing for three or four minutes before
starting his act, and telling the audience, 'Cor, I'm bored now.'[20]

The political boundaries had also been knocked down, not
only because comics could now do politically radical jokes, but also
because the possibility of becoming a comedian became open to a
greater proportion of the population. Alternative comedy produced
women comedians like Pauline Melville, French and Saunders, Jenny
Lecoat and Helen Lederer, gay comics like Simon Fanshawe, Claire
Dowie and Julian Clary, and black comics like Sheila Hyde and Felix.

However, the barriers did not stay down indefinitely. The
artistic experiments of the early days were gradually replaced by a
more solid, professional style of comedy. By the late 1980s, people
had begun to complain about comedians who used exactly the same
set time after time, apparently unable to come up with new material.
The word 'bland' became widely used to describe the increasing
uniformity. The big stars of the current alternative comedy circuit tend
to be young, white, male performers, whose success relies on their
extraordinarily ability to work an audience. Their material tends to be
slight and unchallenging, brought to life only by their highly skilled

performance ability. For example, Alan Davies is one of the most talented of the current crop of performers, and it is interesting to examine footage of his act in front of a less than enthusiastic audience. With a responsive audience, say at Jongleurs in London, what stands out is his remarkable stage presence and audience control, which gives him the ability to create gales of laughter with tiny, insubstantial jokes. However, in front of a quieter crowd at the Edinburgh Fringe, the lack of response does not so much make the jokes seem unfunny, as make them almost disappear. Without the cue of audience laughter, it becomes difficult to distinguish punchlines from build-ups.[21]

The political radicalism of the early days has also subsided. The anarchic political stance of the early days was gradually replaced by a more solid Left position. The first wave of alternative comedians may have introduced Left Wing politics into stand-up, but they also satirised the Left and refused to bow to Left taboos. Alexei Sayle, for example, was vehement in his refusal to observe the Left's embargo on the word 'cunt'.[22] By the mid-1980s, comics like Jeremy Hardy and Mark Steel were taking a more straightforward Left line, and the scene became politically correct, to use the currently fashionable term. The backlash came in the form of a comic called Gerry Sadowitz, who was rather like an Alexei Sayle who has swapped his Marxism for a magic set. His chaotic and aggressive style recalled the early days of alternative comedy, but his targets were more widespread, ignoring the non-sexist, non-racist guidelines. For example, he brought an inflatable sex doll onto the stage and asked, "Any feminists in here tonight?" before pretending to copulate with it. He followed this up with the line: "I bloody hate feminists. They hate men so much, how come they dress like them?" Later in the act, he said he had been working on a character similar to Harry Enfield's Greek-Cypriot kebab shop owner Stavros, and proceeded to present a gross stereotype of a Pakistani:

> Hello, my name is Raj! And I specialise in short-changing people that come into my shop! I wear pyjamas all fucking day! A business suit in bed! I can't go to the toilet without taking my entire family with me!

This was followed by another quick joke: "How do you get fifty Pakistanis in a mini? I've no idea, but they do it, don't they?"[23]

This was the beginning of the end of the Left's influence on alternative comedy. In the wake of Gerry Sadowitz, it became fashionable to target minority groups, albeit less sensitive ones than the Pakistani community. Comics like Jack Dee and Jo Brand, in their different ways, made it possible to make comic attacks on people who are fat and ugly, old people, or people with deformities. As audiences broadened out and were no longer dominated by the Left such easy, casual sickness became more acceptable than polemical material.

The changing politics of alternative comedy has also meant that the trickle of minority groups into stand-up has failed to become a stream. I would estimate that no more than ten percent of alternative comedians are women, a rate which is little better than in variety or club comedy. Similarly, there has been no massive influx of gay comics, and the lack of black comics forging their careers in the alternative circuit has led to the establishment of a separate black comedy circuit.

It should be pointed that the current alternative comedy circuit is not entirely free of radical politics or boundary-stretching innovation, and it is still capable of producing Left Wing comics like Mark Thomas and wildly imaginative innovators like Eddie Izzard or Lee Evans. However, the slick, professional style of the modern alternative comic is far removed from the aggressive anarchy of the first wave of performers. This is perceived as a problem within the circuit itself, and there have been various attempts to recapture the innovation and political edge of the early days: the improvised comedy movement is seen as a return to the innovative side and the Comedy Store's topical material-based Cutting Edge show is an attempt to restore the political aspect.

The cause of this change is undoubtedly the ever-increasing commercialisation of the circuit. Over the fifteen years of its existence, alternative comedy has been transformed from a ramshackle, semi-amateur affair to a lucrative business. It is not Golden Ageism to suggest that the comedians and promoters who kicked the scene into life were motivated more by enthusiasm and the pioneering spirit than financial or careerist motives. In the early days, there really was very little money about. When the Comedy Store first opened, none of the comics got paid, and even Alexei Sayle only got paid five pounds a night for compering.[24]

Now, comics can make a very healthy living playing the circuit and the interest of television means that becoming an alternative comedian can easily become the first stepping stone to media stardom. The scene is equally attractive to promoters. Big venues like The Comedy Store and Jongleurs can entertain several hundred punters in a weekend, each paying around ten pounds on the door. Big alternative comedy agencies like Avalon and Off The Kerb are also thriving; in 1992, Avalon were reported to be earning two million pounds a year from the ten acts on the roster.[25]

Clearly, the unpredictability of the early alternative comics would be inappropriate to this kind of professional environment. Their aim was to break the rules, and to challenge, in the words of Jim Barclay, to dent the prejudices of the audience rather than confirm them.[26] This kind of confrontational attitude inevitably involved an element of danger. Audiences would sometimes respond with silence or would break into fights. Keith Allen was once knocked unconscious by an audience member after making a joke about an IRA bombing.[27] Tony Allen recalls going to the Edinburgh Festival with Alexei Sayle, and having to reverse the order of the show, putting Sayle on second, because his aggressive attitude had been scaring people away.[28] Sayle remembers a review of the same show in a student paper, which expressed total puzzlement at what they were attempting, saying simply, "I don't know what these people are doing."[29]

In the current professionalised circuit, such responses would be undesirable for promoters and comics alike. Promoters want comics who are reliable, so that they can be sure of keeping their audiences, not scaring them away. Comics tend to stick to tried and tested methods and material, aiming to please audiences so as to secure rebookings. The extent of the change in the circuit is encapsulated in an incident related to me by a promoter who runs a chain of small clubs in London. Tony Allen, who is rarely booked in London now because of the unpredictability of audience response to his act, had performed in one of the promoters venues, and had performed a very tight set, starting off with a succession of simple one-liners before moving into his more involved material, which covers such unlikely topics as chaos theory and sub-atomic physics. Allen went down well, but after the show, an audience member approached the promoter and said, "I can see he's very good and everything, but when I get home from work on a Friday night, I don't want that, I want jokes."

Notes

[1] For example, in Roger Wilmut and Peter Rosengard, *Didn't You Kill My Mother-in-Law* (Methuen, 1989)

[2] Author's interview with Tony Allen, 30 September 1988

[3] Bootleg cassette of Alexei Sayle at the Theatre Royal, Nottingham, October 1983

[4] Roger Wilmut, *Kindly Leave the Stage* (Methuen, 1985) p.118

[5] For example, small ads in the back of a 1990 copy of *The Stage* offer "100 Good Strong Club Gags" for £2.00 from Stan and Ken Warby scripts in Blackpool, or a sheet of "1 liners" for £9.95 from The Mercury Group in Oldham

[6] Sally Brockway, "That's not funny! Mike cracks Jack's telly gag", *The Sun* (TV Super Guide), p.5

[7] Lisa Appignanesi, Cabaret (Methuen, 1984), p.186

[8] 20th Century CoVote, on *Fundamental Frolics* (BBC Records, 1981)

[9] Ben Elton, *Motormouth (*Mercury Records, 1987) side 1

[10] Bootleg cassette Of Alexei Sayle at the Theatre Royal, Nottingham, October 1983. "Nick nick" is club comic Jim Davidson's catchphrase, and "Shut that door" is camp comic Larry Grayson's

[11] Alexei Sayle, *Cak (*Springtime Records, 1982) side 2

[12] *Didn't You Kill My Moth er-in Law?* op.cit. p.10 and pp.44-45

[13] Author's interview with Wee Georgie Wheezer, 26 September 1988

[14] *Cak,* side 2

[15] *Motormouth,* side 2

[16] Andy de la Tour on *Let the Children Play* (Panic Records, no date (circa 1984), side 3)

[17] *Cak,* side 1

[18] Pauline Melville on *Let the Children Play***,** side 4

[19] *Didn't You Kill My Mother-in-Law?* p.34

[20] *Didn't You Kill My Mother-in-Law?* pp.157-58

[21] At Jongleurs, *The South Bank Show,* ITV, 15 December 1993. At the Edinburgh Fringe, *Edinburgh Comedy,* BBC2,28 August 1994

[22] "It was a central ideological debate. We used to do a lot of radical venues, and people would come backstage afterwards and say, "Look. Alexei, we really liked the act but..." I became more and more of a resolute cunt-ist, really. I got more and more hard-line." Alexei Sayle, quoted in Lynn Barber, "Offstage it's not so funny," *The Independent on Sunday* (29 September 1991) pp.14-15

[23] Gerry Sadowitz, *The Total Abuse Show*, Virgin Video, 1988

[24] *Didn't You Kill My Mother-in-Law?*, p.11

[25] William Cook, "The Svengalis of stand-up comedy", *The Guardian,* (1 September 1992) p.30

[26] Quoted in Michael Williams, "The new stand-up, put-down comics", *The Sunday Times* (7 October 1984) p.39

[27] *Didn't You Kill My Mother-in-Law?*, p.46

[28] *Didn't You Kill My Mother-in-Law?*, p.47

[29] Author's interview with Alexei Sayle, 5 April 1990

Acklam LRC
Middlesbrough College
Hall Drive
Middlesbrough
TS5 7DY

Ananse's Wealth: Response and Responsibility in African Popular Theatre

Carole-Anne Upton

May I ask you a few questions?...

Do you really consider that a performance is improved by continual interruptions, however complimentary they may be to the actors and the author?

Do you not think that the naturalness of the pre-presentation must be destroyed, and therefore your own pleasure greatly diminished, when the audience insists on taking part in it by shouts of applause and laughter, and the actors have repeatedly to stop acting until the noise is over?

Do you know that...the strain of performing is greatly increased if the performers have to attend to the audience as well as to their parts at the same time?...

Have you noticed that if you laugh loudly and repeatedly for two hours, you get tired and cross, and are sorry next morning that you did not stay at home?...

Would you dream of stopping the performance of a piece of music to applaud every bar that happened to please you? And do you not know that an act of a play is intended, just like a piece of music, to be heard without interruption from beginning to end?

Have you ever told your sons and daughters that little children should be seen and not heard? And have you ever thought how nice theatrical performances would be, and how much sooner you would get away to supper, if parents in the theatre would follow the precepts they give to their children at home?...

Do you know that my plays, as rehearsed, are just the right length, that is, quite as long as you can bear; and that if you delay the performances by loud laughter you will make them half an hour too long?

And finally, will you believe me to be acting sincerely in your own interests in this matter as your faithful servant,

The Author.[1]

The author here is George Bernard Shaw and the questions are, of course, rhetorical. Had they been addressed to an African audience, they would no doubt have been answered with just the loud responses that G.B.Shaw found so infuriating!

For the fundamental underlying principle, the driving force behind African theatre, almost without exception, can be summed up in terms of a *dialogue*. Dialogue, not in the limited sense of a purely verbal exchange, but rather a kind of communication and communion through song, dance, words and action, a reciprocal involvement of all present. This dialogic principle may be regarded as a unifying thread that runs throughout the theatre culture of sub-Saharan Africa, in its various manifestations. Both South Africa and the Northern regions have undergone historical developments that have not rendered them, on the whole, "theatre-friendly", whilst sub-Saharan and in particular West Africa share widespread and often contingent theatrical traditions. Even the most sacred rituals involve a communication with spirits from whom a discernible response is anticipated, whether through the voice and movement of one possessed, or through some palpable change beyond the ritual itself, such as the success of a harvest, the coming of rains, or the conception of a child by a previously barren woman.

In the secular theatre, the interchange is more immediate. Jacques Scherer [2] describes the extreme case of a production in the Central African Republic, where the noise level of the audience grew so great that it became impossible to hear the actors speak. Eventually a loudspeaker in the wings began to bellow repeated pleas of "Silence! Ecoutez! Ne parlez pas tous en même temps!" and so on. This only served to double the din and the performance ended in confusion! He also recalls a more recent performance in Cameroon, during which the audience members called out to the characters by their names, giving them advice, expressing admiration or slipping jokes in between the actors' lines. At the end, he tells us, the whole audience joined in with the dancing, one woman even leaving her seat to jump up on stage and dance with the performers.

Another commentator, on a Ghanaian production of Soyinka's *The Lion and the Jewel* writes:

It occurred to me...as I observed the enthusiasm of the "Zongo" audience clamouring for a repetition of the seduction scene between the Bale and Sidi, that, at long last, we seem to have discovered...a group of theatre entrepreneurs who may give the fillip to the development of the popular theatre in Ghana. [3]

It seems ironic that Soyinka, the doyen of the relatively new literary and above all intellectual drama, should provide the inspiration for such optimism, albeit that *The Lion and the Jewel* is unquestionably his most accessible play. Soyinka himself writes:

> The serious divergences between a traditional African approach to drama and the European will not be found in lines of opposition between creative individualism and communal creativity, nor in the level of noise from the auditorium – this being the supposed gauge of audience-participation – at any given performance.[4]

And further, on ritual mask-drama:

> Overt participation when it comes is channelled through a formalised repertoire of gestures and liturgical responses. The "spontaneous" participant from within the audience does not permit himself to give vent to a bare impulse or a euphoria which might bring him out as a dissociated entity from within the choric mass. If it does happen, as of course it can, the event is an aberration which may imperil the eudaemonic goals of that representation.[5]

According to Soyinka, the role of the audience is nonetheless central. Not only do they constitute a ritual chorus, giving "spiritual strength" and "collective energy" to the protagonists, but moreover, they are integrated and actively involved in the proceedings by virtue of *defining the space,* both physical and metaphysical. Traditional African theatre of both the sacred and secular varieties is usually performed in a setting that requires no more than an open space, and people. Most frequently its "stage" is the village market-place; the dramatic arena being demarcated by the edge of the crowd gathered around the performers. The proscenium arch, despite its recent proliferation in urban cultural centres, has no place in the traditional African ethos of what theatre is all about. Since the Middle Ages this construction, like the portcullis on the Western fortress of dramatic illusion, has safeguarded against the intrusion of any marauding reality from the auditorium. In Jacques Scherer's words it is:

> la construction la plus rigoureuse de l'histoire pour séparer radicalement et en quelque sorte ontologiquement le spectateur de tout ce qui n'est pas lui.[6]

This ontological distinction provides the antithesis of Soyinka's comprehensive cosmos, which is not mimetically represented but actually given material form in African theatre. The so-called spectators provide the concrete apparatus for creating the microcosmic universe which will bring within reach once more the whole gamut of cosmic and temporal "points de repère" that have receded from everyday secular life. The space is sanctified by the participation of this quasi-audience, who are thus able through the re-enactment of chthonic struggles to situate and redefine themselves in relation to the irreducible and timeless truths of existence. Self-apprehension on the part of the collective and the individual becomes the ultimate goal.

As we have seen, Soyinka engages ritual as the basis for his dramatic theory, a theory which in its implicit universality and its emphasis on community involvement is nothing if not popular. However, even the most cursory glance at his dramatic writing would suggest a deep-seated ambiguity with regard to the audience. The erudite English alone necessarily precludes a considerable sector of the potential indigenous audience. The settings usually imply a proscenium arch with decor; hence urban, commercial productions. The content of his more serious works tends to revolve around complex political intrigues which cannot be interpreted as symptomatic of universal truths without undergoing significant reduction.[7] The playwright himself is repeatedly evasive when it comes to identifying his audience:

> Minds out there in the world with whom I can communicate...

143

I think there is a lot of mystique about this business of whom one reaches in one's writings and whom one *ought* to reach ...

We pronounce "Guilty" on all counts, then we leave the rest to the potential reshaping force of society – among which we, the writers, consider ourselves – to work upon. [8]

*A*nd then surprises us with the following, on *A Dance of the Forests*:

What I found personally gratifying, and what I considered the validity of my work, was that the so-called illiterate group of the community, the stewards, the drivers – the really uneducated non-academic world – they were coming to see the show every night.[9]

His most categorical statements on the matter confirm that it is the people of the African continent that are his central concern, with the European audience at the periphery. The international renown of this Nobel prize-winner attests to the existence of an audience with both the inclination, and moreover, the means to listen to his individual voice. But his texts seem to leave little or no space for active participation by any such audience, neither in defining the dramatic arena, nor in expressing the aforementioned "liturgical responses". Furthermore the intellectual, linguistic, and staging demands of his plays leave production exclusively in the hands of a small, though admittedly growing, elite – often university drama groups or companies abroad. Dialogue has been left behind in the village marketplace. Monologue takes its place behind the proscenium arch, with the only concession to integration being the occasional chance to join in with a well-known song or dance. So much for self-apprehension. So much for a popular theatre.

Enticed through years of colonial education with the carrot of Greco-European dramatic paradigms, and beaten with the economic stick of international publishing houses, modern Africa has yielded a new product: literary drama. This cash crop is largely for export or for luxury consumers at home, while more traditional fare is still cultivated for subsistence. Of course, the two are not only produced distinctly side by side, but are also blended and refined in a complex and fascinating process of cross-fertilisation. Paradoxically, in an area where there is not as yet an established sector of aficionados to sustain the theatre as an industry, the ever-increasing number of literary playwrights must seek out ways of popularising their works in order to ensure the revenue that will source an indigenous profession. No matter how great the aesthetic merit or otherwise of the new drama, "bums on seats" are more important than ever now that the seats are there and the theatre has a price:

> For, let us face it, for the theatre to exist and survive in Ghana, the number of people we manage to get into our playhouses is crucial, And when I used the word entrepreneur...above I had in mind a business-like approach which keeps an eye on how to get the crowd into the playhouse, both by the play it chooses and the manner it produces it.[10]

The problems associated with drawing in the crowds are compounded by the fact that most audiences will be multilingual. Religious, political, ethnic and cultural diversity cutting across national boundaries represents in combination a myriad of mythologies to confound even Barthes. Theatre semiotics depend upon a shared cultural background. It seems to me that mass appeal has been ventured in the widest possible interpretation of a common identity through the Negritude movement; though a failure to define the grounds of this commonality within racial, geographical, historical or cultural parameters, together with the adoption of a poetic mode in French (and English) were significant factors in limiting its popular success. Césaire's *Et les Chiens se Taisaient*, though a remarkable work of literature, in stage terms is really none other than the recitation of a rather esoteric poem. There is no apparent attempt to integrate the audience through a proactive experience of the event, other than presumably to inspire a sympathetic urge towards generic revolt against white oppression. In post-independence Africa, the theatre contends with more immediate problems of a specific and localised nature; encompassing, as we shall see, the micro- (rather than the macro-) culture. Césaire's play *Une Tempête* can no longer address the contemporary concerns of an African audience. In Soyinka's words, "the Prospero-Caliban syndrome is, I think, dead".[11]

The widespread appeal of socialist and more especially Marxist political ideology is reflected in an overwhelming trend to establish a dramatic discourse based on class analysis. The concomitant desire to educate and mobilise the poorest illiterate sections of the community with a view to effecting political change also necessitates the popularisation of the theatre. Neo-colonial capitalist structures in Nigeria, to take just one example, that have appropriated theatre institutions for private enterprise leave their closet radical practitioners facing a dilemma; revolutionary drama must address the polarisation of the popular and the literary from within a commercial infrastructure which de facto situates theatre at the elitist end of the spectrum. There seems to be a twofold response to the challenge; firstly, to take theatre away from institutions again, running the risk of lowering artistic standards due to the obvious reduction in resources and facilities and secondly, to institutionalise the indigenous popular traditions that are perceived as the proper cultural heritage of the non-ruling classes.

Despite Soyinka's dismissal of the "lines of opposition between creative individualism and communal creativity," the prevalence of the social function in African theatre is one distinctive feature conducive to popular involvement at the level of production as well as reception. Participatory development theatre is now being used by international aid agencies and in government programmes aimed at educating targeted illiterate communities. This approach may be seen as an extension of the attempts made by the travelling theatres that emerged from certain universities, most notably Ibadan, in the 1960's and 70's to "take theatre to the people", mounting productions based on popular myth and folktale, often adopting local languages and idioms to perform in rural areas and urban townships.

The history of the famous Kamiriithu project under the leadership of Ngugi wa Thiongo and Ngugi wa Mirii serves to illustrate both the success and limitations of such an approach. *I Will Marry When I Want* and *Mother, Sing for Me* were scripted and produced collectively by peasant villagers as part of an adult literacy programme between 1977 and 1981. The final text was given in

Kikuyu, prompting Ngugi's controversial farewell to English[12] as a language for African writing. *I Will Marry When I Want* was banned by the Kenyan authorities after just nine performances, with Ngugi wa Thiongo detained for a year. *Mother, Sing for Me* was refused a performance license, the Kamiriithu Theatre was destroyed by police, and Ngugi along with his colleagues fled into exile:

> We don't look up to individuals and we cannot close the centre if the Ngugis are not here. If they stopped writing we would come together and write something. Group scripting is not something strange and we would do it. These two individuals are not the centre; the centre is the members.[13]

The project undoubtedly inspired its participants to proceed in a renewed spirit of confidence in their own creativity and its attendant power of self-determination. However, the Kamiriithu Community Education and Cultural Centre proved reluctant, in the event, to continue with drama after 1982. Might Ngugi's exile be regarded as a betrayal of a community which he was incapable of leading because of the gulf between his own status as prominent academic and the social situation of the peasant collective? Or does the academic/development officer still play an essential role in the mobilisation of popular theatre in Africa?

One positive view holds that the high profile of Ngugi drew public attention to Kamiriithu and thereby prevented the Kenyan authorities negating its achievements in a silent political repression of its local activities. Censorship in the majority of "Big Man" African states is a ha-ha surrounding the field of participatory theatre, in which anything that strays too far from central propaganda risks disappearing from view.

According to Scherer, responsibility for the suppression of radicalism in the theatre does not lie solely with the authorities, as Ngugi's Marxist philosophy would have us believe:

> Le conservatisme est souvent profondément ancré dans l'écriture dramatique aussi bien que dans la réalisation théâtrale. On peut contester la puissance de la tradition, se

> révolter contre elle, trouver des exceptions aux régles, mais *le*
> *public* ne supporterait pas qu'elle soit rejetée en bloc.[14]

The audience maintains its traditional function, even when confined to the role of receiver, of determining the nature of dramatic presentations. And so we return to the fundamental quest for a suitable form.

The outstanding exponent of popular theatre in Nigeria was the late Chief Hubert Ogunde, an ex-policeman and reputedly the father of contemporary Yoruba theatre. Having established his own professional travelling theatre, made up incidentally of his wives and children, his works were banned by the colonial authorities between 1946 and independence in 1960. In 1964, his *Yoruba Awake!* was also banned by the then government. He was a prolific writer, director, performer and entrepreneur, with a deeply nationalistic outlook, whose productions over the years are "a record in performance of a popular perception of all the major events in Nigeria's history."[15] Blandly sentimental plots on familiar themes of love and betrayal, heroes and corrupt politicians, were presented with all the raucous vitality that characterised his productions. The paying audience, whilst excluded from the rehearsal process, were encouraged quite literally to add their voice to the Yoruba (or pidgin) dialogue:

> The audience talk back, speak, even give you words to speak
> back to them. Here the audience is a part of the show.[16]

Not surprisingly, music and dance provided frequent opportunities for collective affirmation of the Yoruba spirit. Such was the extent of his appeal that his plays have appeared in photocomic book form, part of a veritable Ogunde industry. A consummate entertainer, constantly aware of current sympathies amongst his popular following, it is tempting to surmise that the sheer charisma of this extraordinary figure was at least as much responsible for the success of his operation as was the Protean form he devised. In other words, without Ogunde at its head it seems questionable whether this can provide a cogent paradigm for a popular theatre elsewhere in Africa.

However, if there is one consistent element in Ogunde's stylistic repertoire of operettas, religious musicals, melodramas, political intrigues, concert-parties and neo-traditional presentations, it is this – a close personal rapport with the audience maintained by means of the careful reduction of aesthetic distance.

Empathy, according to Boal, is "the most dangerous weapon in the entire arsenal of the theatre and related arts." Once in its grip:

> the spectator assumes a passive attitude and delegates the power of action to the character. Since the character resembles us (as Aristotle indicates), we live *vicariously* all his stage experiences. Without acting, we feel that we are acting.[17]

Tragedy has never been public property, so to speak. The "noble art" of the isolated tragic hero is particularly alien in societies which place great emphasis on collective responsibility. The African view of the cyclical cosmos with its anthropomorphic gods, who share the realm of the unborn and the ancestors, further intensifies the involvement of the community in all aspects of life; the people – dead, living or not yet born – are not victims of any mysterious meta-human Fate but are themselves to some extent the arbiters of destiny, even if a large section of this total populace is at one remove from the here and now. The psychological tragedy of the individual tends to give place to the more socially motivated arts of comedy/social realism on a broader canvas (often involving a large cast) and offering a greater possibility of change, both within the drama and beyond it, through collective action. Predominant in francophone drama of independence is the celebratory genre of the legendary hero warrior, who is presented as an exemplary affirmation of "people-power." Sympathy is in. Empathy is quite clearly out.

Boal would no doubt approve of the observation made by Robert W. July, that:

> Audiences in Africa regard themselves not as passive spectators but, at the very least, as active commentators and at best as integrated participants. By the same token, the actor never loses sight of his true identity, which he maintains by exchanging asides with the audience as he plays his part.[18]

Emerging from the dialogue – spontaneously interposed – of the traditional theatre, we now find not only the archetypal spect-actor (the acting spectator) but also his opposite number, what we night call the ac-tator (the spectating actor) enshrined within the scripted dialogue of modern dramatic texts.

The Brechtian combination of didacticism and realism is echoed in the dramaturgy of the most ambitious of writers, such as the Nigerian Femi Osofisan, and the influence of Brecht is immediately apparent in *On Joue la Comédie* by the Togolese playwright Senouvo Agbota Zinsou. Alongside familiar epic and anti-illusionist devices, the Brechtian "Not...But..." principle for suggesting alternatives[19] seems to be of central significance. The play presents Chaka, the nineteenth century Zulu hero in comic guise in a satirical attack on the apartheid regime in South Africa. The hero has a twin incarnation; Xuma, the head of the supposed acting troupe, and Chaka, head of a band of freedom-fighters, whose fictitious persona he adopts. Chaka's monopoly of heroic qualities is contested throughout by the opposing traits of Xuma; is it Chaka, or Xuma, or indeed the real actor playing Xuma, (and by implication any "normal" person) who embodies the authentic heroic traits? In the second act, two presenters appear, the first creating an illusion which is destroyed by the second; dramatising the notion of "Not...But..." and at the same time contesting the sole rights to creativity and action in a theatrical metaphor for political activism.

The form of the play derives largely from the Ghanaian Concert Party, which flourished in the 60's and 70's. Originally based upon improvisation around a given topical theme, it was performed without rehearsal in whatever space was available. The performers were all amateur, all male (although there are female roles), and each specialised in a certain stereotype, immediately recognisable by the familiar costume and make-up. "Le bouffon" was an important feature, as was music and dance, and the performance traditionally lasted for up to six hours. Spontaneous audience participation was an important ingredient in this popular jamboree.

Zinsou's self-reflexive transformation of the genre into a literary mode exploits the participatory element in order to present disparate viewpoints which situate the historical enactment in a contemporary "reality":

> *De la salle monte un vieillard...*
>
> LE VIEILLARD: On m'a dit qu'ici c'est le théâtre où tout le monde a droit à la parole.
> LE PRESENTATEUR: Qui vous a dit ça?
> LE VIEILLARD: Quelqu'un a l'entree, [...]
> LE PRESENTATEUR: *(Aux spectateurs)* C'est un comédien.
> LE VIEILLARD: Qui? Moi, je suis comédien?
> LE PRESENTATEUR: Non, pas vous. Nous.[20]

The Prologue is full of such interventions by agents provocateurs. One demands a refund at the suggestion that the piece should be improvised, on the grounds that this is not proper theatre; another disputes the relevance of a historical play in addressing contemporary problems. As the play goes on there are fewer such interventions, and they remain within the diegetic narrative. The dialogue is not between actor and audience but rather between two characters, one on stage and the other in the auditorium.

Zinsou has injected vitality into the piece by attempting to recreate artificially a rhythm of spontaneity. The dramatic space is extended into the auditorium by this device, thus ostensibly incorporating the audience. Given roles include actors playing actors, in turn playing characters, as well as actors playing spectators of the play within a play. What is noticeably absent from the work is spectators playing anything but a passive role. The Presenter's request for spectators to "participer à notre modeste comédie qui fait un grand effort pour sortir du sous-développement"[21] is clearly, and comically, disingenuous, in complete contrast to the final moments of the play, which give an ironic twist to the question of free speech:

> Ce soir, nous avons ouvert des prisons, brisé des chaînes, libéré des détenus, tout en riant, mais nos frères sont encores dans les prisons d'Afrique du Sud, parce qu'ils ont osé prononcer ce mot précieux: Liberté! Et vous, êtes-vous prêts ce soir à réclamer avec nous, non seuiement en paroles, mais aussi en

actes? Si oui, criez avec nous! Liberté! Liberté! Criez-le dans
toutes les langues, dans tous les lieux, jusqu'à la libération
totale de notre peuple! *Liberté! Liberté! sera répété par tous les
disciples sure la scene et dans la salle par des spectateurs.*[22]

This somewhat bathetic call to arms serves as a reminder that for the
duration of the play and despite all the anti-illusionist devices, the real
audience have lived *vicariously* the stage experiences. They have felt
that they were acting, without acting. In Zinsou's transposition of the
popular form, the responsibility for active participation is transferred
from the dramatic to the political arena.

One final peculiarity demands attention with regard to this
text. It is written in French, the language of officialdom, treats a South
African subject with a pan-African rally cry, and yet it contains literal
translations of local Togolese idioms from the ewe and mina
languages that are unintelligible to the non-native speaker. All of
which raises the vexed question of whom this play is addressing.

Another play which employs the device of planting actors
amongst the audience is the Nigerian Sam Ukala's *Akpakaland*,
described by the author as "a one-act folkscript". The Dramatis
Personae include M.O.A. or Members of the Audience. In this case
the technique is employed amidst a number of other strategies taken
directly from oral folk narration, in a more straightforward attempt to
imbue a literary piece with the flavour and appeal of popular culture.

A significant difference, however, between Ukala's
development of the participatory convention and Zinsou's is that
Ukala uses the M.O.A. as a stimulus for genuine audience
participation. The initial stage directions have the Narrator "*leading
the audience in the opening song*" which is repeated "*until the
auditorium has been warmed up and Narrator and some members of
the audience have danced.*" Later, when the narrator addresses a
political question directly to the M.O.A, he "*pauses for reactions
from the public audience.*" Again we have the device of calling for
supposed audience members to come forward to take roles in the
fictional narrative; the narrator pauses to ask their names, thus
seeming to narrow the distance between actors and audience whilst
placing the fiction at a further critical remove from reality by

highlighting the "true" identity of the players. The focus of the event is redirected into the auditorium by objectifying the fiction of the stage world. The lines spoken by M.O.A. bear a resemblance to those liturgical choric responses described by Soyinka; ritualistic repetitions ("and we'll see the arse of the hen" for example) punctuate the action, offering encouragement and passing comment. Again we have the impression of complicity between actors and audience, but the public experience is not entirely vicarious. Ukala suggests that genuine audience participation is to be elicited following the liberating example of his agents provocateurs, but the very structured nature of the M.O.A. responses limit spontaneity and the result is a highly controlled level of active participation. [23]

The Contest by Ugandan Mukotani Rugyendo challenges our very concept of literary drama. His text, published by Heinemann Education no less, can hardly be described as a script at all. Described in a production note as "an experiment...to explore what can possibly be done to maintain the *popular* nature of theatre"[24], the scant text is interspersed with extensive stage directions suggesting a high degree of improvisation on the part of both designated performers and so-called spectators:

> First there is a lot of drumming from far off. Then the drumming draws nearer until the drummer appears, well-attired, as if for a ceremony. The drumming can be discerned as summoning the people to collect in the square. As the drummer reaches the square his drumming becomes louder and he starts dancing to the rhythm of his drumming all around the square. The people start coming to the square. Men and women come individually or in twos. Some walk all around the square and take their seats on the edges. Others dance around or across it to the rhythm of the drumming and do all sorts of funny gymnastics with their bodies to the amusement of all the others. The drummer becomes wild in his drumming and dancing and the people get captured by the whole thing.[25]

This integration of "the people" into the very fabric of the event implies not only public familiarity with the conventions of the form, in this case the local "heroic recitation", but also great skill on the part of the performers in arousing and controlling their responses:

> *Their arms, shoulders, and heads particularly will have to be relied on for the gestures and movements which match the leaping and strutting of the feet, and help to involve the people in the action. Throughout the contest the people will be participating effectively, throwing in comments on what they think of the performers and what they are saying. The people will also occasionally drive home what the hero has said with a loud "Yeee..." or "Hmm..." in the manner of active participation. The heroes, therefore, must always make logical pauses according to the strength of what they have said and create the right atmosphere to make the people's assent acceptable.[26]*

The rationale behind the use of the popular participatory form is expounded in the production note, and reflects a Marxist view of culture. The class structure which is a product of colonialism has alienated the people from that rich cultural heritage which previously embodied the African life-force. Rugyendo talks of the "magic" and "dynamism" of traditional African art forms as a vital source of popular strength in the political struggle against oppression and exploitation. Once again, the social function of popular art takes it beyond the cause of entertainment pure and simple. Song and dance are invigorating to the point of being dangerous. Not simply a release mechanism, such vigorous group performances signal the potential existence of a loud collective voice outside the dramatic arena as well as within it. Action is no longer to be accepted as the prerogative of a chosen few. The play, written in the `70's is contemporary with Boal's *Theatre of the Oppressed*:

> The *poetics of the oppressed* is essentially the poetics of liberation: the spectator no longer delegates power to the characters either to think or to act in his place. The spectator frees himself; he thinks and acts for himself! Theatre is action! Perhaps the theatre is not revolutionary in itself; but have no doubts, it is a rehearsal of revolution![27]

Since the collapse of communism in Eastern Europe we might find it difficult to share the ideological optimism underlying both these works. However, unless one is prepared to accept the residing political status quo in many parts of Africa – and recent events in South Africa are proof to the contrary – it is essential that the theatre should continue to provide an outlet for the popular voice.

In theatrical terms, *The Contest* "aspires to minimise to the lowest degree the hollow distance between actors and the silent audience in modern theatre."[28] It is an aspiration towards the popular that marks the works of many modern African playwrights, as we have seen. The distinction between involvement at the point of production or reception is significantly blurred by such experiments in which the production ceases to exist independently of its public.

Extensive scholarship has concentrated on the influence of Western forms in African drama. It seems almost too obvious for words that a century of colonialism should have left its imprint on indigenous culture. Indeed, European contemporary trends are now adopting the very syncretic and synthetic approach to art, now referred to as post-modern, which characterises the most ancient of African and other aboriginal traditions. The dialogic principle is also being reinstated; one has only to think of interactive television.

It is my suggestion that the most consequential Western legacy in African theatre is not primarily artistic but economic. The commercialisation of the theatre means that a conscious effort has to be made in order to avoid the devalorisation of popular theatre in the face of a literary hegemony enjoying the financial support of commercial institutions. Brecht wrote in the 1930's:

> When considering what slogans to set up for German literature today one must remember that anything with a claim to be considered as literature is printed exclusively abroad, and with a few exceptions can only be read there. This gives a peculiar twist to the slogan of *Volkstümlichkeit* [or *popularity*] in literature.[29]

The imperative towards a text-based theatre in Africa is attractive in terns of artistic status, access to facilities including specialised practitioners, and a degree of financial reward. On the other hand, the problems of identifying, attracting, and addressing a popular audience, of transcending divisions of class and ethnicity, have led to the reclamation of age-old traditions in a new dimension. The proud reappropriation of indigenous forms that began under the auspices of Negritude finds a new internal stimulus in the popularisation of an indigenous literary theatre.

There are, however, inherent contradictions in the process. J.P. Clark's adaptation of the Ozidi saga is a case in point. The saga belongs to an Ijaw tradition, in which the story is told over seven days, actively involving the local community, and led by a dexterous storyteller. Clark, concerned to preserve the ancient oral tradition, set about recording it and subsequently writing a play version, in English, entitled *Ozidi*.[30] Admittedly, Clark makes no claim, to my knowledge, to a popular theatre with this work, which eliminates the participatory element. Nevertheless, if this may be described as the transference of a popular form into a literary drama, the general danger becomes apparent. In attempting to popularise the literary theatre by reference to traditional forms, it is possible to have the opposite effect; what was once popular becomes literary and loses its authentic voice. Furthermore, one might argue that the Urtext, for want of a better word, of these evolving oral traditions is somehow petrified through publication. It becomes retrogressive and self-defeating if deprived of its ongoing capacity to adapt to topical circumstances.

Multi-culturalism is the harmonious face of separatism. In drama, what we might call *specific universality,* by which I mean an appeal to the universal truths of a given ethnic community, social class, or linguistic group rather than of humanity in general, may offer a key to popular involvement within a targeted audience. In the absence of an operational network however, there is a danger of ghettoisation which runs contrary to any aspirations towards unified national culture.

Participation is a convention of popular theatre culture across Africa that might be cited as evidence of its prominent position of responsibility within society. The convention goes beyond mere theatricality by drawing the community into the event, and vice-versa. But it would appear that it is the extrapolated principle that is transferable, not the wholesale tradition with all its original trappings. A 1962 Nigerian production of *The Taming of the Shrew* by the travelling theatre of the University of Ibadan adopted the pretence of an impromptu performance by members of the audience, the company having supposedly been held up en route to the theatre. Of course, these so-called audience members turned out to be none other than the missing actors themselves. Geoffrey Axworthy, the first director of the University Arts Theatre and School of Drama, describes the liberating effect of the technique:

> A whisper passes around the hall, growing into an overwhelming wave of laughter, which stops the play. Such audiences love a practical joke and by this time are truly hooked. They even carry on the pretence. When Katherina, in the closing scene, drops back into her original character of an emancipated Nigerian girl...and refuses to do the submission speech, the actors, and then perhaps the whole audience, may beg her to carry on, for the sake of the show. She agrees, it being understood that no self-respecting Nigerian woman would behave like this nowadays.[31]

The collective oral culture bears no copyright. By contrast, the modern theatre is governed by individual impresarios, a fact which perhaps offers a bright artistic future of an African theatre culture nurtured by trained specialists. Scherer makes the point that the communal "triomphe de l'émotion socialisée" has the disadvantage of excluding talent; "devant les sonnailles de centaines de danseurs, il n'y a pas de Nijinski possible"[32]. But the evidence shows that the most participatory of forms is not an anarchic free-for-all but a careful structure which allows for spontaneity controlled by the drummer, storyteller, or leading performers. Zinsou's spoof of the old man above demonstrates the point. In any case, what Scherer seems to ignore is that *being* a dancer, even a mediocre one, is just as important as watching a brilliant one. It is the responsibility of the talented minority to get the less able majority on its feet.

And so at last to Ananse. In Ghana, Efua Sutherland has developed a system of participatory literary theatre which has proved extremely popular, and which she has called 'Anansegoro'. It is inspired by the Ananse storytelling tradition of the Akan people, and is informed, especially in *The Marriage of Anansewa*, by a healthy principle of dialogue between actors and audience. Her explanation of Ananse's significance is germane to the core of our argument; perhaps we might even see in Ananse not just a fictional character, but an apt metaphor for the popular African theatre itself?

Who is Ananse, and why should so many stories be told about him? Ananse appears to represent a kind of Everyman, artistically exaggerated and distorted to serve society as a medium for self-examination. He has a penetrating awareness of the nature and psychology of human beings and animals. He is also made to mirror in his behaviour fundamental human passions, ambitions and follies as revealed in contemporary situations. Significantly, laughter is the main social response to Ananse as a character. In addition, it is in the verbal comments which often underscore the laughter that society's attitude to him is clarified. Of these the most representative is "Ananse's wealth!" – a sarcastic expression for successes and triumphs which are not likely to last. Indeed most of Ananse's successes are doubtful and temporary. By constantly over-reaching himself he ruins his schemes and ends up impoverished. That Ananse is, artistically, a medium for society to criticise itself can be seen in the expression, "Exterminate Ananse, and society will be ruined." [33]

Notes

[1] G.B.Shaw, "To the Audience at the Kingsway Theatre" in *John Bull's Other Island* (Penguin, 1984) pp.165-6

[2] Jacques Scherer, *Le Théâtre en Afrique Noire Francophone* (Presses Universitaires de France, 1990) p.51

[3] K.E.Senanu, "Thoughts on Creating the Popular Theatre" in James Gibbs (ed.), *Critical Perspectives on Wole Soyinka* (Three Continents Press, 1981) pp.75-78

[4] Wole Soyinka, *Myth, Literature and the African World* (C.U.P., 1976) p. 37

[5] Ibid. p.39

[6] Scherer (op. cit.) p.31

[7] In a note to *Death and the King's Horseman*, Soyinka tells us that "the colonial factor is an incident, a catalytic incident merely. The confrontation in the play is largely metaphysical, contained in the human vehicle which is Elesian and the Universe of the Yoruba mind." The metaphysical significance of the long parody of English manners in Scene 3 is, however, elusive.

[8] Interview with Biodun Jeyifo in Wole Soyinka, *Six Plays* (Methuen, 1984); Foreword to *Opera Wonyosi*, ibid.

[9] D.Duerden and C.Pieterse (eds.), Interview with Lewis Nkosi, *African Writers Talking* (Heinemann, n.d.) pp. 169-177

[10] Senanu (op.cit.)

[11] Wole Soyinka, *Six Plays* (op. cit.)

[12] See Ngugi wa Thiongo, *Decolonising the Mind* and "The Language of African Literature", *New Left Review* 125 (1985): "African literature can only be written in the African languages of the peasantry and working class, the major alliance of classes in each of our nationalities and the agency for the coming revolutionary break with neo-colonialism."

[13] W.Mutahi, "Drama Behind the Drama", *Daily Nation* (22nd January 1982)

[14] Scherer (op. cit.) p.41

[15] Martin Banham et al (eds.), *The Cambridge Guide to African and Caribbean Theatre* (Cambridge University Press, 1994) p.76

[16] Ogunde, interviewed in BBC TV documentary, 1980

[17] Augusto Boal, *Theatre of the Oppressed* (Pluto, 1979) p.113 & p.34

[18] Robert W. July, *An African Voice: The Role of the Humanities in African Independence* (Duke University Press, 1987)

[19] John Willett (ed.), *Brecht on Theatre* (Methuen, 1964) p.197

[20] Senouvo Agbota Zinsou, *On Joue La Comédie* (Editions Haho, 1984) pp.10-11

[21] Ibid. p.18

[22] Ibid. p.62

[23] Sam Ukala, *Akpakaland* in *Five Plays: ANA/British Council Prizewinners* (Heinemann, 1990) p.3, p.33, p.36

[24] Mukotani Rugyendo, *The Barbed Wire and Other Plays* (Heinemann Educational, 1977) pp.36-38.

[25] Ibid. p.39

[26] Ibid. p.44

[27] Boal (op. cit.) p.155

[28] Rugyendo (op. cit.) p.38

[29] John Willett (op.cit.) p.197

[30] J.P.Clark, *Ozidi* (Oxford University Press, 1966)
[31] July (op. cit.) pp.61-62
[32] Scherer (op. cit.) p.36
[33] Efua Sutherland, *The Marriage of Anansewa and Edufa* (Longman, 1987) p.3

From Art to Stage: Performance Codes in the Drawings of Dario Fo

Christopher Cairns

The connection between art and theatre has long been abundantly clear to those who have sought to record the directly-lived experience of theatre-going.[1] From the original records of *Commedia dell'Arte* performance down to more modern records, the artist has sought to record what struck him most. The energy and style of the Callot military stereotypes comes down to us only in the famous *Capricci,* and who can tell how far these celebrated actual performance, and how far they were a nostalgic memory.[2] We recall also the clearly expressed element of dance in these illustrations[3], expressing movement, which also recalls that much more modem celebration of movement in the *Dancers* of Matisse. Then again, there is the famous cartoon example of the *Death of Harlequin,* where several stages in time are reduced to episodes in a single plane[4], and, still with the *Commedia dell'Arte,* the example of the *Receuil Fossard,*[5] which modem scholarship is locating within a recognisable performance sequence. And finally we have the example of the influence of iconography on performance, again precisely within the long history of *Commedia*: here is one of the oldest images of Mezzettino, on all fours, and here is a twentieth-century version, clearly influenced by the image (Carlo Boso's *Scaramuccia,* performed in Trier in Germany, in 1986)[6] . And this reminds us yet again that Ben Jonson's Masques (so often thought to be memories of the *Commedia dell'Arte* in performance) are now known to be memories of it in the iconography of Callot – far from the realities of actual performance.[7]

But if the artist is also the theatre practitioner, as is the case with a number of significant practitioners – in our own day, from Ionesco to Federico Fellini – we have the possibility of the visual image as a building brick in the playwriting or directing process. All the above examples have been moving us closer to Dario Fo, a self-confessed inheritor of the traditions of the *Commedia dell'Arte,*[8] and this latter is certainly the case with him. When I interviewed him for the *Guardian* at Heathrow some years ago, he stated in answer to a questionnaire that he considered himself first an artist, and second and third, playwright and actor.[9] In context, this was meant half as a joke, but it remains true that his formal training was as a draughtsman and artist, at the Brera in Milan, and that he has consistently brought his own individual touch to theatre production by designing most of his own productions himself, as well as designing costumes and set for those productions (for example Molière's *Le Médecin malgré lui* and *Le Médecin volant* at the Comédie francaise, 1991 and Rossini's *L'Italiana in Algeri,* at Pesaro, 1994) where he was invited to direct a production.[10] This is why the present contribution concentrates less on Dario Fo's plays, less on his talents as an actor, exclusively, perhaps more on productions in which he was director and designer.

From the foregoing, I hope that it will become clear how Dario Fo uses drawing as a preparatory stage in the directing process, either as an image in the mind of the audience which the practitioner is to create on stage, movement, which the drawing may anticipate just as a cartoon creates the illusion by representing successive stages in an action, or by creating, in the artist's medium, an effect, machine or theatrical device which may become three-dimensional reality on stage. All theatre is art effect: visual design on a single plane may be represented as painting or drawing, just as three – dimensional effects may be shown by perspective or sculpture. Only film may recapture as full an expression of life-related action in a single medium. All this, I think, is to state the obvious. One or two illustrations may clarify quickly what I mean. First, the image created by the artist may represent literally what the audience is to imagine. The image may be created in the spectator's mind by a number of theatrical tricks – the actor may **mime** the effect to create the image in the mind of the audience, (and physically he may be very different from the image itself, but what he does may create that image in the mind of the spectator). Second, the artist may **represent actually what the spectator sees** (a prop or machine, whose outlines are exactly the same as what the theatre spectator sees, or a costume sketch which approximates, more or less exactly, to what the spectator sees). Thirdly, the **illusion of movement** may be created in a sketch by the representation on a single plane of successive stages in time in the theatre, which is what we have already seen with Mezzettino.

I want to examine the ways in which Dario Fo uses his art in these three distinct ways to direct and design theatre by comparing his sketches with rehearsal stills of the final results in the theatrical production.[11] Of course he uses similar methods in his direction and design of his <u>own</u> plays, in which he also appears as principal actor (and this has been confirmed as a lifelong habit quite recently)[12] but scholarly attention has been directed rather less to his work as director/designer, so perhaps it is here that we shall be able to investigate the function of images in the design of the theatrical process. And, unlike some modem theatre directors and designers, it becomes clear at once that Dario Fo prepares meticulously for the directing process by imagining the physical and three-dimensional reality of many scenes in advance. This in itself militates against the concept of theatre growing from the rehearsal process. But I also want to show just how far what was conceived as a drawing in the mind of an experienced and talented director **was not used in final production** because it clearly did not work (or the actors failed to realise it) in the conditions of the theatre. Thus, the existence of a drawing does not mean predestination. No-one more than he is alive to the immediate reality of live theatre as an organism created from the rehearsal process; no-one more than he knows the immediate impact of what is theatrically effective and what is not. So the drawing is never a fixed prescription. It is a **possible** performance code, pre-existing in the mind of the director, which may, or may not, come to life in production.[13]

Since 1985, I believe that Fo's art for the theatre has moved through four identifiably distinct phases. By 1985, it was the stimulus of the *Commedia dell'Arte* tradition (with its long iconographical history, as we have seen) which prompted him to build a show from his own sketches of classical and modem *lazzi* derived from academic research. These were brief notations, a collection of illustrative sketches, many of which were never incorporated into performance, but were published by his son in the in-house magazine, *Alcatraz News*. These are more illustrations than working models, research notes, perhaps, based on the academic work of Delia Gambelli.[14]

The second stage was perhaps his design and direction of Molière's *Médecin Malgré lui* and *Médecin volant* at the Comédie Francaise in 1991, a production which was hugely successful and built on the relationship between Moliere and the *Commedia dell'Arte*. Drawing has by now become a formula for action and part of the directing process, a performance code in embryo, a fact recognised by Fo himself in publishing his text – created by an expert in a kind of grammelot Rabelaisian French – surrounded "in a close-knit harmony by the drawings themselves."[15] Quite clearly, the illustrated book, combining sketches and text, is an additional artefact born from this process.

A third stage may be identified when we come to the production, in 1992, of Fo's *Zitti, Stiamo Precipitando (Hush, We're Falling!)*, since the greatest concentration of drawings illustrates the theatrical device, illusion or surreal theatrical set-piece (obviously enjoyed for itself), where the execution in the theatre needs careful preparation of props and precise timing in rehearsal. There are numerous examples, but a few must suffice.[16] By now, almost every detail that could be called **visual** is represented by a drawing – and in practical terms, directing apart, the sketches may simply be passed to the costume -maker, set-builder, and whoever creates props.

Johan Padan a la Descoverta de le Americhe (Johan Padan discovers the Americas) has become the worthy successor to the celebrated *Mistero Buffo*, a one-man-show devoted to satirical treatment of the Columbus celebrations in 1992, a fable of adventure in the New World by a Venetian stowaway aboard Columbus's ships.[17] This performance is a tour-de-force of Dario Fo's mime skills, but was created through drawings, is prompted in performance by a large book of drawings, which never leaves the stage and can be consulted by audience members near enough. So the drawings are **illustrations** of the fable (images in the minds of the audience to be created by the actor using other means), **prompt process** (he consults it often in performance, or pretends to)[18], **souvenir** (every copy of the text carries them) and

charitable initiative (Fo was selling "prints" each one of which he made himself in aid of a good cause in the theatre).[19]

So the drawn image has become not only the audience's image to be created theatrically on stage, but part of the act itself as a prop. The process is carried a stage further with the issue of text-plus-art which we saw with the Molière,[20] now significantly evolved, as the artefact has entered the stage itself. We shall find this mixture of image and acting again **in** the theatrical use of silhouettes in Fo's directing of Rossini's *L'Italiana in Algeri* (Pesaro, 1994), and in this production, it seems that the drawing has taken on all four of my functions.

Now let us come to the images: **first** the **illustration,** in set and costume designs,[21] **second** the **theatrical devices,** surreal set-pieces, the swing, Islamic and Christian moveable temples, the carriage and substitution devices using look-alike dummies, like Lindoro's lyrical projection of his heart's desire as a dummy to accompany his aria, and Mustafa's very different "merchandising" of her as a marionette made up entirely of vegetables.[22] **Third, action scenes** in the directing process have their first life as drawings (getting up from the swing)[23] and **fourth,** an example of **silhouettes** used as images imported into the action, but created by the actors.[24]

In more detail, the point is illustrated by the Rossini overture visualised by Dario Fo. The shipwreck is **graphically** created, (fishes and drowning sailors respond to accents in the music), seagulls fly realistically as marionettes on flexible poles, and the tide wins the struggle against the rowers.[25] The temple of the Bey of Algeria is a magic box, a mosque on wheels, from which the arrogance of male absolutism issues forth.[26] The Lion (a pantomime lion used before in *Harlequin,* as we have seen), here mocks the seriousness of the passionate Lindoro when he sings of the pains of love in the chains of slavery. The lion joins the zoo with leonine music, and follows the singer in a grotesque mime of the vocal acrobatics of grand opera. Now, the Bey reconstitutes the ideal woman in marriage before the eyes of Lindoro (in vegetables), and the "merchandise" acquires life by theatrical substitution.[27] The first of two silhouette sequences shows the appearance of images on stage created by the actors, a commentary on, and backcloth to, the downstage action.[28] Here, the artist creates his image within the stage space and the image has become part of the theatrical action itself. The substitution of the actor for a dummy depicts the flight of fancy of Mustafa, as his carriage leaves the ground and flies freely in the stage space. The clash of cultures comes out in the wooing of Isabella by Mustafa: the Islamic mosque carriage is counterpointed by the gondola-cum-fairground merry-go-round boat, perhaps doubtfully representing western christianity, and we recall that this image was sown in the minds of the audience during the shipwreck of the overture. Image as recurring leitmotif, therefore.[29] Now the fears of Isabella's "uncle" are also represented on-stage by a recurring image: the motif of the "*palo*" or stake are expressed by the use of chorus actors who bring on various sizes of stake, upstage and downstage, with a giant example to strike fear into the audience.[30] Again, the flights of fantasy of Lindoro, the young lover, are represented by Fo as a dummy, with whom he wrestles during his key aria.[31] And finally, the mirror scene triplicates the image of the heroine, Isabella by means of two mirrors: actresses mime her undressing and aria, until, in a surreal flourish, the images step out of their mirrors, as Alice had done, and are joined by the actress playing Isabella.[32]

Lastly the importation of the image into the theatrical action itself could, of course, evolve no further than the issue of a book (Molière) and the use of it as prop (*Johan Padan*). Fo capped this in the only way left: an exhibition of many of the preparatory drawings for his *regia* of *L'Italiana in Algeri* in the theatre itself, in Pesaro, invites the audience to participate at its leisure in the translation of art into theatre. Finally, the art process has itself become theatre – as valid a product of the director's vision as the show itself, to be "consumed", if he so wishes, by the spectator, for as long as the opera itself in performance.

Notes

[1] The use of iconographical evidence for the understanding and interpretation of theatrical performance is now recognised as a growing

field of research. A society and possible journal are under discussion, for which see Prof. Robert Erenstein, Theatre Studies, University of Amsterdam and the "European Performance Iconography: a multi-disciplinary initiative project". A conference was held in Amsterdam on this in June, 1995, at which many examples of this process were discussed, and at which a concentrated summary of part of the present contribution was given.

[2] They certainly became a kind of visual constant for later generations. See K.Richards, "Inigo Jones and the *Commedia dell'Arte*" in C.Cairns (ed.), *The Commedia dell'Arte from the Renaissance to Dario Fo* (Edwin Mellen Press, 1989) pp. 209-225

[3] See fig. 1, reproduced from Cesare Molinari, *La Commedia dell'Arte*, Milano, Mondadori pp.126-7, and I am grateful to Prof. Molinari for permission to reproduce this and other illustrations from his volume.

[4] Fig. 2 *La Morte d'Arlecchino*, Venice, Museo Correr, engraving reproduced from Molinari (op.cit.) p.162

[5] Fig. 3; an example from the *Receuil Fossard*, see Molinari (op.cit.) p.73. Most recently, the researches of M.A.Katrizky are paving the way towards a fuller understanding of the performance origin of this intriguing series. See, for example, "The *Receuil Fossard* 1928-88: A Review and Three Reconstructions" in C.Cairns (op.cit.) pp.99-117. For comparison, fig. 3a shows one of Dario Fo's preparatory drawings for his 1985 *Harlequin*, for which see also C.Cairns, "Dario Fo and the *Commedia dell'Arte*" in D.J.George and C.J.Gossip (eds.), *Studies in the Commedia dell'Arte* (University of Wales Press, 1993) pp.247-265.

[6] Of course, it cannot be proved that this modern performance detail is a memory of the classical pose from iconography, but Tag Teatro seeks to research and reproduce a "strict tempo" *Commedia*, and at least an unconscious memory is highly likely. Compare figs 4 & 5 (reproduced respectively from Molinari (op. cit.) p.100 and the surviving videotape of the Tag Teatro performance of *Scaramuccia*, Triers, 1986).

[7] See note 2 for source.

[8] Interpreted interview conducted with Dario Fo in London, November, 1988, tape held by writer. See also interviews with Ferruccio Marotti collected in *Alcatraz News*, Perugia, 1985.

[9] *Weekend Guardian*, about October 1992

[10] The Moliére farces, performed in a Rabelaisian form of grammelot, and influenced (as the originals must have been) by the physical acting styles of the *Commedia dell'Arte*, were performed to great critical acclaim at the Comedie Francaise in Paris 1991. Rossinni's *L'Italiana in Algeri*, designed and directed by Dario Fo, opened for a short season in Pesaro in August 1994,

afterwards transferring to the Opera House in Amsterdam and broadcast on Dutch television in 1995.

[11] It goes without saying that the lecture on which this is based used video.

[12] Interview with Dario Fo, Milan, April 1995. In another interview recently, Dario Fo outlined the kind of artistic atmosphere in which he moved as a young architect, stressing his autonomy and freedom from involvement with "schools": "Sï, ho fatte parte del cosidetto postcubismo figurativo, ma non accettavo il realismo socialista...Ero legato a interessi di tipo culturale, con pittori come Peverelli, Morlotti, Tadini, Bobo Piccoli...non si dipinegeva con spirito di gruppo, non esisteva un "movimento" di pittori." See interview with Franco Quadri published in the publicity leaflet, Teatro Astra, Stagione di Prosa, 1992-3, Forlĭ.

[13] In April 1994, I put precisely this point to him, and, in reply, he stressed the importance of the rehearsal process in arriving at the final performance.

[14] See figs. 6,7 and 8 for this type of illustration, from *Alcatraz News* (op.cit.) p.68, and more recent drawings for Rossini's *L'Italiana in Algeri*. The researches of Delia Gambelli were known to Fo in 1985 from two journal articles in Biblioteca teatrale published in the 1970's. These are now collected as *Arlecchino a Parigi: Dall'Inferno alla corte del Re sole*, volume III of the series *La Commedia dell'Arte: Storia testi, documenti* (a cura di Ferruccio Marotti, Roma Bulzoni, 1993). the lion is emblematic (or just a favourite image?) since it appears as a pantomime lion in *Harlequin* (from Aesop's *Fables*, 1985), again as the same (in fact the same skin) in *L'Italiana in Algeri* and the "Earthly Paradise" backdrop which he designed for Franca Rame's one woman *Sesso? Grazie, tanto per gradire!* (1995). Fig. 9 shows the scene in rehearsal.

[15] The script was published as *Molière, Le Mèdecin malgrè lui, Le Mèdecin volant: illustrations de Dario Fo, tirees de ses carnets de mise en scene* (Imprimerie nationale, 1991). Fig. 10 (the drawing for the fight scene in Act 2, scene 2, p.46) shows the scene had clearly been visualised as a "cartoon" continuation of action, as we saw in the *Morte di Arlecchino* (fig. 2 above).

[16] Fig. 10 (a drawing of Fo's plans for the dwarf trick – one actor plays the arms, the other uses his arms as the dwarf's legs etc.) is published in the performance script of *Zitti! Stiamo precipitando!* (Copione di scena, 1990), facing p.18. An indication of the drawing as a working performance code is in the caption: "Far fabricare un pupazzo prototipo"

(have a prototype dummy made) which shows that the actors will be substituted by a dummy, which will then be thrown about the stage.

[17] Dario Fo had planned to perform an updated version of this sell-out success in various European cities in 1996, but has been unable to do so. The original Italian edition is available commercially on videotape, and an edition with English subtitles by the present writer and Antonio Scuderi is held by me.

[18] This is becoming a trademark of the one-man (woman) shows of Dario Fo and Franca Rame: a heavily carved lectern is placed near centre stage, and the "promptbook" is placed there for consultation by the actor. Often not needed, obviously, but he (she) will turn over several pages to symbolise the passage of time. These were present both for Franca Rame's Sesso.. and *Dario Fo's Dario Fo recita Ruzzante* in 1995, and are consulted by the curious during the interval. Significantly, for the present argument, the prompt process (when needed) is accomplished by images as often as not.

[19] When I saw *Johan Padan*... in Pistoia, he was "printing" individual copies of the script by impressing a template by hand on every single copy backstage before the show began. These were sold for charity, and he referred to it during the performance.

[20] See the edition cited above at note 15.

[21] Fig. 12 show Dario Fo's drawings of costume designs. I am indebted to Dario Fo for permission to photograph the originals in Milan at Easter 1995.

[22] Compare drawings (figs. 13 & 14) with rehearsal stills (figs. 15 & 16). Fig. 15 shows the "vegetable marionettes" (Dario Fo observes from the wings), while fig. 16 shows the actress who has been substituted (Dario Fo is teaching her how to move, left of the picture).

[23] See fig. 17 (also published in Rossini, *L'Italiana in Algeri,* Rossini Opera Festival, Pesaro, 1994 p.36), clearly prepared as a performance code for production, but I can find no scene in the final production which represents an actor pulling another from the swing device. Here is an example therefore (and there were doubtless many) of the practicalities of rehearsal. Whether the scene was theatrically ineffective, or (as in this case we may assume) was dangerous to the actors, the result was that the performance code was abandoned.

[24] Here is an example of a monotone image, created by the actors, but stepping away from realism for theatrical effect. Fig. 18 shows the image seen by the audience, while fig. 19, a disrobing shot from backstage, shows how the effect was achieved. Typical of Fo is the device where the actors pass from view behind the screen and then back into view, allowing the audience to fully perceive the theatrical effect.

So, this is an example of the techniques of drawing actually imported into theatrical action: the artist "creates" within the proscenium arch itself, and there were no preparatory drawings.

[25] And we have a rehearsal photograph showing Dario Fo teaching the actors the rowers' movements (fig. 20). In performance, the overture was a fine blend of music, ballet and theatrical special effect as image. For example, seagulls on flexible poles were made to swoop low over the front audience stalls, streamers descended to simulate rain, fishes on sticks jumped out of the sea in time with accents in the music and a range of three-dimensional "boat" images moved across the stage.

[26] Compare fig. 21 (drawing) with figs. 22 (Dario Fo observes from the wings) and 23 (performance). Here again, the image of the "mosque" is both a cultural and religious signifier (representing Muslim religious values, to be contrasted with Western Christian ones) and a theatrical jack-in-box special effect, housing the Bey of Algeria, which rotates in space, is moved by the eunuchs, and, in one scene, is carried horizontally (with aggressive, even sexual overtones) echoing the imagery of the "palo" (for which see below). Its shape and its symbolism perhaps need no further elucidation, made even clearer in the drawing which originated the device, an image of Mustafa's male prowess.

[27] Compare Fig. 38 with Fig. 39. The theatrical substitution of a puppet with a live actor is a favourite device of Dario Fo's, having appeared in many previous plays. In *L'Italiana in Algeri* it is repeated with the carriage in which the eunuchs carry the Bey (which achieves violent and dizzy movements in space by disappearing offstage; a replica carrying a dummy appears and the aria is sung from the wings; this is then repeated with the actor back in place.) Extremely effective in the Pesaro production, this device was then cut from the Amsterdam staging, though is celebrated in the colour drawing (fig. 24), and was clearly a much-prized special effect. The device was used in Dario Fo's direction of The *Barber of Seville*, where a character is tossed in a blanket, substituted by a dummy, which then falls on the stage.

[28] The silhouette devices were performed behind a screen (a boat sail in the scene's realism) in which disrobing and "circus" acts are perceived by the audience in monotone. Action comes to "life" when the sail is lowered. See figs. 18 and 19 above.

[29] The wooing of Isabella by the Bey contrasts two cultures (Muslim and Christian) by the encounter between their representatives (Mustafa and Isabella) each transported by massive carriages which move and gyrate in space. Isabella is enclosed in a structure resembling a gondola

or fairground merry-go-round boat, while Mustafa's carriage has an ogival shaped canopy signifying the "mosque" shape of Muslim architecture. Compare the drawings for this recurring image motif (figs. 25 & 26) with stills from the rehearsal (figs. 27 &28). Many drawings survive testifying to the fascination these complex moving structures had for Dario Fo and revealing their evolution.
[30] Fig. 29 (drawing) and 30-32 (performance). The performance images are derived from video. This is a notable example of the image originating in drawings and being reduced to a miniaturised version for comic effect (an actor enters with a tiny stake strapped to his head as a hat), and the multiple effects of the giant stake image in its theatrical possibilities (it is carried across stage in many sizes, it is sharpened, as a pencil, by an actor on a ladder; it enters horizontally into the action with multiple symbolical overtones). Finally the comedy of the image depends on the anachronistic and the grotesque when it appears to rise into the sky as a rocket with Taddeo strapped to it. All this, of course, creates comedy from the centuries-old horror of Italians of the (Turkish) practice of impaling. All is perfectly consistent with Rossini's libretto, since Taddeo is threatened with impaling.

[31] See figs. 33 (a rehearsal still, which shows Fo teaching the tenor how to operate the device) and 34 (performance, the version of the dummy which takes flight). The surrogate woman is in this case a tailor's dummy, and the previous scene has prepared the audience for this. The actor pushes the dummy which rotates and moves independently on wheels, suspended from the flies. It is then replicated by a flying version, and the remoteness of two separated lovers is poignantly (yet comically) evoked. The final touch is a dance between an actor on stilts and the "flying version" in the air.

[32] See this scene in rehearsal (fig. 35). The comic impact of theatrical palm trees which "grow" into an erection as she undresses, which much amused Pesaro audiences, was not repeated in the Amsterdam staging. Fig 36 is a backstage shot showing the structure which held the "mirrors" (Dario Fo seen through the opening).

Fig.1: The famous Callot *Commedia*-related images
in which the dance element is clearly predominant.

Fig 2: *The Death of Harlequin*: images
in sequence which tell a story in the same plane.

Fig. 3: *Commedia dell'Arte* episode
from the *Receuil Fossard.*

Fig. 3A: Preparatory Drawing for
Dario Fo's Harlequin (1985)

Fig. 4: *Fossard* image: Mezzrttino
on all fours

Fig. 5: Tag Teatro's *Scaramuccia*
(Trier, 1986), Mezzettino on all fours

Fig 6: The preparatory drawings for the Lion in Dario Fo's *Harlequin*, 1985.

Fig 7: Drawing for the Lion in L'Italiana...1984

Fig. 8: Drawing of zoo animals for *L'Italiana in Algeri*

Fig 9: *L'Italiana in Algeri* in rehearsal: the lion mimics the vocal gymnastics of the tenor, Lindoro. (Photo: Amati-Bacciardi, Rossini Opera Fetival, Pesaro)

Fig 10: Drawing for the fight
scene in *Le Medecin Malgre Lui*

Fig 11: The Dwarf in
Zitti! Stiamo precitando

Fig 12: Drawings for costumes, *L'Italiana in Algeri*

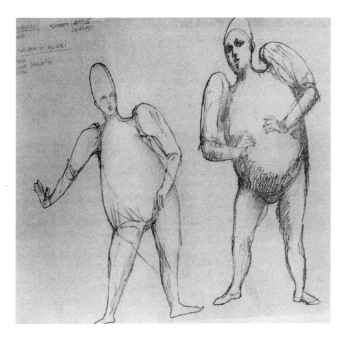

Fig 13: Drawing for the "vegetables" scene

Fig 14: The Eunnuchs carry off the marionette
(to be replaced by a real actor); drawing

Fig 15: Lindoro "composes" a bride from vegetables
(Photo: Amati-Bacciardi, Rossini Opera Festival, Pesaro)

Fig 16: The 'vegetable-marionette" has become flesh: Dario Fo (left) teaches the
actress how to move (Photo: Amati-Bacciardi, Rossini Opera Festival, Pesaro)

Fig.17: Drawing for action on the "swing"

Fig.18: The silhouette disrobing scene as viewed by the audience
(Photo: Amati-Bacciardi, Rossini Opera Festival, Pesaro).

Fig.20: Dario Fo teaches the rowers in preparation for the storm at sea in the ouverture (Photo: Amati-Bacciardi, Rossini Opera Festival, Pesaro).

Fig 19: How the effect was achieved (seen from backstage)
(Photo: Amat i-Bacciardi, Rossini Opera Festival, Pesaro)

Fig 21: Drawing for Mustafa's "box" showing it open to reveal him

Fig 22: Dario Fo observes from the wings while eunuchs move Mustafa's "box"
(Photo: Amati-Bacciardi, Rossini Opera Festival, Pesaro)

Fig 23: Another image of the "box"
(Photo: Amati-Bacciardi, Rossini Opera Festival, Pesaro)

Fig 24: Drawing for the carriage for the Bey
(who is substituted for a dummy)

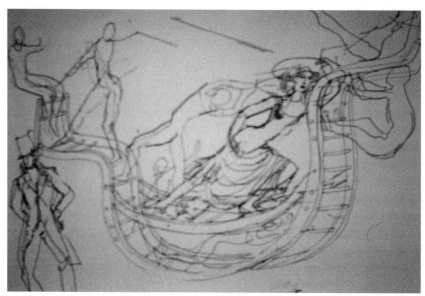

Fig 25: Drawing for Isabella's "gondola" carriage (showing only actors as weights)

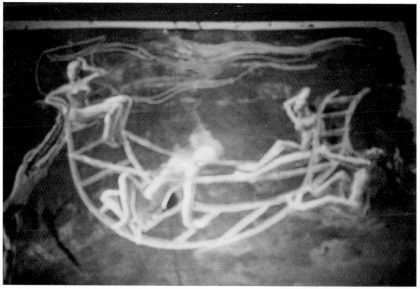

Fig 26: Final drawing of the "gondola"

Fig 27: Isabella's "gondola carriage" in rehearsal
(Photo: Amati-Bacciardi, Rossini Opera Festival, Pesaro)

Fig 28: Anoyher image, with Isabella installed
(Photo: Amati-Bacciardi, Rossini Opera Festival, Pesaro)

Fig 29: Drawing for the *palo* (Note example where Taddeo is carried on it)

Fig 30: The miniature *palo* as a hat worn by an actor

Fig 31: The stake sharpened as a pencil by actors on a ladder

Fig 32: The *palo* rises as if it were a rocket (dummy Taddeo strapped to it)

Fig 33: Dario Fo teachers the tenor how to manipulate the dummy
(Photo: Amati-Bacciardi, Rossini Opera Festival, Pesaro)

Fig 34: Lindoro and the flying dummy in rehearsal
(Photo: Amati-Bacciardi, Rossini Opera Festival, Pesaro)

Fig 35: Isabella at her mirrows (actresses mime her movements)
(Photo: Amati-Bacciardi, Rossini Opera Festival, Pesaro)

Fig 36: Behind the same scene (Dario Fo framed in the distance)
(Photo: Amati-Bacciardi, Rossini Opera Festival, Pesaro)

"Théâtre Populaire": Ideology and Tradition in French Popular Theatre from Copeau to Mnouchkine

Nigel Ward

In 1941 Jacques Copeau tried to define the "Théâtre populaire". He wrote at a very particular moment in French history. France had just been invaded by Germany, the idea of French nationhood itself was in doubt and, in defining what popular theatre should be for France, Copeau sought to help define national values.

As always Copeau was as much interested in the tradition out of which the popular theatre had arisen as any possible future he might discover for it. He defined two periods as high water marks of the kind of popular theatre he dreamt of: Classical Greece and the Middle Ages. Both of these periods saw a theatre which appealed across class boundaries, a theatre with a recognised social function. Indeed, a theatre answering a social need. In both cases the theatre had developed out of and retained strong links with religious ritual. The rules by which society lived were tested, through debate and example, or temporarily subverted in carnivalesque disorder.

This kind of theatre was made possible, in Copeau's view, by the society's shared beliefs and conventions, above all its shared religious faith. The problem for his own times lay in the breakdown of these conventions. If popular theatre was based on religious ritual for a united society, it stood little chance of reaffirming itself in a secular, fragmented modern world. The fragmentation of theatre audiences was merely the most obvious sign of a much deeper fragmentation of society itself. Parisian theatre had splintered into the boulevard and the arts theatres, one appealing to a portion of the middle classes, the other to intellectuals. Popular audiences had been so far marginalised as to find their entertainment away from the conventional theatre altogether, in circuses, music halls and the cinema.

Copeau became interested in the forms that had once attracted popular audiences, including *commedia dell arte* and music. He saw their parallel in circus acts, such as the Fratellini brothers or in film performers like Chaplin. Chaplin seemed to Copeau to have stumbled instinctively upon the traditions of the *commedia,* with a comic form that could operate across linguistic boundaries. The two men met, and on one occasion Copeau took Chaplin to the circus and discovered just what popularity might mean:

> Now I saw the whole crowd get up, from top to bottom of the stands and, with one movement, 3000 people surged into the ring and crowded round the little actor until he was almost smothered. The police had to intervene to extricate him. We went out into the street, the crowd went out with us. We quickened our pace, they did too. We began to run, they ran ahead of us and turned back to surround us.[1]

One of the difficulties of popular theatre for Copeau lay in his mistrust of people. Copeau's work seems to have been at war with the modern world whose spirit was responsible for the decay that the theatre experienced. After having tried and failed to build a popular audience at the Vieux-Colombier, Copeau reacted against the city. Debased theatre was Parisian theatre. If the theatre moved out from the centre, out of the city, it might be able to rediscover its roots in a society which had been less touched by the modern world. Moving to an agricultural community in Burgundy, Copeau was not simply displaying a commitment to regional theatre, but retreating from the spread of modernity. Previously there had been attempts, like Gemier's with the Théâtre National Ambulant, to create touring companies to bring work to communities with limited experience of the theatre. But what Copeau intended was to involve his company in the life of a particular community, to develop work of direct relevance to it.

The retreat also allowed the possibility of developing the skills of performers away from the commercial pressures of performance, to establish a theatre laboratory rather than a theatre factory. With collaborators including his nephew Michel St Denis, Copeau explored mime, the *commedia* and improvisation, all of which contributed to a general exploration of the training of the actor. The contemporary tradition of French mime benefits from this period of experimentation; Etienne Decroux learned mime with Copeau, going on to train Marcel Marceau and Jean-Louis Barrault. Performances were developed for the local community based around popular music, mime, mask and improvisation. From all accounts these were well received, perhaps Copeau's own attempts to write and perform for these events was less so.

Much has been made of Copeau's Catholicism and there is no doubt that he regarded the work with his actors with something like religious zeal. The devotional, almost monastic commitment to theatre that may be seen in a Grotowski was prefigured in the work of Copeau. Copeau's rejection of modernity owed much to a rejection of the material, of the worldly:

> Souvent c'est le degoût, degoût des êtres, degoût des choses. Je souffre des platitudes, des petitesses, des vilenies qui m'entourent, me pressent et m'ulcèrent même dans ma chair... L'alle de nôtre rêve se brise trop souvent aux angles de la realité. [2]

The conflict was between a utopian popular theatre of the imagination, which could be contemplated abstractly through writing, or tested in the sealed environment of the theatrical workshop, and the demands of reality, the reality of the crowd and of modern life. The rural idylls could not last: training had to have a point, the company would have to re-engage with the world at some stage for the work to have had a function. If the problem for theatre lay in society then the theatre would have to address that problem by engaging with society.

This was the difficulty Copeau dealt with in his 1941 pamphlet. In a society now more fragmented than ever he speculated on the possible future for the theatre. He describes being at a conference in 1934 at the Volta Congress in Rome first quoting the Russian representative, Alexander Taïrov, describing the theatrical benefits of the Russian Revolution:

> It instilled an ideological discipline into our theatre by banishing moral indifference and opportunism from the stage once and for all. It chased away from our audiences the spectator who would come to the theatre in order to stimulate the digestion of his

dinner. It introduced a new public to our theatres, the one which made the October revolution and is now looking to the theatre for answers to its problems, a public which is building a new society and which also communicates its creative energy to the theatre.[3]

Copeau's response acknowledged the force of this argument:

> The question is not in knowing whether today's theatre will draw its appeal from this or that experimentation, its strength from the authority of one director or another. I think we must ask ourselves whether it will be Marxist or Christian. For it must be living, that is to say, popular. To be living, it must give man reasons to believe, to hope, to grow.[4]

On the one hand Taïrov, as the representative of Soviet culture, on the other Copeau, the devout Catholic. Both with a common aim for the theatre and, in Copeau's view, both with a common method. They agree that the theatre needs to redefine itself in terms of its popularity and they agree that this is not something that can happen spontaneously from within the theatre, the change needs to be in society. Clearly this implies the possibility of political activism within the theatre; if the world has to change then theatre can play its part in that change. Many post-war efforts to create a popular theatre, by Mnouchkine or Littlewood or Planchon, have involved this ideological element. Theatre as a catalyst to social change. This was nothing new. Political theatre had already put down strong roots in Germany, Russia, even Britain. The new element that Copeau offers is that of a religious theatre, addressing spiritual as well as social needs.

If we were to redefine the terms slightly, Marxist as political theatre in general and Christian as theatre with a sense of religious ritual we begin to see the accuracy of Copeau's prophecy. The avant garde of the following years would find itself increasingly pulled between these two poles – political activism and the rediscovery of ritual.

Perhaps, though, there need not be a dichotomy between these two? As Copeau showed, they at least have the shared aim of ameliorating the human condition, of uniting audiences in a shared experience to reinforce social cohesion, even of affecting audiences, so that the work of the theatre is turned outwards, to engage with the world. Perhaps the two could be complimentary, one addressing external social needs, the other internal development, especially if, as I have suggested, we do not take the call for Christian theatre literally. Christianity is clearly at odds with Marxism, but perhaps spiritual theatre need not be at odds with political theatre.

Typically the spiritual theatre is interested in a return to theatrical roots, based on a romantic notion of the cultural ascendancy of the primitive, it seeks to avoid the moral degeneracy of contemporary western theatre. Thus the fascination of Copeau with the Middle Ages, or of Craig with the Greek theatre. Another form of this attraction to the past is the interest in other cultures, where, again the assumed primitivism is seductive. So Artaud's fascination with Balinese dance and Mexican peyote rituals, or today the appeal of the Orient to Mnouchkine or Grotowski, Barba or Brook, all have their origins in this same rejection of a western theatre. Typically these directors have rejected naturalism as the supreme example of the bourgeois, materialist theatre. Craig in particular develops a neo-Platonic alternative, derived in part from the Symbolist theatre, in which external reality is merely a block to the presentation on stage of spiritual truths.

This notion of primitive theatre, while meant as a tribute, can become merely patronising. The search for non-Western styles of theatre so often derives from Orientalist prejudices, however kindly meant. When Artaud wrote about Balinese dance in *The Theatre and Its Double* he glossed over a massive ignorance of both the society that had produced it and its intended effect. Grotowski kindly describes Artaud's view of Balinese dance as "a crystal ball for a fortune teller. It brought forth a totally different performance which slumbered in the depths".[5] "The depths" presumably were those of Artaud's own imagination. He had never visited Indonesia. He wrote based on viewing a single performance, in Paris in 1931, at a colonial exhibition. Artaud took the dance to be "purely popular, non-religious", whereas in Bali dance music and performance have almost no place except as a function of religious ritual. Many of the narratives for dance drama, as for wayang kulit, the shadow puppet plays, are taken from Hindu mythology, principally from *The Mahabharata* and *The Ramayana*. When Artaud looked at the dance of Bali he saw perhaps not quite the crystal ball that Grotowski describes, but a mirror reflecting his own concerns and dreams of what the theatre could be. He would not be troubled if the actual dance he described failed to match the one he wished to see. His was a dance of the imagination.

Artaud wished to see a "non-religious" theatre coming out of Bali to reflect his own objections to organised religion. Yet Artaud himself was one of the first to promulgate the sense of spiritual theatre. Brook, Barrault and Grotowski would take much of their inspiration from him. He located the association of the avant-garde with the quest for a theatre innocent of the corrupting influence of the west. He rejected political theatre because, like the theatre of naturalism, it focused on the external. For Artaud the revolution that was necessary was not one that would rearrange the economy or the structures of power, but one which would transform the individual, reconstituting the human spirit and breaking down the Cartesian distinction between mind and body.

Much distinguishes the aspirations of Artaud from those of Copeau: one an ardent enemy of Christianity, the other a devout Catholic, one consumed by a hatred of literary tradition, the other devoted to the classics. But both aspire towards a vision of theatre where it has regained its centrality in the public imagination through a return to its origins as sacred rite, a mystical ritual.

The central difference between the political and the holy theatres lies in this tension between the external and the internal. Socialist theatre's concentration on ideological conflict played out through examinations of class, economics and power structures as against holy theatre's exploration of ritual and the power of theatre to transform audiences from within.

Yet this dichotomy has at times been blurred in post-war theatre. While someone like Planchon or Barrault may be clearly seen to fall into one category or another, other directors have attempted to draw the two traditions together.

Thus Brook has been a student of Brecht as well as of Artaud. For a time in the sixties it might have seemed that he was a director with a genuine commitment to political theatre with *Marat/Sade.* The tensions between the political and Brook's Holy Theatre are well illustrated by a story told by actor Yoshi Oida in *An Actor Adrift.* Brook was invited in 1968 to mount a production at the Odeon, at that time being run by Barrault. The original choice of play was Genet's *Le Balcon,* which in the context of the imminent *evenements* could have proved an inspired offering. Instead, though, Brook chose to work on *The Tempest.* Rehearsals were disrupted by French Equity's decision to strike to support the students and workers. The strike would forbid any further rehearsals taking place. Brook decided to appeal directly to the leaders of the students:

> Brook stated: "We are not satisfied with the current theatre situation in the West. This is why our group, including actors from four different countries, has gathered together. We want to re-evaluate theatre. Since what we intend to do is in the spirit of your revolution, will you let us continue our activities during your strike?..."[6]

Brook was overtaken by events as Barrault, in an attempt to show solidarity with the students turned the Odeon over to them, causing him to lose his job. The students turned down Brook's request. In his own display of solidarity Brook arranged for the company to be flown out of Paris by the RAF and the production reconvened in London. The spirit of revolution could, it would seem, be impractical.

By comparison we might consider the work of Ariane Mnouchkine. While the political overtones of Brook's work were short lived and might seem modish, Mnouchkine has been much more deeply committed to a political stance. While Brook's work was being banned by the students in 1968, Mnouchkine was invited to bring her production of Wesker's *The Kitchen* to striking factories. Yet here too we might detect a contradiction between radical beginnings, culminating in the productions *1789* and *1793,* and an increasing fascination with the classics and with theatre styles of the Orient in *La Nuit des Rois* or *Les Atrides.* The early commitment to collective creation represented an attempt to democratise the theatrical process. Increasingly though it has given way to work not simply on texts but on major classics: Shakespeare, Euripides and Aeschylus. These productions have attempted to bring some of the radical performance style to bear on conventional notions of these works, but nevertheless they must represent some kind of concession to the bourgeois audiences who will travel to see Mnouchkine's work at international festivals. As the ideological content may be said to have softened, so the commitment to non-western theatre styles, and to ritualistic theatre have increased. *Les Atrides* represented an attempt to use Greek texts in order to revive a notion of Greek theatre very close to that offered by Copeau. In the absence of an audience with a shared vocabulary of music and movement, Mnouchkine sought to create her own conventions, incorporating styles from a variety of traditions, which would nevertheless be easily recognisable to western audiences. Yet it fails Copeau's final test – just as Copeau's own work did. It fails to find popular audiences, appealing instead to the conventional theatre audiences. When *Les Atrides* visited England it was hard to spot a face in the audience not belonging to theatre professionals or academics. The Théâtre du Soleil retains some of its radical stance, in particular its democratic structure and apportioning of jobs within the company, as well as its emphasis on the ensemble. Yet the radical edge may be said to have softened since the mid 1970's.

Perhaps Copeau was right, the theatre would have to choose between the ideological and the spiritual. To try to combine the two reveals the sharp distinctions between the traditions. It is worth examining the context of Copeau's prediction. Writing in a France that was already under Nazi rule he assesses, with some sympathy, the use that National Socialism had put theatrical devices to. There was a genuine effort to create spectacles for mass audiences, with striking results. He writes:

> Those who have attended the multitudinous *mises en scene* that Mr Hitler has proliferated throughout his empire... agree in praising the grandiose éclat and thrill which they produce... However, theatre should not, even if it tends towards the mystical, take its example from these

spectacular displays for which it is not fitted. It should avoid confusing what falls within the domain of the procession, parades and festivals with what is in the essence of drama.

Theatre *for* the masses is not necessarily theatre of the masses.[7]

The difficulty with the Nazi rallies is not their content, but the fact that they do not quite adhere to Copeau's sense of what constitutes drama. Though it is difficult to know whether the Greeks or the audiences of the Middle Ages would have been quite so clear on the distinction between drama and "processions, parades and festivals".

Writing in Paris in 1941 Copeau recalled the conference in Rome in 1934. So the prediction about the Marxist or Christian future of the theatre was made in Mussolini's Italy and recalled in Hitler's France. Copeau hits on a distinction between two opposing but powerful ideologies. To many in the 1930's the two ideologies which offered some prospect of social change were Marxism and Fascism. Perhaps there is a sense in which Copeau's sense of Catholicism might find echoes in the Fascist philosophy, with its appeal to history and tradition, its hierarchical vision of society and the shared "mystical" content that Copeau perceived as being part of Hitler's appeal.

Copeau would not be alone in this. Many artists in the 1930's were compelled by the choice between Communism and Fascism. Both Craig and Artaud were impressed by Fascist Italy and both made approaches to Mussolini's government as a potential sponsor of their work. Artaud, perhaps with the excuse of insanity, dedicated poems to Hitler and was attracted to an apocalyptic vision of society based on the philosophy of Nietzsche.

Obviously the view of popular theatre that was possible before the war would have to change, with the changing appreciation of the dangers of both Fascism and Communism. But perhaps the tensions that have underpinned the popular theatre of the post-war period derive from its attempts to reconcile the philosophies of left and right, even as the philosophy of the right was disguised in mysticism and romanticism. While popular theatre continues to struggle in the way that it did in Copeau's time, theatre which would attempt to break conventions may still feel the same impulses, in a continued recognition that if theatre is to be popular there must first be a society for which theatre is essential.

In the aftermath of the break up of Communism and the continued decline of organised religion Copeau's prediction might seem more pertinent than ever. In order to be popular the theatre must fulfil a social need. It cannot simply be imposed on society based on some vague claim to be "a good thing".

Just as Taïrov discovered the theatre answering a social need in post-revolutionary Moscow, so today the theatre may answer similar needs in post-Soviet states. Peter Stein's most recent production of *Orestia* showed an ancient Greek text dealing with the emergence of a new kind of state – based on democracy and new standards of justice – displaying urgent relevance to a Russia undergoing a similar transformation.

Copeau thought he felt a spiritual vacuum in the post-Christian west. The work of Artaud, Barrault, Grotowski or Brook would seem to be addressing this vacuum, creating ritual for a secular audience. *The Mahabharata* was at least in part an attempt to approach a sacred text that was not burdened by over-familiarity for its western audiences. These audiences might have balked at being presented with Christian dogma, but were happy to accept a philosophy they only partially recognised. Accusations of Orientalism really miss the point: *The Mahabharata* is an eastern myth put to the service of a western theatre whose own myths have become debased.

What Copeau suggests to us is that popularity cannot reside simply in a theatre as entertainment, that solutions to a declining audience are not to be found in solipsistic regard to programming or style. Theatrical engagement with society, depending not only on particular dogmatic creeds or ideologies, but on an active attempt to necessarily define and debate those things which bind a society, is not a luxury, or an activity for the leisured classes. A theatre without vision cannot answer the needs of a society without vision and until the theatre recognises the social and spiritual needs of its audiences it will not find the hunger that will make popular theatre a demand rather than an imposition.

Notes

[1] John Rudlin & Norman H Paul, *Copeau: Texts on Theatre* (Methuen, 1990) p.184

[2] France Anders, *Jacques Copeau et le Cartel des Quatres* (Nizet, 1959) p.57

[3] Rudlin and Paul (op. cit.) p.189

[4] Ibid. p.189

[5] Jerzy Grotowski, *Towards a Poor Theatre* (Methuen, 1969) p.88

[6] Yoshi Oida, *An Actor Adrift* (Methuen, 1992) p.19

[7] Rudlin and Paul (op.cit.), p.194

"Rude Mechanicals": Popular Theatre in the Elizabethan Playhouse

Lisa Hopkins

When Hamlet wants to ascertain whether his uncle is guilty of the murder of his father, it seems to him logical to stage a play. The theatre company which has fortuitously arrived at Elsinore at the very time when they will be useful to him have fallen on slightly hard times: the sudden popularity of child actors has impacted their takings, the boy who takes the role of female lead is growing alarmingly – but they are, nevertheless, clearly recognisable as representatives of what the Elizabethans would have thought of as serious theatre. Their repertoire includes a speech about Pyrrhus which is very clearly reminiscent of Shakespeare's great predecessor Marlowe, whose "mighty line" inaugurated the tragedy of state; and the play which they perform in the hopes of ensnaring King Claudius is another tragedy, albeit one with some extemporary lines interpolated for the purpose by Hamlet himself. The scheme is successful: moved beyond self-control by the fictional drama unfolding before him, Claudius unwittingly confirms his own role in a "real-life" drama to those in the know amongst the audience. Such tales of the power of plays to win confessions from the guilty were fairly commonly recounted in Elizabethan and Jacobean times, almost always, as might be expected, in connection with the "higher" genre of tragedy, and can serve as useful – and rare – evidence for the ways in which the theatre and theatregoing were popularly regarded at the time. They suggest that it was accorded a degree at least of serious respect, an idea which may perhaps be rather more equivocally reinforced by the anecdote told of Burbage's appearance in Shakespeare's *Richard III*, that a female citizen found him so attractive in the role that she sent a note backstage with her address and an invitation to visit her that evening. Shakespeare, however, is said to have read the note first, and when Burbage arrived and sent in his name he was duly greeted by the information that "William the Conqueror was before Richard the Third."

Both these Shakespearean episodes suggest that serious drama seriously acted was thought capable of having a genuine impact on the lives of those who watched it. The same is certainly true of the numerous instances where inset plays or masques turn to real instruments of revenge. This happens in *The Spanish Tragedy*, where Hieronimo, unable to find vengeance for the murder of his son by any other method, stages a play which, bizarrely and symbolically, uses a babel of different languages to represent the cross-purposes of the court. During it, characters depart from their scheduled roles to bring about for real the violence they are supposed only to enact. The same happens in – to name only a few – *Women Beware Women, The Revenger's Tragedy,* and *'Tis Pity She's a Whore,* in each of which the device of a play-within-the-play proves crucial to both plot and theme, as it not only enables the furthering of the action but also prompts us to reflection on reality and pretence, acting and imposture, identity and role.

In all four of these non-Shakespearean tragedies, there is a variation on the pattern of *Hamlet* in that the performers in the plays-within-the-play are all amateurs, members of the court who are enlisted or who volunteer to act in masques or what are, in effect, home theatricals. This pattern is also used by Shakespeare in *A Midsummer Night's Dream,* but there it is to very different effect. The tragedy of Pyramus and Thisbe is performed not by educated members of the court but by the rude mechanicals who service the household needs of the citizens of Athens, weaving their clothes and mending their bellows. They suffer from all the worst nightmares of amateur dramatics, from the man who wants to play all the parts to the man whose rendering of the lines is so bad that they are reduced to gibberish (though of course their all-male composition would itself render them virtually unrecognisable in terms of modern-day groups of amateur actors). Their lack of education and of performance skills leads them to render this potentially touching story as merely laughable. It is not only the very different social status of the performers that leads the play-within-the-play to have so markedly different an effect in *A Midsummer Night's Dream* from that achieved in *Hamlet,* however; we also have to take into account the widely differing genres of the host plays. Tragedies, it seems, enhance tragedies, like *Hamlet* and *The Spanish Tragedy*, but become merely ridiculous in comedies. The suggestion that it is the genre shift as much as the ineptness of the actors which is responsible for the failure of the piece gains reinforcement from the fact that Shakespeare seems so clearly to be mocking his own tragedy, *Romeo and Juliet*: it, like *Pyramus and Thisbe*, had a prologue in sonnet form, or "eight and six", it told of lovers separated through parental quarrels, and in *Romeo and Juliet* as in *Pyramus and Thisbe* the heroine kills herself in the mistaken belief that the hero is already dead. Comedy, it seems, cannot easily house tragedy within itself. It may perhaps be instructive to compare here two other instances of a sort of popular theatre contained within a Shakespearean comedy: the horn dance in *As You Like It* and the masque of Herne the Hunter in *The Merry Wives of Windsor*, which, with their emphases on continuity and fertility rather than waste and loss, energise the plays which house them rather than merely contributing to incidental mirth.

But if tragedy sits ill in comedy, the insertion of episodes of popular comic theatre into tragedies can work to very different effect. Although *King Lear* and *Othello* both lack a full-blown play-within-the-play, each can be seen as drawing on this tradition. The Clown in Othello is in essence a street entertainer; the Fool in *King Lear*, who is of course so closely allied with his counterpart in *Twelfth Night*, is a crucial presence at a mock-trial where Lear pretends to misrecognise a stool for his erring daughter Goneril. This most basic form of acting – pretending that something is what it is not – has clear links to the play-within-the-play in *A Midsummer Night's Dream*. In both there is much concern about the use and effectiveness of props; the rude mechanicals are much agitated about the representation of the moon and the wall, while the Fool turns on its head the traditional jokey apology for accidentally ignoring someone, "Cry you mercy, I took you for a jointstool", when he says it to the actual joint-stool which Lear is pretending is Goneril. The confusions between pretence and reality here are precisely analogous to the first rehearsal scene in *A Midsummer Night's Dream*, where the mechanicals, gesturing to the stage, say "This green plot shall be our stage", and, gesturing to the tiring-house, declare that "this bush shall be our tiring-house". In each case the audience's own imagination is so implicated in the double layers of the joke that we, too, become accessories to the theatrical game of pretending that things are what they are not.

A similar effect can be achieved in a Shakespearean history play, in the impromptu role-playing of Falstaff and Hal in *Henry IV Part One*. As Hal and his surrogate father take it in turns to act out the role of his real father, serious psychological work, analogous to Freud's idea of dream-work, can clearly be seen to be unfolding, although it is being carried on by (supposedly) unskilled performers with the minimum of plots and setting. This ultimate "poor stage" in the Eastcheap tavern of The Boar's Head may provide a deeply ironic commentary on the development of Shakespeare's own company from the Elizabethan theatre's origins in inn-yard performances to the expensively equipped Globe and, ultimately, the even more elaborately accoutred Blackfriars. Although Shakespeare towards the end of his career acquiesced in creating plays which could be staged at both the Globe and the Blackfriars, there is no suggestion that he preferred the ostensibly classier venue. Indeed when he apparently makes use of its facilities in *Antony and Cleopatra* to have his dying hero drawn up to Cleopatra's monument he accompanies the moment with a telling commentary on Antony's weight and the technical cost of producing this spectacular effect.

Other writers beside Shakespeare made use of popular forms within their own more erudite structures. When John Webster, disappointed after the poor reception afforded to *The White Devil*, tried his luck again with the less baroquely complex plot of *The Duchess of Malfi*, he punctuated his tale of perfidy and incestuous desire in the sophisticated ducal court of Amalfi with one of the most basic of all popular forms of performance, the charivari. The embittered Duke Ferdinand, whose unacknowledged sexual interest in his own twin sister will eventually drive him to lycanthropy, visits that sister in the confinement to which he has condemned her with various forms of acting and pretence. Having first subjected her to viewing wax models of her husband and children in order to convince her that they are dead (and to give a further twist here, those models, to be convincing and practicable, must surely have been not wax at all but the actors themselves), Ferdinand then arranges for a masque of madmen to visit her. As Inga-Stina Ewbank pointed out several years ago, this is directly analogous to the charivari, immortalised by Thomas Hardy as the skimmington-ride, the rustic show which condemns a marriage perceived as ill-advised by parading the bride and groom in effigy tied on to a horse. It could also serve to remind an Elizabethan audience of one of the most popular spectacles of all, that of the insane at Bridewell, who were regularly visited by the sane in much the same spirit as we when we were children might have gone to the zoo. Their impromptu and unpredictable antics seem to have been received as some of the most exciting of performance art, and are alluded to not only here but also in the masque of madmen in Middleton and Rowley's *The Changeling*, and perhaps even in *King Lear*, where Edgar's plan for his father to regain his patience by a simulated fall from a cliff may in fact have been a remedy actually tried in seventeenth-century treatment of the insane.

John Ford also makes use of forms of popular theatre in his otherwise notably serious and *recherché* plays. In *The Witch of Edmonton*, which he co-authored with Thomas Dekker and William Rowley early in his career, the rustic ritual of the morris dancing in the sub-plot (also referred to in *A Midsummer Night's Dream*) provides an important counterpoint to the bigamy, murder and witchcraft of the two main plots. While Mother Sawyer conjures up the devil with the help of her familiar Black Tom and while Frank Thorney stages a kind of play of his own by his pretence of having been tied up and forced to witness the abduction of the wife whom he has in fact murdered himself, the country people devote their energies in rather more healthy fashion to the preparation of the morris dance. Though not without its attendant intrigues – there is an unfortunate moment when everyone forgets that the part of the hobby-horse always goes to Cuddy Banks – it is, nevertheless, notable that those who are involved in the morris dance escape the disasters which overtake so many others of the characters in the play. In particular, Cuddy Banks is directly tempted by the witch's familiar, the talking Black Dog Tom, but because he treats him simply as a dog, whom he uses kindly, he proves quite immune to his snares and escapes scatheless from his encounters with the animal, unlike both Mother Sawyer and Frank Thorney.

Although Ford and Dekker will of course have had a say in overall plotting, it seems to have been Rowley who actually wrote the morris-dancing scenes in *The Witch of Edmonton*; but there can be no doubt of Ford's hand in the comedy scenes of his chronicle history play of *Perkin Warbeck*. His treatment of this story is unusual in that, unlike the majority of Tudor and early Stuart chroniclers, he never affirms that Perkin Warbeck was in fact an impostor, and indeed his treatment of the story leaves us in little doubt that the young man himself seems to believe in his own veracity. Although Ford does not openly condemn him, however, he does tar him by association, because Perkin is accompanied throughout his quest for the throne by a set of Irish counsellors and followers, who would undoubtedly have been viewed with the deepest distrust by the eyes of his audience, educated to perceive the Irish as anathema to civilisation. Shortly after Warbeck has been married to the high-born and high-minded Lady Katherine Gordon, the occasion is celebrated by a masque. It is described in the stage directions (which, in Ford's case, are almost invariably authorial), as follows:

> Enter at one door four Scottish Antics accordingly habited; enter at another four wild Irish trowses, long-haired, and accordingly habited. Music. The Masquers dance.
> (III.ii.112-4)

Described by a sceptical member of the on-stage audience as "kingly bug's words" (III.ii.111), these eight masquers form an interesting visual gloss on a crucial stage in the action. Although the description of their appearance is so brief, we should not underestimate the vital effect which visual effects so often have in Ford's plays. Here, the Scotch antics and the wild Irish appear both as a comment on Perkin's marriage, which has united a Scotswoman to a man who has just come from Ireland, and also stand in striking contrast to the deadly earnest of the military preparations which Henry VII is making for the suppression of the threat posed by Perkin. While the English king musters his army, the implication might well be, the Scottish king and the pretender have nothing better to rely on than their woefully accoutred native troops. Most interestingly of all, however, the masque is concluded by Warbeck saying "In the next room / Take your own shapes again" (III.ii.115-6), which clearly reveals that the supposed Scotch antics and wild Irish are in fact only masquerading as such – a fascinating comment on the questions of imposture and nature which haunt so much of the play. Whereas in comedy, then, popular performances of tragic interludes prove merely grist to the comic mill, tragedy can use popular forms of masquing, mumming, role playing and improvisation to add weight to its own themes and outlook. My concentration on questions of form has allowed no time for consideration of Bakhtinian or carnivalesque approaches, but might nevertheless lead to a suggestion that the use of popular forms in tragedy can provide telling comment on the aspirations of the main characters to heroic individuality, by a contrasting assertion of the overriding power of community and continuity invoked by these popular forms, with their stress on the fluidity and pretence implied in identity rather than the stability to which tragedy aspires.

Staging the British Empire under Charles Dibdin the Younger at Sadler's Wells 1800-1819

Anita Shir-Jacob

At the beginning of the nineteenth century during the time of the Napoleonic Wars, Sadler's Wells was one of eight theatres in London, including the Theatres Royal, Drury Lane and Covent Garden, that was actively dramatising the ideology of British imperialism. The theatres, potentially subversive agents of unrest, were licensed as if they were public houses so that if they became too riotous or insubordinate, their licenses could be taken away. The cumulative impact of the theatrical licensing laws of 1737, 1752 and 1755 had the effect of making the control of British society one of the most important functions of the theatres. The trials of the archetypal British sailor of working-class origins, Jack Tar and his landlubber equivalent, John Bull, against hostile foes in foreign lands were dramatised in such a way that they were perceived to be of direct advantage to each individual within the imperial nation. The audiences at Sadler's Wells were strongly identified with the sailor hero whom Dibdin dramatised as the backbone of the empire, eminently suited to rule over subject races. The largely working class audiences, who saw themselves not merely represented as a nation on the stage but constitutive of that nation, felt that their self interest was materially served within the structure of the pantomimes and aquatic pieces.

This paper examines the way in which Charles Dibdin the Younger (1768-1833),[1] manager, author and machinist at Sadler's Wells from 1800 to 1819, portrayed, through the medium of popular theatre and specifically the aquatic drama, battles fought against Napoleonic and other forces in order to naturalize the imperial policies of the British Government. In 1804 water from the reservoir of the New River Head, adjacent to the theatre, was piped into a tank under the stage. When the stage was raised a sheet of water, 90 feet in length, from 10 to 24 feet wide and three to four feet in depth, covered the stage area. "Real" naval spectacles on a grand scale were presented on his theatrical ocean. On eight thousand cubic feet of water, ships, gun boats, floating batteries, built on a scale of one inch to a foot, and manned by five to six inch high mariners, celebrated Jack Tar, defending Britannia against the despised "Boney" In the downstage area of the tank, regular boats and stage smoke screened the ships upstage. Actors and water-boys tumbled about in the water and engaged with one another, in the words of a contemporary theatrical correspondent, in "life-like skirmishes."

Connecting a Class and Ethnic Identity to a British and Imperial Identity

J. S. Bratton's analysis of imperialism in the theatre, in the collaboratively authored *Acts of Supremacy: The British Empire and the Stage, 1790-1930*, opens up a whole new perspective on how imperialism was naturalized on the stage.[2] Her insights offer a methodology that can usefully be applied to Dibdin's presentations at the Wells. A nationalist discourse interconnected with an imperialist discourse as Dibdin validated Britain's right to colonize other nations. During the nineteen year period that he was manager at the Wells, a substantial immigration into London included large numbers of Scots, Irish and Welsh while from abroad came the Germans, the Dutch, the French and thousands of Jews from Russia and Poland. Many of these new immigrants, denied residence in the City, moved to the northern suburbs and settled in the neighbourhood of Sadler's Wells in the parish of St. James, Clerkenwell. Within the narrative of his pieces Dibdin regularly included each of these groups, and most specifically the working classes of these groups, as members and builders of the British Empire. In this way a class and ethnic identity was transformed by Dibdin's popular theatre into an imperial identity: local and regional allegiances and any other national loyalties that might prove to be seditious were thus effectively subordinated on the stage.[3]

In his serious-comic pantomime, *Ko and Zoa* (1803), Dibdin dramatises the incorporation within the hegemonic group of Leonard O'Leary, an Irish sailor from Kilkenny who has been shipwrecked on the Indian shore. O'Leary, who has long resided with the "savages," informs the audience in the opening song that he had undertaken to "civilize" the natives:

How d' ye think I came over each tawny fac'd rogue?
Why, English I taught with an Irish brogue

O'Leary makes no attempt to converse with the indigenous inhabitants in their own language. Within the action of the pantomime it is O'Leary's initiative that first saves Ko, an Indian Chief and then Zoa, his wife, from insurgents within the tribe who want to kill them. He is the arbitrator who sees that justice is done and who is directly involved in the structural melodramatic formula of the production that ends, in Dibdin's words, with "a picture, expressive of the happiness of the virtuous, the punishment of vice, and the joy of the Indians." [4] O'Leary's "Irish brogue" with which he spoke and taught English was good for a laugh and it disarmed the audience but what was significantly dramatized, was how natural it was for the British to take control. While O'Leary's regional peculiarities, his class, and his potential allegiance to a different history were acknowledged, what was paramount was his membership of the British Empire/ Club.

Dibdin's dramatic treatment of the volunteer system in the burletta spectacle, *British Amazons; or, Army without Reserve* in 1803 is part of this same discourse of power as it interconnected with class and regional discourses. The formation of the Volunteer Associations, sponsored by the government had been established in 1797. It was generally agreed that the volunteers, men and women drawn from all classes and groups, were intended as a civilian police force to act as an auxiliary defence force against the enemy from without. But the real purpose of these brightly uniformed and drilled civilian troops was to combat sedition from within. In 1803 their numbers were increased to 300, 000 and they were divided into 11 regiments of infantry and one corps of cavalry. Colourful parades of volunteers whipped up strong national feeling and in October 1803 there was a brilliant parade of Volunteers in Hyde Park. Dibdin incorporated actions in *British Amazons* that were satisfactory from both a dramatic and an hegemonic point of view. The piece opens with John Bull scoffing at the "Corsican Chief" whom he and his accompanying chorus label, after Aesop's tale, the "Ass in a Lion's skin." Scene 2 then follows with a recruiting sergeant paying tribute to the patriotism of the citizens from whose number he cannot muster up any recruits because everyone <u>of all classes</u> has joined the volunteers:

> I offer them money, but offer in vain,
> They cry, "<u>We're all soldiers for glory</u> not gain;"
> A crown and a guinea I offer them down,
> They the guinea refuse but stand up for the *Crown*.

In the next scene reference is made to the female divisions of the volunteer corps in which class differences are again subsumed within a collective identity:

> Then since Amazon means,
> Women, (<u>Peasants, or Queens</u>)
> Who, than life, prizing honour far more,
> Resist foes that invade,
> May she die an old maid,
> Who wouldn't belong to our corps.

A rousing cry of "Old England for ever, and God save the King!" in the finale is followed by a chorus of male and female volunteers representing a cross section of the citizens, carolling "Britannia! George! and Liberty!" Dibdin enjoyed an excellent relationship with the Middlesex magistrates "whose Word," he professed, "was always Law with us," – and who issued him with an annual licence to present entertainments at the Wells. Their support for him was directly attributable to the global world, "liberated" by the British, which he presented within the framework of his proscenium arch. The connections which Dibdin's audiences made between the stage world at the Wells and the "real" world earned him many public commendations of "patriotic loyalty and philanthropic benevolence."

Documentary Connections

In the immediate aftermath of World War Two, the theatre historian, Edward Dent called attention to the fact that the battle pieces represented at Sadler's Wells during the Napoleonic period, "fulfilled exactly the same requirements for that generation as the war-propaganda films do for certain types of audience to-day."[5] Britain's role as a formidable sea power, a favourite theme before Dibdin developed the aquatic theatre, became an even greater attraction once the tank was installed. In an age without cinema and television and with almost no direct reporting from the battlefront (the electric telegraph had not yet been invented), the naval representations at Sadler's Wells not only disseminated information but connected and shaped that information as part of an imperialist discourse. Representations and re-enactments of naval battles on the stage at Sadler's Wells were widely held to be documentary and authentic. More importantly Dibdin's pieces complemented the meaning of Empire as it was interpreted by politicians, military and economic reports, news coverage, official documents and commercial expectations.[6] Theatrical correspondents claimed that the aquatic exhibitions were *drawn from facts*. Dibdin himself wondered at the suspension of disbelief that never saw the "glaring abandonment of perspective, proportion and scenic propriety." The "credulity" of the audience resulted on a number of occasions in spectators shinning down from the gallery onto the stage and into the water, to "show Õem as tight work as we did under his honour, Admiral Nelson." [7] During this period of war, members of the audience broke theatrical conventions by invading the stage space, as they expressed their agreement with the "reality "of the *feelings and facts* that the entertainments evoked. Theatre reviewers, referring to the exhibitions at Sadler's Wells, appeared to be much impressed by their verisimiltude. The observation that these water shows were the "greatest proof of the excellence of an Entertainment which could so far interest the passions of a spectator as to betray him an idea of its being a reality," exemplifies a conventional response to the spectacles in the tank.[8] The distinction between fact and fiction on the Wells stage had become irrelevant. What was most "real" in these productions was not the real/artificial theatrical situation to which the reviewers referred, but a shared ideology, or in other words the connections that Dibdin was making between the stage world and the world outside. At this point however, it is worth noting that the spectators were often sodden with drink, especially those in the gallery, of whom the majority were frequently sailors home on leave or employees in the Port of London. According to Joseph Grimaldi, the most popular clown in London and employed at Sadler's Wells, the Wells was "at that time a famous place or resort with the blue-jackets, the gallery being sometimes almost solely occupied by seamen and their female companions."[9]

How Dibdin's Productions Connected With an Imperialist Discourse

In order to depict Britain within his presentations as the natural leader of the world, Dibdin employed various dramatic techniques and strategies to effect his naturalisation of Britain's right to rule: past history was called up to legitimate the present; he presented the British colonizer as the anti-hero and/or the underdog to gain the sympathy of the audience and to draw attention away from the conqueror as aggressor to the victim as aggressor; he frequently introduced oriental characters and settings that were restructured within the imperial discourse; he employed a pastoral convention that sanctified the hearth and home but in which the subtext was clearly the propagation of imperialism; he manipulated the melodramtic formula of stereotyping in which good was pitted against evil to appeal to the "British" sense of fair play; he freely indulged in talismanic stimuli in the form of rousing songs, cannons on stage and displays of the British flag to stir up patriotic sentiments.

Making Connections Between the Past and the Present

A few examples of how Dibdin placed the imperial discourse in the past to validate his country's expansionist policies in the present, include the "grand military pantomime spectacle" of *The Old Man of the Mountains; or, Gorthmund the Cruel* (1803), the "burletta spectacle," *British Amazons; or, Army without Reserve* (1803) and the pantomime, *London; or, Harlequin and Time* (1813). In *The Old Man of the Mountains,* representatives of the various Christian powers assemble under Richard the Lionhearted to "help" the muslim Saracen "to rescue Palestine." The parallel that Dibdin drew between Gorthmund's "atheistic" oppression and Britain's "Christian" liberation of the pagan world was an analogue for the conflict between

195

Britain and France during the Napoleonic wars. In the following recitative Dibdin describes the "wicked old devil," Gorthmund, (Napoleon) in his mountain stronghold:

> He kill's (sic) in cold blood, it one's patience provokes,
> Jews, Christians, and Turks, great and small;
> So I fancy, like some of our monstrous great folks,
> He's of no *religion* at all.

Dibdin's presentation of British incursions into foreign lands was set in an historical context that naturalized Britain's control of the present and future. In scene 10, at the Temple of Death, Richard, together with the Sultan, Saladin, and their combined forces of Saracen and Christian soldiers make themselves "masters of the Mountain and Castle." Within the structure of this pantomime Britain's imperialist intentions are covert. What was dramatized instead was the peace keeping mission of Richard as he assisted the Saracens in getting rid of Gorthmund. The piece concluded with an "appropriate picture and scroll with MAY THE ARMS OF THE KING OF ENGLAND PROCURE PEACE. In fact, so entrenched were prevailing beliefs about Britain's right to rule, that the subject for a university prize essay at Fort William College in 1813 was "The probable design of the Divine Providence in subjecting so large a portion of Asia to the British Dominion." [10]

On a most obvious level the connections in Dibdin's productions in these early years created and propagated a tradition of the "nation." But a possible invasion by the French also enabled Britain to justify her imperialist policy to herself: she could mimic Napoleon's imperialism or rout him. She did both and continued to expand her domination after 1815. In the comic pantomime, *Castles in the Air; or, Columbine Cowslip* (1812) the continuity and growth of the British Empire was theatricalized by a number of chairs multiplying on stage while a song in honour of the late Nelson emphasised how (very probably burlesquing the apparition of Banquo's descendants in the mirror) he would continue to be replicated: "His fame shall British Tars inspire;/While future Nelsons catch his fire, /For tho' one valiant Nelson falls, /Our Navy many a

Nelson knows ..." Ultimately the dramatization of the self interest of the individual sailor/soldier is seen to be served best in and to be inseparably connected with the interests of the Empire. Britain was consistently dramatised as a natural leader of the Second and Third Coalitions formed against Napoleon who threatened the sovereignty of other nations. Yet even as Napoleon was being demonized on stage, Britain's presence in America, Malta, Gibraltar, India and China was unexamined.

Connecting the Conqueror to the Underdog and/or Anti-Hero

Dibdin's concern with a moral commitment in the pantomime, "every thinking writer knows that he is compromising his duty, if *Moral* (sic) be not the foundation of his Superstructure;..." was carried by Harlequin and Columbine (on stage) to the far corners of the globe, to India, China and Persia, where they taught the local inhabitants a thing or two about British justice. Clown, an important person in the pantomimes of the nineteenth century was usually an anti-heroic figure, but one who significantly dramatized aspects of the self which theatregoers were obliged to repress. As in all discourses of power with subversive characters, Clown was routinely presented in order to be overcome and contained. Dibdin explained in his memoirs that, "In order to emphasise morality, "every *immorality* (sic) committed by that half-idiotic, crafty, shameless, incorrigible, emblem of gross sensuality, the Clown, was almost invariably followed by some appropriate punishment, through the agency of Harlequin which served as a striking antidote to the Crime."[11] The characters in the plays – and the audience – come to terms with a governing pattern through experimentation and adjustment. Dibdin's pantomimes were a teaching tool which articulated and represented the adjustments made not only by outsiders but also by Harlequin, Columbine, Pantaloon and their fellows as part of a social, emotional and intellectual education.

In almost all his productions which dramatized the imperial discourse, Dibdin consistently reversed the roles of aggressors and victims so that the British expatriate was usually presented as a bumbling fool who was hopelessly outnumbered by physically stronger opponents. But Bull and Tar were always victorious in the name of liberty, king and country. They "saved" and then incorporated the natives into their world. In 1808 in his "New Grand Aquatic Melo-Dramatic Spectacle, the *White Witch; or, the Cataract of Amazonia* Dibdin introduces "an English Woman, who has been Shipwrecked on the Coast (of Amazonia in South America) with her Relation Pedagogue, an ignorant pedantic School Master, ...who impose(s) his Cousin upon the Superstitious Natives, as a Powerful Witch... (while he) opens a School to teach the Natives English." Their situation is reminiscent of Leonard O' Leary's in the earlier production of *Ko and Zoa* (1803) who is caught in a feud between two different factions of the natives. English Woman, after having had a narrow escape from a perilous conspiracy against her, proves to be more than a match for her Amazonian sisters and, in Dibdin's words, at the "Annual Sacrifice of the Amazonians to the *Spirit of the Cataract* ...Innocence triumphs." Most importantly the good spirit of the tribe, Pulkawulka (played by Mrs. Dibdin) appears in the final tableau showing gratitude to Pedagogue and his cousin, English Woman for protecting her tribe...and the Piece concludes with Pulkawulka exhibiting a Scroll signifying that *"Virtue is Heaven's peculiar Care."* Dibdin presented the two marooned British travellers in an unsympathetic light: they set out to deceive the Amazons and the "Intelligence he (Pedagogue) communicates to her (his cousin, English Woman) enables her to carry on the deceit ..." They are transformed into decent folk in the action of the piece as they learn to trust the natives. Dibdin's presentation of these two representatives of Empire and their obvious vulnerability which almost ends in the death of English Woman, gave the audience a sense of fair play.

Dibdin wrote that when he adapted Byron's poem, *The Corsair* (1814) "as a good subject for an Aqua-Drama," he had been obliged to make changes for "Stage Effect (as that which *reads* well, does not always *act* well) (sic) and therefore it "occasioned (him) in the construction of this Piece, materially to differ from parts of his Lordship's Story." But as Byron had done before him, Dibdin represented the British as lovers of liberty rather than imperialists. Conrad, a pirate chief, leaves his island home to make sorties on powerful opponents who are enemies of freedom. He trounces them not only in the public sphere but also in the personal one. Gulnare, the mistress of Seyd, Conrad's opponent, tells Conrad in Byron's version of the events, that "I felt — I feel — love dwells with — the free."(Canto the second-xiv) and aligns herself to Conrad after helping him to kill Seyd. (Dibdin, anxious not to offend the magistrates by whom his theatre was annually licensed, cut this scene). In the opening of Canto 1 in which Byron's Corsair unites the concepts of home and empire he is no more a pirate than he is a Jacobin. He is rather a red necked imperialist whose engagement with the discourse of the ruling classes readily lent itself to the kind of material dramatized at Sadler's Wells:

> O'er the glad waters of the dark blue sea,
> Our thoughts as boundless and our souls as free,
> Far as the breeze can bear, the billows foam,
> Survey our empire and behold our home!
> These are our realms, no limit to their sway
> Our flag the sceptre all who meet obey.

The aquatic drama, *The Gheber; or, the Fire Worshippers* (1818) that Dibdin based on one of the tales in the Irish poet's Thomas Moore's best selling *Lalla Rookh* is a later example of Dibdin's method of dramatizing the naturalization of the Empire through the deliberate manipulation of the aggressor/victim-victim/aggressor opposition. Feramorz, a slave of Lalla Rookh, with whom she is secretly in love tells her in Moore's version, in response to her question about the history of a tower, that "the tower was the remains of an ancient Fire-Temple, built by the Ghebers or Persians of the the old religion, who, many hundred years since, had fled hither from their Arab conquerors, preferring liberty and their altars in a foreign land to the alternative of apostasy or persecution in their own." [12] Feramorz added that it was impossible not to feel sympathy with the sufferings of the persecuted Ghebers. In adapting this widely popular story to the stage, Dibdin connected it with recent events. Napoleon was safely out of the way but the threat of a French invasion a few years earlier was still fresh in the minds of his audiences at Sadler's Wells. In the aquatic adaptation, the British were not, as one might expect, likened to the oppressive Arabs but to the freedom-loving Persians/Ghebers who had fled their land rather than suffer the yoke of the oppressor. (Ironically, Moore's tale was really allegorical of the predicament of Irish nationalists under the yoke of British domination). The picturesque setting described in Moore's narrative – "In the middle of the lawn where the pavilion stood there was a tank surrounded by small mangoe-trees, on the clear cold waters on which floated multitudes of the beautiful red lotus; while at a distance stood the ruins of a strange and awful-looking tower, which seemed old enough to have been the temple of some religion no longer known ..." – was magnificently staged at the Wells where Dibdin spared no expense that season to mount three extravagant aquatic dramas.[13] Within this mise en scene Britain was mythologized, fighting against great odds for her survival and freedom when in reality she had emerged triumphant from a war against the French whose fleet was inferior to hers.

Orientalism and Imperialism

Nigel Leask refers to Byron who in 1813 wrote in a letter to Thomas Moore that Madame De Stael had advised him (Byron) to "stick to the East," and that the "public are orientalizing."[14] The British acculturation of Egyptian originals (and Indian and Chinese) as objets d'art, furniture, accessories, and as material for the theatre, became part of a systematic connection of Britain with the Orient, defined in Said's seminal work on orientalism as "a Western style for dominating, restructuring and having authority over the Orient."[15] Sybil Rosenfeld describes an album of scenes at the Wells, now in the collection of the Garrick Club, that she believes was a record book for the theatre. In addition to the watercolour paintings of new and stock scenes there are engraved aquatints of "Gothic, Egyptian and Chinese halls, furniture, ceilings and decorative motives (sic) which would have been useful to the scene designers, particularly for the exotic scenes which were so often called for in Dibdin's melodramas."[16]

Presentations at Dibdin's popular theatre, a mass medium for its period, were characterised by their eastern settings and characters that were part of the wider cultural concern with imperialism. Some of these presentations were comic pantomimes such as *Anthony and Cleopatra; or, Harlequin Nilus* (1804), *Castles in the Air; or*

Columbine Cowslip (1809) and *The Brachman; or, The Oriental Harlequin* (1813), the last mentioned founded on the "Brachman of Visapour" in the Persian Tales. The orientalism in the comic pantomimes, rather than being mere background, is constitutive of an imperial hegemony. In *Anthony and Cleopatra* where Egyptian landscapes form a prominent feature of the scenery, scene one opens with startling effects: in the interior of an Egyptian catacomb "the tomb bursts open with thunder and lightning, and the Mummy of Nilus appears, moves forward, and *receives homage* (my emphasis) from other Mummies in the Sepulchre" in a dance that Dibdin records, became very popular with the audiences at the Wells. In *Castles in the Air,* Cowslip, a small farmer's daughter, dissatisfied with her rank in society, is magically transformed into Columbine and escapes with Harlequin. After a series of wanderings through England, she and Harlequin arrive, in scene 8, in China, at which point the audiences were entertained with a mime sequence that included "animated tea equipage." The landscape views of China are the backdrop for the hair-breadth escape of the Lovers from Columbine's pursuing parents who have been transformed into Pantaloon and Pantalina. The setting of this scene is not contextually related to the plot in any logical way but is specifically there to familiarize the audience with Britain's authority and presence in the Orient. *The Brachman* tells the story of Canfou the Brachman, a "hoary Brachman, skill'd in Magic lore," who falls in love with a fair lady who does not return his love until the final aquatic scene when the Brachman is changed into a handsome Persian prince. Scene 2 depicts a view of the Ruins of Palmyra, an ancient city in Syria on the north side of the desert, while scene 3 is described as a "Fancy Scene, Exhibiting Specimens of various Asiatic Fruits, Flowers, Shells, &c."

A central figure within the action of the *Magic Minstrel; or, Fairy Lake* (1808) based on Shakespeare's Titania and Oberon, with Persian characters and with views and landscapes of Persia figuring largely in the scenery, is Paddy Abdallah, an Irish retainer of Saed, the son of a Persian merchant. Abdallah, who is an Irishman and Persian rolled into one, helps the plot move briskly forward to the final denouement, when boats, dragons and sorcerers plunge in and out of the water to vindicate the supremacy of the good. Abdallah's crucial role to validate British hegemony is offset by his buffoonery that is meant to allay doubts about Britain's real intentions. Dramatic interaction between the characters was placed in a global setting which extended conceptual boundaries so that within the action of these pieces, the exotic was familiarized and incorporated into an English context. The presence of foreign characters and settings was almost certainly even more substantial than is revealed by the evidence that is currently available from the extant songbooks and scripts, many of which are fragmentary and incomplete.

Pastoral Convention: Connecting the Exile with his Homeland

Britain is allegorized as immediate family within the imperial discourse. In a sketch of his serio-comic pantomime, *Philip Quarll; or, the English Hermit* (1803) which Dibdin claimed was based on a novel describing an actual event of a man stranded for a number of years on an exotic island, [17] he dramatized the yearning for being part of the British family. He pits the wits of his protagonist against several blacks who come to "explore the Island in search of game." Pirates are also introduced and they function dramatically as the shadow self, the subversive other. Quarll and the pirates are "saved" by the timely arrival of Britannia in the form, to quote Dibdin, "of an English ship, whose Lieutenant and some Sailors land, (and whose help) occasions their deliverance. The Lieutenant is discovered to be Quarll's son, and the Curtain drops during the picture of astonishment, gratitude and joy formed by the several characters." Quarll is significantly united with his family and country, inseparable in the single persona of an officer of the British navy, emphasising the father/fatherland connection/relationship. The blacks are destroyed, the pirates decide to drown themselves instead of being a burden on the law, and Quarll and his son return together across the seas to Britannia. By connecting new and dislocating encounters with the familiar, these encounters assumed the form of a safe home, and the aggression and the intrusion of the British were regularly denied.

Talismanic Triggers

Dibdin freely indulged in talismanic triggers in the form of rousing songs, military bands, cannons rolling on and off the stage, and displays of the British flag to evoke the victorious Britons on the battlefields. The audience bestowed value and meaning on these signs which not only had the same meaning for everyone, but the same potential meaning. Connections were therefore elaborated by self sufficient spectators during the process of performance in ways that were wholly predictable. In 1801 a reviewer commented rather fulsomely on the realness of the flag in a new musical spectacular, *Egyptian Laurels*, that "had all the appearances of reality...is an exact copy of the real one in all its original splendour ...." Given the ingenuity of the early nineteenth century machinists and scene painters, the achievement of recreating a flag could not have been so extraordinary. It would seem that it was not the *literal* "reality" of the flag and the battle scenes to which Dibdin owed his success but the connections that the audiences made between these representations and what was "real" in war-time England. The semiotic representation of the flag in this piece that evoked the defeat of the French at Aboukir Bay in 1798, in which the British forces captured the French flag, was intended to be evocative of all the battles in which Britain engaged. Since major battles occurred on average more than once a week from 1792-1814 on one or another of the several fronts where campaigns were in progress, the flag on stage came to be consistently connected with the nation at war. The final scene of the pieces often concluded with a military ballet, martial music and the illumination of the Horse Guards or some other ceremonial symbol of Britsh rule. Under Dibdin the Wells therefore became a theatre in which everything was predictable and clearly codified and the spectators became accustomed to decodifying the performances very precisely.

Conclusion

  Between 1800 and 1819 the Wells, under Dibdin's management, was evidently a crucial tool in making connections between an ideology that justified Britain's imperial policies and the tangible economic benefits accruing from that imperialism. In 1821, a year after Dibdin had resigned from the management, Sadler's Wells was one of the theatres chosen as a venue by King George IV to mark his coronation. The "theatres of Drury Lane, Covent Garden, the English Opera House, the Surrey, Sadler's Wells, &c. were, by command of his Majesty, thrown open to the public..." *Free* tickets were issued and the theatres were soon filled to overflowing. Journalists observed that at these public gatherings, "[t]he loyalty evinced by the audiences at each Theatre shewed the estimation in which our Monarch is held by his people. God save the King was sung amidst acclamations." [18] Despite the gushing blurb of this particular publication, George was at this time the target of severe public censure for his conduct to his estranged wife, Queen Caroline. His selection of the theatres as venues to affirm popular sovereignty even when the people had lost their confidence in him, lent weight to the connections made in the theatres as they propagated an imperial discourse. The coronation celebrations were in fact a logical extension and fuller expression of the communal singing of the royal anthem by performers and spectators at the commencement of the entertainment, a custom which London theatregoers, until fairly recently, continued to practise.

Notes

[1] Dibdin was the elder of two illegitimate sons born to Charles Dibdin the Elder (1745-1814), a song writer and dramatist and Harriet Pitt, an actress in Covent Garden. His younger brother, Thomas John Dibdin (1771-1841), was also a popular and prolific playwright and composer who was employed in the London circuit of theatres. His mother was the daughter of Ann Pitt, a popular comic actress. In 1775 he was adopted by his maternal uncle, Cecil Pitt Esq, a household goods broker who made Charls adopt his name of Pitt. His expectations of being his uncle's heir never materialised and he resumed the name of Dibdin in 1796 when he made his debut on the stage.

[2] "British Heroism and Melodrama" in J.S.Bratton et al (eds.), *Acts of Supremacy and the Stage, 1790-1930* (Manchester University Press, 1991) pp.18-59; intro. pp.1-16

[3] Bratton (op.cit.) refers to the precedent set by Shakespeare in *Henry V* where the English are a "band of brothers" drawn from the four kingdoms, bickering together like a family, but united against a threat from overwhelming outside forces. See p.25

[4] Charles Dibdin, New seio-comic pantomime Ko and Zoa, 1803. This pantomime is bound in *The Writings for the Theatre of Charles Issac Mungo Dibdin (1768-1833) known as Charles Dibdin the Younger*, 2 vols, collected and recorded by his grandson Edward Rimbault Dibdin, Liverpool, 1919. Theatre Museum, London. All the pantomimes and aquatic pieces referred to in this paper, unless otherwise stated are from this same collection.

[5] Edward J. Dent, *A Theatre for Everybody* (Boardman, 1945) p.15

[6] Bratton, op. cit.

[7] Records of the Great Playhouses, Series One: *The Sadler's Wells Archives from Finsbury Central Library* (Harvester Microform Collection, 1988), 12 reels. "Scenes and Criticisms 1783-1803", reel 9.

[8] Ibid.

[9] "Boz" (ed.), *Memoirs of Joseph Grimaldi* (Routledge [1838]) p.138

[10] S.E.Ayling, *The Georgian Century* 1714-1837 (Harrap, 1966) p285

[11] "Boz" (op. cit.) p.89

[12] Thomas Moore, *Lalla Rookh, An Oriental Romance* 5th ed. (Longman, 1817) p169-287. Moore's publishers had commissioned this piece for 3000 guineas.

[13] To date no extant version of Dibdin's dramatic adaptation of *The Gheber* has come to light. Announcements in playbills and the newspapers give descriptions of it and Dibdin's memoirs and theatrical reviews make references to the scenery.

[14] Nigel Leask, *British Romantic Writers and the East: Anxieties of Empire* (Cambridge University Press, 1992) p.13

[15] Edward Said, *Orientalism* (Vintage, 1979) p.3

[16] Sybil Rosenfield, "A Sadler's Wells Scene Book", *Theatre Notebook* 15 (1961) pp. 57-62

[17] Peter Longueville, *The Hermit; or, the Unparalleled Sufferings and Surprising Adventures of Mr Philip Quarll, an Englishman*, 1727 (Garland, 1972). Quarll was discovered by a Mr Dorrington, a Bristol merchant on an uninhabited island in the "South-Sea" where he had apparently lived for fifty years.

[18] Percival Collection, *London: Sadler's Wells Theatre*, 1683-1848. Crach. 1. Tab. 4.b.4/4. Mic. 19293-306. (British Library Reproductions, 1993) 6 reels. Reel 4, p.150

Space and Popular Theatre

Sophie Nield

Popular performance and notions of the popular are frequently discussed in terms of high/low art divisions, examinations of audience taste, and class-specific cultural practice. This article does not seek to undermine these inquiries; rather the aim is to take into consideration a different and challenging area of analysis – that of the production of space – and bring it to bear upon an area of documented theatre practice – that of the monumental theatre spaces of the mid to late nineteenth century.

Obviously, the study of space is hardly a new concern in the discipline of theatre study. In addition to work on the scenic and representational space of the drama, issues of architecture and location have begun to be addressed, notably by Steven Mullaney, in his sustained examination of the location of playhouses in the Elizabethan age, and by Ian Mackintosh in his recent *Architecture, Actor and Audience*.[1]

The theorisations I wish to address here, however, have developed in the course of a dialogue between the disciplines of geography and social theory, and derive from the recently traced development of a materialist interpretation of spatiality.

One of its foremost theorists, the geographer Edward Soja, categorises this as a "transformative retheorisation" of "the socially produced geographical configurations and spatial relations which give material form and expression to society."[2] Soja uses the term "spatiality" in a deliberate way to refer specifically to "socially produced space" and it is this sense of a space created and recreated through human interaction, relationships and intent which is significant here.

That space was somehow marginal to the study of social interaction seems to have come from prejudices in both geography and social theory. Soja writes that:

> Throughout its history, the institutionalised discipline of geography has repeatedly sought philosophical legitimacy in its

distinctive, if not unique perspective, often using this sustaining legitimisation as a means of confining geographical analysis to pure description of phenomenal forms regardless of their causal origins.[3]

This tended to cause social space to be analysed and interpreted as if it were physical space, and spatial analysis remained static, and tangential to developments within philosophy, historiography and social theory.

Space was also, it seemed, distrusted by social sciences keen on avoiding traces of "geographical determinism" in their work. The rapprochement seems to have been inspired, in part, by the seminal work of Henri Lefebvre, *The Production of Space,* whose translation into English in 1991 has evidently invigorated so much of this work. The key concept is that space, whether urban, rural or architectural, is not merely inherited from the past, or nature, but is actively shaped through human intentions and practices: it exists both as a concrete set of material spaces, and as a set of relations between individuals and groups.

Spatial structures can be seen as the material form of social structures and relations, social relations made manifest, rather than their incidental reflection:

> To be alive is to participate in the social production of space, to shape, and be shaped by, a constantly evolving spatiality which constitutes and concretises social action and relationship.[4]

These actions and relationships, in our society, take place within the context of capital and, therefore, the spaces in which we live, and the spatiality we experience, is that of capitalist relations and their reproduction.

Since the social relations are political and ideological, it follows that the spatial relations are political and ideological, because:

> the social relations of production have a social existence only as far as they exist spatially; they project themselves into a space, they inscribe themselves into a space while producing it.[5]

As we have seen, the production of space and spatiality is no once-and-for-all fixed event. The reinforcement and restructuring of capitalist spatiality is a continual source of contradiction and conflict. And thus, as socially-produced space (space produced and created through casual or intentional use) is simultaneously the product of a transformation process (the evolution of society) and is transformable itself, it follows that any social struggle, including of course class struggle, must also be consciously and politically engaged in spatial struggle, to gain control over the social production of space.

This theorisation of space as a participatory and *affectable* factor in social and by extension, cultural change, therefore, becomes significant in any social or cultural history, including the particularly energetic and lively social histories of popular performance. The ability to control and determine the production of space is recognised as being an indicator of social power. This can be done in many ways: materially, imaginatively, through the creation of maps, or borders, or spatially expressed statements of authority such as exclusive places, or places of punishment.

The key divisions relevant to this inquiry are the production of what Lefebvre termed "abstract" and "absolute" spaces. "Abstract" space is a space of domination, put to the service of some abstract purpose such as state power, ideology, the reproduction of capital or, in this context, the production and presentation of art. "Absolute" space is appropriated space, space bent to the uses and needs of those who live in it. It can be appropriated through a conscious "counter-using" of abstract space, but more commonly emerges organically out of the routines and practices of everyday life.

Obviously, the concerns of geography extend to all manifestations of spatial practice – private homes, urban environments, business districts, landscape etc.

However, within the rather tighter frame of reference of the social history of the theatre, examples can be found which support this division.

Richard Wagner opened his Festspielhaus in Bayreuth in 1876. This event is recognised as being a key moment in the birth of the modern movement.[6] The Festspielhaus had a fan-shaped, or circular-section auditorium, a single tier and boxes for Wagner's patron, King Ludwig. Mackintosh refers to the description of this form as democratic, albeit with some reservations. His reluctance is borne out by Julius Posener, who recognises the semi-circular amphitheatre as the truly democratic experiment in theatre architecture.[7] He argues that this was transcended by the fan-shaped hall, which not only continued the absence of the tiers of boxes which had highlighted the divisions between social classes, but also prevented the self-celebration which the public enjoyed in the amphitheatre. And' indeed, although perhaps maintaining economic democracy, in that all the seats were the same, this theatre does not seem to have been intended to promote a "democratic" experience of the drama. Rather, the aim was to promote a particular kind of relationship between the spectator and the representation on the stage.

Wagner wrote of the need of the theatre to:

> channel ..sight itself to the careful perception of an image, something which may only be brought about by completely deviating the sight organ from the perception of any reality that may lie in between, like that of the technical apparatus that evokes the image itself.

This requires a strict adherence to the rules of perspective and sight lines determined by the position of the proscenium:

> As soon as the spectator has occupied his seat, he immediately finds himself in a real, life-size "theatron"..a place created exclusively for looking, and for looking in the direction in which his seat points to.[8]

Thus is the gaze of the spectator compelled and controlled by the construction of the spatial environment in which she finds herself. The space is produced as coercive.

This has some important consequences in terms of the experience of the viewer. Arnold Zweig, in *Theater, Menge, Mensch* wrote:

> The spectator is alone in front of the show: a closed relationship is created, jealous and perfect, between him and

the object. It is unimportant if there are thousands of spectators who turn their eyes onto that single curtain which is about to go up... it is not the mass who will see Malvolio or Cassandra, but the single, thousands of singles.[9]

Thus, argues Posener, the almighty power of art dissolves all social bonds.

It could rather be argued that the almighty power of produced and constructed spatial experience places vast distances between people in actual physical proximity. The relationship ceases to be that of members of an audience to each other (on whatever terms), but becomes that of individuals and art itself.

The theatre becomes, under these circumstances, a spatial structure in service of an abstract ideal, that of the transcendence of the aesthetic/cathartic experience; rather in the same way that a cathedral is a spatial structure for the experiencing of the ideas of religion.

Here, I wish to address a form of "appropriated" or "absolute" space. It is my contention that moments of "popular" theatre, moments at which there is a sense of freedom of use of theatre and entertainment spaces, occur when the "totalised" nature of the space, so to speak, is not a given. The audience does not find itself entirely constructed on the space's terms. This space is appropriated in more than the sense of a counter-using of established space; rather the appropriation takes place through the exercise of economic force determined by the ways in which it is wished to use the space, and to experience the self within that space.

The early to mid nineteenth century is well-documented as a period of vast expansion in theatre-going by a varied and popular audience.[10] Although Booth reminds us that it is risky to generalise about the composition of nineteenth-century theatre audiences, it is nevertheless certain that entertainment provision for lower-middle and working class audiences was on a larger scale than at any time previously.

Of course, a large part of the explanation for this is the massive increase in urban population due to increased living standards, rising birthrates and rural emigration to the new industrial centres such as Manchester, Leeds, Glasgow and London. The population of London trebled between 1801 and 1851, then doubled again by the end of the century to stand at 6,000,000 in 1901. From being the only town with a population of over 100,000 in 1801, London became one of thirty of that size and over by 1901. Booth cites the 1851 census, which states that in the middle of the century, 79% of the population of London was working-class, and this statistic remains true of the 1890's. We can reasonably assume that in 1851 there was an urban working-class in London of nearly 2.5 million, and by 1901 somewhere in the region of 5 million. It is suggested that in 1892, venues in London offered accommodation for more than half a million people nightly.

In response to this newly available audience, a spate of theatre building, or adaptation of saloons and drinking clubs into music halls, began in the 1810's and 20's. Theatre building stalled for a while between 1840 and 1866, but music halls continued to be inaugurated until quite late in the century. These new places of entertainment were often located adjacent to the areas in which their potential audience lived. The Palace, in Manchester, is on Oxford Street, directly opposite the areas which Engels wrote about in *The Condition of the Working Class in England 1844*. The Tivoli, in Hull, stood on the corner of the populous Beverley Road, not far from the railway terminus. A substantial number of buildings were opened in the East End of London in the early part of the nineteenth century, although theatre-goers from here still travelled to fill the pits and galleries of the West-End theatres and Halls.

Certainly, plenty of theatres were adapted by enterprising managers from existing halls, pavilions or bazaars. In their rebuilding and restructuring, however, they seem to share certain aspects of architecture and decor with the new constructions. This can be recognised as their "monumentality". This description, coined by Daniel Rabreau, is more than metaphorical:

> Unlike the impromptu boxes set up at fairs, unlike the aristocratic theatre built up against a palace, the monumental urban theatre in the nineteenth century was created to satisfy a

need for a permanent building, proof of urban growth and civic maturity.[11]

Theatres and entertainment halls separated themselves visually from the rest of the increasingly complex and evolving urban environment by their size, impressive frontages, and eclectic architectural "quoting". The way in which an audience member approached the theatre building was in itself theatrical; climbing a grand stone staircase, passing through imposing, column-flanked doors, travelling down ornate passageways.

The Royal Panopticon of Science and Art, which opened in 1854 and later became the Alhambra Palace Music Hall in 1860 was detailed in the *Illustrated London News* on the 31st January 1854 as:

> a...specimen of the Saracenic style of architecture...the splendid remains at Cairo have afforded much that is here reproduced; and it is from an actual Daguerrotype of one of the mosques that the dome has been taken...The imposing *facade* which this structure will present to Leicester Square will be by no means diminished by the two lofty minarets which rise on either side to a height of...100 feet. [12]

The Oxford, which opened on the 26th March 1861, was described in *The Era* of the 31st:

> The entrance, from Oxford Street, is through a bold Corinthian portico, thence by a passage, 12 feet wide, 38 feet long and 16 feet high; the architectural treatment of which consists in detached Doric columns, supporting the entablature, over which spring semi-circular arches. These divide the entrance into so many bays, seen in perspective from the street...at the end of the passage is the grand staircase. [13]

And the Strand Musick Hall, opened on the 15th October 1864 in what was then a most disreputable area of courts, alleys and a warren of little streets, boasted "Continental Gothic" as the basis of "this eclectic design."[14]

The architects of the British theatres were making reference to grand traditions in these buildings: first of all the classical architecture of Greece and Rome, and secondly the architecture of the wide-spread British Empire. The Victorian theatre-goer was reminded at all times of the fact that London sat at the centre of a mighty Empire, and that he or she may enter freely into the monumental buildings which represented it. This of course is also true of the many libraries and museums inaugurated at the time, but it was, in fact, the nineteenth century which created permanent spaces for public entertainment which expressed certain aspects of the cultural identity of the evolving community.

The opulence of the interiors serves a similar purpose. Ornamentation and allegorical scenes feature in the descriptions of the Alhambra of 1860 as follows:

> ...the...paintings in the dome comprise – The Court of Lions in the Alhambra, the Lion Fight of the Moor, Last Sigh of the Moor, Almed on the Banks of the Darro and the Last Look on the Vermilion Tower. The Proscenium presents in the compartments; Tacadora, The Toilet of the Queen, Boar Hunt, Rise of the Moor, Battle of Vega, the Gardens of Sinderaxa, and the Tower of Camaras[15]

Weston's of 1857 is perhaps more typical:

> The front of the commodious gallery...is highly embellished with ornamental work in relief, representing natural foliage, and at intervals emblazoned shields, with monograms on their fronts, and surrounded by scroll-work relieved by gilding. The walls throughout are decorated with panel-painting...beyond the proscenium...is a large semi-circular arch...(over which) is a tasteful representation of Tragedy and Comedy. The hall is lighted with five magnificent chandeliers...the central one weighs nearly one ton, and is eleven feet in diameter.[16]

Again, what we see in these descriptions is not particularly (despite what they say) taste, but opulence and extravagance.

These buildings speak of power: economic power, colonial power and cultural power. But what of power over the production of space?

It is important to note that although having qualities of monumentality similar to the great institutional buildings of the nineteenth century, the production of the huge and imposing spaces of popular entertainment is based on a reciprocal relationship, a commercial dialogue between management and customer, between capital and consumer. And therefore, by dint of sheer economic weight, the audiences of the popular theatre are able, for a time, to appropriate and produce the space toward their own desires.

Architecture and decor are only part of the story – what is needed is a way of examining the ongoing *production* of these spaces, which evolve over time. A useful distinction is provided by Michel Foucault:

> Architecture is only taken as an element of support, to ensure a certain allocation of people in spaces, a *canalisation* of their circulation, as well as the coding of their reciprocal relations. So it is not only considered as an element in space, but is especially thought of as a plunge into the field of social relations in which it brings about some specific effects.[17]

So if we take this as a starting point, how do people move in the space? How are they encouraged, and how do they demand to experience it, and through it, themselves?

First of all, there is the question of access to the building. Although some of the buildings were originally constructed with only one entrance (for example, the Alhambra), these tended to add extra entrances and exits in the course of alteration and rebuilding. The theatres tended to have separate entrances for the pit and the gallery (those for the Holborn Theatre Royal in 1866 were round the corner from the main entrance on High Holborn, in Brownlow Street). It would seem however that in the 1860's this segregation did not as yet continue into the main body of the buildings. *The Era* of 16th October 1864 reported that:

the Strand (Musick Hall)...contains besides the spacious corridors and grand staircase saloon (forming communications from the Strand with all parts of the building), commodious and elegant dining and smoking rooms...and lavatory and dressing rooms for visitors to each.

Even after the Strand was reopened as the Gaiety Theatre in 1868, *The Era* of 13th February was able to tell its readers that "the rooms over the (new) entrance, and the new building extending along the Strand...will form the 'Restaurant' entirely distinct from the Theatre, but with a corridor of access from every tier of the Theatre."

Part of these concerns, to do with relative freedom of movement once inside the building, as well as the number of entrance and exit routes, is undoubtedly connected with the fires that razed so many theatres to the ground, often with loss of life. It may be that these concerns aided a substantial alteration in the ways in which these spaces were used and, by extension, how they were produced. This has to do with the separation of the various functions and rooms in the buildings. As we have seen, the Strand provided separate dining and smoking rooms. The Alhambra reopened under new management in 1871, and:

the rows of tables which filled the basement have given way to a number of elegant and luxurious chairs...The refreshment bars have disappeared from their wonted sites, and are now to be found in snug nooks and sly corners out of view of the stage. Smoking is conspicuous by its absence, except in the large and commodious smoke-room.[18]

This is certainly an attempt to curtail the practice of selling food directly to the patrons of the pit, and later the stalls. It was not, as yet, an attempt to create the buildings solely in the service of art. They are sold very much in terms of the range of entertainments available (food being quite high on the agenda), together with the range of spaces in which they could be sampled.

As I have argued, what is interesting about popular space, and these spaces in particular, is the level of reciprocity in their production: changes initiated by managements have to find some level

215

of acceptance or approval from their patrons, who will otherwise take their money elsewhere. Clearly, the range of spaces made available by the division of entertainment, dining, and smoking was pleasing to the audience, and architectural changes were made with an eye on the uses and demands which the public made on the buildings.

The Oxford burned down in 1872 and, on its reopening, *The Era* notes:

> Among the changes and improvements may be mentioned a splendid promenade in place of the boxes at the back of the balcony. This makes a most agreeable lounge for those who prefer freedom of action and wish to gossip with their friends between the pauses of the entertainment.

A spate of theatre building and rebuilding in the 1880's, now controlled by fire safety legislation passed in 1878, continued these developments. Promenades were added to the Alhambra in 1882 and the new Tivoli in 1890. The Tivoli also had several rooms on the second floor, and several dining rooms on the third floor. The Empire, in 1884, had a real novelty:

> A feature in the construction is comparatively novel in an English theatre, that is the foyer so generally popular on the continent. The foyer at the Empire is in reality a splendid saloon nearly fifty feet square.[19]

What becomes clear from these accounts is that the audience evidently expects to have freedom of movement, to be able to choose from a range of spaces and entertainments, and to direct the course of their own time. In spatial terms, they do not wish to entirely construct themselves in terms of the space, to subjugate themselves to its requirements. Rather, the space itself is produced in terms of the interaction of the person with the space, in terms of how you can expect to experience yourself in the space.

Theatres are aware of this, and publicise themselves accordingly. Illustrations, advertisements, programme fronts all offer images of the various spaces of their buildings, as well as the entertainments which the audience could expect to enjoy. Often figures are included in the drawings to give some sense of scale, certainly, but also to suggest to the audience an image of themselves in the space, experiencing themselves through the cipher of the space, defining both it and themselves in doing so.

At a time when the middle-class is producing space for itself in the private sphere, in the home and in recreational life (day room, breakfast room, nursery and so on), the same scope is not offered to the working-class and lower-middle class in private. They are circumscribed by working practices, overcrowding and so on, and it is in public that their recreational space exists. Their exclusion from this space, which, although trends were apparent, occurred finally in the last decades of the century, took place along three trajectories.

Firstly, there was the literal spatial exclusion. Following the increasing segregation within the theatres of the less salubrious members of the audience into their own entrances and refreshment spaces, the pit and the gallery actually shrank and diminished towards the turn of the century. The St. James was built in 1869 with no pit accommodation, and the trend culminated in 1888 when the Bancrofts laid out the whole floor of the Haymarket with stall seats. Decor began to approximate more and more the colours and intimacy of the bourgeois home until, in 1881, Percy Fitzgerald was able to comment that Irving's Lyceum had "an air of drawing room comfort"[20]

Secondly, the increasing concern with sightlines, and the use of steel cantilevers in theatre construction in the 1880's, drew theatres closer to the experience, if not the design, of Wagners Festspielhaus, detailed earlier. The buildings were increasingly dedicated to the service of art, and the atomisation of the collective audience was further enhanced by the dimming of house-lights during the performance.

The third trajectory was the gradual change in the production of space. Since the audience which took over the production of space had different expectations of comfort and experience, as before, the space was shaped accordingly. Yet the force that did the shaping, the bourgeois audience, was itself constrained, and this restricted the production of popular space.

For in addition to the formalising of the artistic experience which serves to destroy the relationship between members of the audience, a certain formalising of cultural habits was also taking place – a system of "knowing how to behave" – the real cultural exclusion which, hand in hand with price, supports the increasing spatial exclusion of the popular audience. Bourgeoisification of theatre spaces occurred as freedom of movement, of cultural expression and self-determination was restricted, and as cultural expectations positioned and fixed spectators and consumers.

The key difference is that what we begin to see is a public space that is the extension of private space. As opposed to truly public space, in the sense that it exists nowhere else, the formalised relationships of these audiences to themselves and each other extended into all areas of their lives. The theatres form only a part of a lived experience dictated by codes and practices of behaviour.

Therefore, we are again in the realm of "abstract" space – in this instance, space in service of late Victorian bourgeois manners and routines. The heightening in cultural value of the entertainments they witnessed, and the adaptations of space in support of this detailed earlier, served these interests. Dominating space is not always tyrannical. It can be conspired with.

In conclusion, then, it seems to me that theories of the production of space offer a means of investigating the construction of theatre spaces. Popular theatre can be interpreted in terms of the influence and requirements of its users, as a reciprocal production of popular space.

Notes

[1] See Steven Mullaney *The Place of The Stage* (University of Chicago, 1988) and Ian Mackintosh *Architecture, Actor and Audience* (Routledge 1993).

[2] Edward Soja "The Spatiality of Social Life: Towards a Transformative Retheoriation" in Gregory and Urry (eds) *Social Relations and Spatial Structures* (Macmillan, 1985) p.90.

[3] Ibid., p.101.

[4] Ibid., p.90.

[5] Henri Lefebvre The Production of Space (Blackwells, 1991) p.152.

[6] Ian Mackintosh Architecture, Actor and Audience (Routledge, 1993) p.41.

[7] Julius Posener "Theatre Construction in Berlin from Gilly to Poelzig" in *Zodiac 2* (1988) p.16

[8] Richard Wagner *Das Buhnenfestspielhaus* (Munich,1906) p.34.

[9] Arnold Zweig *Theatre, Menge, Mensch* (Berlin,1920) p.35.

[10] See Michael Booth *Theatre in the Victorian Age* (Cambridge University Press, 1992) and GeorgeRowell *The Victorian Theatre: A Survey* (Oxford University Press, 1956).

[11] Daniel Rabreau "The Theatre Monument: A Century of French Typology" in *Zodiac 2* (1988) p.45.

[12] Raymond Mander and Joe Mitchenson *The Lost Theatres of London* (1968)

[13] Ibid.

[14] *The Era* 16/10/64.

[15] *The Era* 2/12/60.

[16] *The Era* 17/11/57.

[17] Michel Foucault "Space, Power, Knowledge" in Simon During (ed) *The Cultural Studies Reader* (1993) p.163

[19] *The Era* 17/4/84.

[20] Fitzgerald,1881in Booth (op cit) p.58.

Acklam LRC
Middlesbrough College
Hall Drive
Middlesbrough
TS5 7DY

Oh No It Isn't
A Functionalist Re-Definition of Pantomime

Robert Cheesmond

The title of this paper itself illustrates a curiosity which has been an enduring characteristic of English pantomime since the early years of its development. To my present knowledge, and with only one exception, there is no other theatrical genre of which the "definition" has been such an obsession of critic, practitioner and audience alike.

The one exception is, of course, melodrama, but the thirst for a formulaic definition which characterised most of the earlier books on melodrama is largely confined to the scholars and critics who wrote and read those books.

In the case of pantomime, on the other hand, the weight of evidence is that consciousness of what constitutes a "proper" pantomime (the phrase has even found its way into common speech) is an intrinsic part of the pantomime experience. Disappointment at a particular performance is expressed, not merely at whether it was "good" or "bad", but at whether it conformed to the criteria making it a "true" or "proper" pantomime.

This is proof, as far as it goes, of what we all already know, that Pantomime has come to partake of the nature of religious ritual; attendance at the prescribed occasion is an act of observance, carrying with it its own satisfaction and fulfillment, providing certain criteria are met.

The paradox is that no other theatrical form has been so mutable over so long a period. Contemporary pantomime contains features which date back beyond the invention of the genre (notably the figure of the Dame, which, though as old at least as Aristophanes, did not finally enter the Pantomime tradition until the mid-nineteenth century) as well as others which, though recent, are revered equally as "traditional".

As any student of English theatre history knows very well, the recorded history of pantomime is punctuated by outbursts of sentimental regret at what pantomime "used to be", often combined with moral outrage at what it "has become". From Garrick's mealy-mouthed eulogies of the dead John Rich, through Planche's bilious fulminations at the success of Beverly's scenery, Blanchard, Dickens, Leigh Hunt, Palgrave-Simpson, Davenport Adams, H.J.Byron, and a host of newspaper writers, perpetuated a continually regenerating myth of a lost Golden Age of Pantomime, located in each case in his (they are all men) own childhood.

Very recently (September '94) a theatre manager with whom I was discussing the subject commented on the present gradual loss of a generation of pantomime performers (most recently the death of Terry Scott) and wondered whether it would be possible for the "true" old style pantomime to survive.

By way of illustration of the general drift I have chosen Leopold Wagner[1], whose catalogue of complaints is perhaps the most comprehensive:

> There was a time, alas! when Pantomime was something very different to the now-a-day entertainment of that name, which has been described as "a mass of insane absurdity and senseless incongruity", a time when reason and fanciful invention were called into requisition, to produce results as dignified as they were pleasing. Those were the days when visiting the theatre during the coldest nights of January might be regarded as a real treat; when the Pantomime was built upon a story or legend, intelligible to the merest child; when genuine delight was depicted on every countenance; when the jokes were new and practical; when acting was in earnest, and singing rendered with due regard to vocal harmony; when knockabout niggers, clog dancers, gymnasts, contortionists, Whitechapel songsters, and other music-hall "novelties" were not considered indispensable for success; and when pageants and processions, realistic representations of farm-yards with their live stock, cataracts of real water, and extravagant ballet scenes, with the limelight directed upon an army of palpably naked thighs, which decency should require to be covered with skirts- were as yet unheard-of....
>
> ... Now-a-days we can little enough appreciate what a real, down-right, mirth-provoking pantomime should be. The business of the librettist has become monopolized by a parcel of

literary hacks and third-rate reporters, – we here refer to the majority of Provincial pantomimes – who buy up an old collection of "books of words" of past years, then proceed to grind up the ingredients of several into a grand *ORIGINAL* whole, or cut up, adapt and improve the work of a deceased playwright, with a plentiful introduction of local skits, outrageous puns, ribald songs, and trade advertisements, whenever such can put an extra crown in their pockets. In London we have yet one or two Pantomime writers of untarnished reputation; but whence it is that scarcely half-a-dozen nursery tales, with three contributions from THE ARABIAN NIGHTS, not forgetting ROBINSON CRUSOE, can be found to furnish the dramatic elements of an entertainment of this kind, has more than once prompted us to question their literary knowledge or inventive powers.

In the present decade Pantomime has continued to offend; the moral outrage of the nineteenth century, focused largely upon the amorality of Clown, and the "vulgarity" of music-hall stars and chorus girls, has been largely replaced by feminist rejection of the misogynistic fantasy seen in the figures of the Dame and Principal Boy, and a more general objection to such politically unacceptable features as the Seven Dwarfs, Man Friday, and so on.

An address to these problems lay behind a production at Hull University written and produced by my colleague Sarah-Jane Dickenson; in the companion paper to this she outlines her approach to the adaptation, and the thinking behind her rejection of some of the forms of Pantomime most usually encountered.

The present article is the result of the sense prompted by that production, that there might, after all, be value in attempting a re-definition of the phenomenon about and of which so many commentators had felt sufficiently sure as to make so many lofty pronouncements. With no dissatisfaction at the quality of the presentation or performances, I felt that what I had attended was "not a pantomime". This of course begs the question why I thought it should have been, since it was never formally described as such in any publicity, and, as Ms. Dickenson makes clear, the piece was a deliberately-proposed alternative to "traditional" pantomime.

Nevertheless, the title was *Whittington and the Cat*, the performances were timed as closely as possible for Christmas, and the project was referred to universally as "the pantomime".

In the nineteenth century the "definitive" characteristic of the Pantomime was, of course, the Harlequinade. As Leopold Wagner makes clear (see above) by the end of the century, as the Harlequinade dwindled, some dozen or so stories were themselves coming to be regarded as definitive of the genre.

Nowadays, we all "know" that *Aladdin* and *Jack and the Beanstalk* are pantomimes, whereas *A Christmas Carol* and *The Snow Queen* are not.

Walt Disney Studios are making considerable headway in returning us to the early 19th century position, in which the stories were performed as ballets, operas, melodramas, and so on. Pantomime has no monopoly. It is still the case, however, that in this country certain stories are thought of as Pantomime stories. What they have in common to make this so is matter for a separate enquiry.[2] For my present purpose I make the assumption that we all "know" *Dick Whittington* is a pantomime.

Of course, to trace the development of the features of Pantomime so as to arrive at a historically substantiated "norm" would be part of a longer study than this. Also, as is the case with Melodrama, as soon as some sort of norm is suggested, it is found that no individual example wholly conforms to it. Therefore, to expedite matters, I give the following list of aspects of the Hull production merely as those which prompted my present enquiry:

1) Although the part of Dick's mother was played comically, she was played by an actress in a relatively "straight" comic style, without significant physical clowning. She was not played as a "Dame".

2) Dick was played by an actress but, unlike the more usual Principal Boy, was kept at a pre-adolescent stage of development reminiscent of Richmal Crompton's William. Apart from gags about "playing doctors and nurses", there was little reference to adult sexuality, and no emphasis whatever upon the (female) sexuality of the actress playing the part.

3)There was a marked absence of "mess". A water-fight was introduced toward the end, along with other slapstick passages, but these were tightly controlled, and did not approximate to the mayhem of the traditional "slosh" scene.

4) Much less tangibly, the performance style, and the staging, were alike direct and straightforward, without self-parody or subversion.

To express this in more general terms, the train of thought thus started fetched up at the following as of pivotal importance:

1 The matrix of characters at the heart of the story
2 The casting and playing of those characters
3 The significance of slosh scenes
4 Subversion

It will be noted that my list does not include the story, or plot structure.[3] This is because, in this context, and in spite of the evidence from production statistics, this emerged as a less important element in my (personal) definition than I would have thought before undertaking this enquiry, notwithstanding the central importance of the Harlequinade structure to the Pantomime of the last century..

Twenty years ago, in advance of the huge outpouring of psychoanalytic criticism generated (initially) by feminist scholarship, it did not seem a statement of the obvious for David Mayer [4] to suggest that:

> ... much fantasy, including pantomime's, is a mechanism for dealing with real and immediate and acute anxieties in disguised form. Pantomime fantasy...confronts not the reality of the objective world, with its identifiable traumas, but answers the psychological realities generated by events in the tangible, verifiable world.

Mayer poses the significant question:

Why, for 120 years or longer, from approximately 1750 to 1870 – when literally thousands of pantomimes were performed and competition for pantomime audiences was an incentive to novelty – should audiences find so psychologically satisfying the same harlequinade characters and the same plot which twice enacts the loss and restoration of male potency?

As well as the basic plot structure, Mayer establishes the basis in fantasy of three of the central matrix of characters – Harlequin, Pantaloon, Columbine (the fourth, of course, being Clown), who made up the Harlequinade. He provides a convincing account of the anxieties generating the fantasy, and how those anxieties, mutating along with the economic circumstances of the poor and middle classes, gave rise to the transition from the characters of the Harlequinade into the Principal Boy and Dame of contemporary Pantomime.[5] The point is well made that both of these are expressions of male fantasy, and are essentially misogynistic. He suggests four points of foundation for the figure of the Dame:

> The first is that to dress as a woman is temporarily to become one, and in becoming a woman one both controls "her" and briefly comprehends the mysteries of female psychology and anatomy...
>
> The second premise is that impersonation permits the audience to express its own hostility in sanctioning aggressive acts against women...The dame role affords occasion for outrageous, aggressive parody of female behaviour even as it invites momentary sympathy and insight...In the fact that the dame, with rare exceptions, is represented as middle-aged, plain (if not painfully unattractive) and inept in her dealings with men, we discover the third premise: the dame is a means of dispelling the threat implied by the mother's sexuality...Finally, for some members of the audience...the dame is the embodiment of the "phallic mother".

The discussion has been taken up on television by Victoria Wood, and of course forms part of the much wider considerations of cross-dressing and gender representation opened out by Richard Dyer, Marjorie Garber, Lesley Ferris, among others.

An interesting additional insight, complementary rather than contradictory to Mayer's analysis, is afforded by Tony Green's account of the popularity of the "Betsy", the man/woman of the English Mummers' Play, as a reflection of nineteenth century socioeconomic concerns. Green's understanding of popular as a categorizing term would eliminate an entertainment on such a large commercial scale as nineteenth century Pantomime, and opens up questions concerning the relation of the "commercial" to the "popular" with which there is not scope to deal in the present paper.[6]

Mayer's analysis does not extend to a consideration of the appeal of the Dame figure to the women in the audience, and of course, such an account would demand to be historically contextualized.

An alternative *contemporary* response to the ideological rejection of the Dame figure was suggested to me by a group of female students, who were asked to consider why, developed feminists as they were, and aware of the arguments, they could nevertheless be wholehearted in their enjoyment.

Stated briefly, their position was that the Dame, in attempting so grotesquely to fulfill the requirements and conform to the constraints (physical allure, sartorial fashion etc.) imposed on women by a patriarchal culture, was not so much to be taken as a masculine attack upon women as, in effect, giving them a voice, or, at least, an opportunity to participate in therapeutic mockery. What may have begun, or been subconsciously intended, as ridicule of women's social behaviour, is here re-appropriated by a female audience, and inflected as comedic protest.

Clearly, the Dame figure is susceptible to either response. No clearer case could be found of the inscription of significance by the audience, rather than the performer, writer or director. Not, of course, that the figure is merely neutral. The Dame takes his/her place alongside the myriad safety-valve inversions of authority provided by popular entertainment forms. Throw a custard-pie at the boss, it's all good, harmless fun.

In the case of the Principal Boy, Mayer points out the increasing emphasis on the female sexuality of the Principal Boy from the early androgynous figures of Eliza Povey and Eliza Poole into the amply padded stars of the later nineteenth century, and suggests how s/he was aligned with the male Harlequin in a mechanism for the relief of male anxiety:

> By bringing the principal boy into pantomime, arrangers, (no doubt unconsciously) devised a fantasy means for coming to terms with the woman whose earning power equals or exceeds that of a man...the role of Principal boy, a creation of male anxiety, allows both men and women to confront and to contemplate female power, to admit in fantasy that an aggressive woman rivals a man, even to the point of pursuing the girl who is to become Columbine...However, when at the transformation scene the principal boy is about to be transformed into Harlequin, the actress is replaced by an actor....The transformation in sexual identity is from neutered female to potent male. It is Harlequin with his bat who gets Columbine, not the principal boy. Thus male anxiety is reassured. And, very likely, female anxiety is similarly dispelled, for the principal boy may raise guilt or anxiety that the male has been castrated or damaged.

This explanation works well for Harlequinade pantomimes, but must be taken further to explain the continuation of the Principal Boy in contemporary Pantomime. That s/he has continued is apparent, in spite of sporadic instances of the male lead being played by a male actor.[7]

The strong emphasis on female sexuality in the costume has continued in all of the examples I have seen in recent years, some of which are described in the appendix.

Here are, however, two sites of contradiction.

The production of *Aladdin* at Hull New Theatre 1992/3 opened with the police in full pursuit of Aladdin for scrumping apples from the emperor's orchard; a distinctly juvenile misdemeanour. Throughout the pantomime Abanazer proclaimed the variety of punishments he intended to mete out to "that brat".

When Aladdin first appeared it was as a jack-the-lad adolescent leading a rousing chorus of villagers. Within two scenes s/he had become – and, of course, remained – "credible" as a sexually mature suitor to the princess. Throughout, s/he was dressed in high heeled shoes, and a tunic so brief as to offend some American students whose first pantomime this was. This Aladdin (like, very often, Jack and Dick) was ambivalent in age as well as gender, though the former was quickly forgotten as the pantomime progressed.

There has been considerable recent discussion – to which I have scope to make only a passing reference here – of the role of woman-as-hero in male fantasy drama. The films *Thelma and Louise, Nikita* and *Blue Steel* are the most recent in a line which stretches back through Westerns such as *Hannie Caulder, Rancho Notorious, Johhny Guitar*,(and now, *Bad Girls*) in each of which the heroic status of a gun-wielding woman is subverted by a demonstrated vulnerability; the warrior-women of the sword-and sandal epics (*Red Sonja, Conan the Barbarian*) are dressed in "armour" which is entirely dysfunctional as protection, but arranged for maximum sexual appeal. Even the leather worn by Honor Blackman and Diana Rigg in *The Avengers* owed more to Sixties notions of kinkiness than to combat efficiency.

That the Principal Boy is not intended to appear even remotely convincing as a combative male hero is clearly indicated by the costume. Denial of male potency is even further emphasised than by the plain fact that the man is a woman. She is a woman whose femaleness is expressed as a male-defined femininity.

The *Cinderella* at Sheffield 1993/4 featured a Prince Charming whose costumes (red satin tunic, thigh-high high-heeled red suede boots) might have been designed for the character of a street prostitute in an American cop show. (*Miami Vice* springs to mind).

David Mayer is manifestly correct in identifying the Principal Boy as "pantomime's chief excursion into sex" (by which he means, of course, male sexual fantasy).One question not raised in his 1974 article, but currently of interest in the light of contemporary fashion in entertainment, is the extent to which the suggestion of lesbianism, covert or overt, conscious or subconscious, in the relationship of the Principal Boy and Girl is significant.

Part of the difficulty in discussing this lies in the fact that it has never been acknowledged in the plots or structure of pantomimes, but would always depend entirely upon the nuances of performance.

The love-duet sung at Sheffield by Cinderella and Prince Charming, wearing the costume I have described, left me in no doubt, in spite of the studied innocence of the performances, that the suggestion of a lesbian relationship is, at least unconsciously, an ingredient of the underlying fantasy sustaining the continued existence of the Principal Boy figure.

What is more, although the plots of pantomimes may continue to bring the characters to a point of crisis correspondent to the "dark scene", there is no longer so overt a reference to male potency as Harlequin's bat, its loss, or its restoration. The Principal Boy doesn't have a bat to begin with.

It is for this reason that I omit any reference to the plot, or the story, from the list of features mentioned earlier as pivotal in this attempt to re-define pantomime. The sexual fantasy sustained by the Principal Boy in contemporary pantomime does not lie in a sequence of symbolic events featuring a male figure. It is not located in the stories at all, many of which are now available as animated films. These have their own significance. It is located in the figure of a woman masquerading as, but manifestly failing to function efficiently as, a man *from the outset*, and parading as an object of female sexual display at the same time.[8]

In the 1993/4 pantomime season a student following a study course in pantomime wrote a comparative study of three separate productions of *Dick Whittington*, one of them featuring a male actor in the lead. He made the observation that, at the point when Dick is falsely accused of stealing, there was in the audience a much less tangible sense of sympathy with Dick as played by a man than when as a Principal Boy. There was a clear feeling that a man – a real man – ought to be able to sort things out for himself.

Furthermore, it is clear that the masquerade is what is significant, rather than the sexual display, whatever may have been the case in the nineteenth century. Then, the pantomime represented a rare opportunity for the male voyeur to gaze upon a publicly-displayed pair of female legs. Nowadays, there is much more explicit sexual display freely available in daily newspapers, TV dramas, films, most of which are not even thought of as pornographic, and therefore illicit.

It cannot be, therefore, that the appeal of the Principal Boy, even in red suede boots, is straightforwardly sexual.

However, in the manifestation of sexuality in the context of innocence, in the "pretty story – a nursery tale – dramatically told"[9], we have yet another site of contradiction.

It was perhaps inevitable, and not even entirely to be explained by reference to fantasy or anxiety, that once the Dame figure became popular, Clown, as a discrete character, would disappear. The Clown and the Dame naturally elide.

There is a great deal to be said of the fantasy sustaining the Clown figure proper throughout his history, but in a consideration of contemporary Pantomime there is space only for a few relevant observations.

The clown embodied a particular strain of humour, anarchic, violent, visceral, which made him, and Pantomime in general, an obvious target for nineteenth century moralists[10]. In his greed, skill as a thief, defiance of authority and downright impudence, Clown was held to set an undesirable example to the young, at whom the said moralists deluded themselves that pantomime was aimed. As David Mayer points out, the majority attending pantomimes until the late nineteenth century were adults. This may be true, even today. In any case, as Jacqueline Rose[11] has argued, there is no such thing as a "children's entertainment". The child in this context is a construct of the adult. It therefore makes little sense to seek to account for pantomime fantasy by much reference to children.

Nevertheless, the figure who was introduced more and more into the pantomimes of the late nineteenth century, and is now a central figure, is that member of the current matrix of characters who most relates to children, and whose creation and continued popularity depend upon the function of pantomime as entertainment for children. One might term this character the "feminised man".

As, sometimes, brother to the Principal Boy, sometimes hopeless admirer of the Principal Girl, this character, as Wishee Washee, Buttons, Silly Billy, Idle Jack, has become the principal link with the audience, and the usual voice of kindness, compassion, selflessness. Pathetically and comically not "macho", his "impotence" mirrors the false male "potency" of the Principal Boy, and contrasts with the machismo of the other "real" man in the line-up, the villain. Much more than in the case of the Principal Boy, this character is ambivalent in age, and might easily be generically christened the "child/man".

Significantly, whoever he is, Buttons, Wishee Washee, Billy, the child/man comes to terms by the end of the pantomime with the limitations imposed by his age and status upon his aspirations. The Wishee Washee of the Hull *Aladdin* 1992/3 (played by the female partner of The Krankies, of which more is to be said later[12]) resigned himself to wait to grow up to marry the princess's (mute) serving-woman; Buttons invariably settles for Cinderella's friendship and, importantly, her happiness in denial of his own. For this character, the pantomime story is one of "growing up".
Martin Barrass, playing this part in successive years at York Theatre Royal, uses catch-phrases referring to his being/becoming a "manly man" and, as Silly Billy, proclaimed triumphantly at the end of *Jack and the Beanstalk*: "Now I'm eighteen I can go out wi' girls at neet".

Most often connected by family to one or both of the Dame and Principal Boy, it is clear that the "child/man" or "feminised man" could only exist and function in this system of ambivalence and contradiction. Interacting with a "real" male hero, and a "real" mother, he would emerge as an unsympathetic wimp.

There is no character corresponding to Buttons in the basic story of *Cinderella*, and no Wishee Washee in *Aladdin*. Neither do they appear in the Walt Disney films. This figure is peculiar to pantomime, and his ubiquity in contemporary performances is a further strong argument that the true significance of pantomime lies in the character matrix, rather than the individual story.

The next step, to seek an explanation for the emergence and continued popularity of this figure by reference to contemporary socioeconomic factors, is outside the scope of this paper. Tempting as the emergent figure of the reconstructed male, the new man, might be as an explanatory model, he is far too recent, and it is probably best to refrain from guesswork until after a more thorough investigation.

Two other "real" men figure in the contemporary line-up. The father-figure often remains, but has lost most of his significance as "heavy" father, and is more often than not benevolent, rather than threatening.

The villain is grotesquely threatening, with an enjoyment of his villainy which – importantly – amounts to self-parody, and therefore subversion. Truly frightening, on the other hand (and I speak from the experience of attending the pantomime in the company of young children) is the principle female villain in the pantomime pantheon, the Queen in *Snow White*.

This character has importance in the present discussion in that she is not usually presented with the leavening of self-parody which characterises the male villain (most of us are familiar with the notoriously disturbing Queen of the Walt Disney film). The obvious inference is that the female villain is too psychologically powerful a figure not to be taken entirely seriously.

It is also traditional for much comic by-play to take place between the villain and the Dame; frequently there is the suggestion of a sexual pursuit of the villain by the Dame. The confrontation of a female villain with the Principal Boy is similarly problematic. Once again, there is further work to be done here in aligning the figure of the female villain with male, and female, notions of clowning.[13] (Since this paper was presented Marina Warner's *From the Beast to the Blonde* has brilliantly synthesised and expanded upon the corpus of psychoanalytical research into the folktales which provide pantomime plots, and has established the importance to them of social and historical circumstances, in particular with reference to women. Her comments on wicked stepmothers are germane.)

In conclusion to this part of the argument, I suggest that though on the one hand the central matrix of characters has become less rigidly prescribed in contemporary pantomime than in the Harlequinade, the quality of ambivalence has been increased, and extended to more of them. With the exception of the Principal Girl, who has continued as an ingenue in direct descent from Columbine, practically no characteristic is exhibited which is not to some extent qualified, even contradicted.

In this tension between contradictory signifiers we find the quintessential dialectic of pantomime; fundamentally, I suggest, its defining characteristic.

The character-types of the pantomime, as opposed to the characters themselves, entice the spectator into a bungee-jump of the imagination, a leap into the fantastic dark, truly forbidden territory, with the self-evident contradictions and ambivalences as the elastic.

There is no danger. It's all perfectly safe, provided the elastic doesn't break.

Slapstick, Subversion and Slosh.

The phrase "a proper pantomime" (an oxymoron if ever there were one) connotes in common speech an event or experience which is thoroughly mismanaged, or disorganised. It suggests, in other words, a state of chaos.

The anarchic humour of the pantomime clown, like that of his modern Circus descendant, repeatedly demonstrated the consequences of an abrogation of the normal rules both of social behaviour and of natural science. The catalogue of "lazze" bequeathed by Grimaldi to his successors features most, if not all, of the Seven Deadly Sins, in a spirit of glorious, if disastrous, indulgence. Inanimate objects are subjected to impossible transformations, or brought to life to act with their own – usually malign – intelligence.

There is, however, an irony in the fact that Clown and his world of chaos were so violently objected-to, in such moral terms, and with so direct an invocation of his -putative – effect upon children.

The most superficial cross-cultural examination of clowning traditions is sufficient to demonstrate that it is in the very inversion of moral and social values, and the display of physical and behavioural grotesquerie, that the clown most forcefully asserts the rules and morals of society.

Particularly once it had become so firmly tied to a specific point in the calendar we may see in pantomime an English Saturnalia. It is not so much the child, as the adult, who revels in the fantasy of direct sensory gratification, with no social or moral restraints. pantomime therefore satisfies, or at least assuages, the adult yearning for a lost infancy.

Significant also, in the light of what follows concerning the sociopolitical constituency of pantomime, is the fact that the Saturnalia was a feast for the common people, and the slaves.

Clown, in applying his poker to the unfortunate policeman, acted surely for an audience with a developed understanding of authority, however much children may have delighted – and still do – in the mayhem.

Repression of this form of collective therapy in an attempt to impose an excessive degree of social and moral control was, of course, a prime characteristic of what we now identify as Victorianism. It amounts to social hybris – a denial of the imminence – and immanence – of chaos.

In contemporary traditional pantomime there is usually to be found at least one passage in which chaos is made manifest. The "slosh" scene, whether in the kitchen, or decorating the parlour, in Widow Twankay's laundry or the Ugly Sisters' boudoir, features uninhibited violence, glorious incompetence, and, by the end, unbridled malice as the scene descends into a custard-pie or wallpaper-paste war between the (usually two) protagonists. It is a reminder of how brittle is our control over our lives, our world, and ourselves.

Coming as it does in the middle of the action of a pantomime, it is also a safeguard. We are brought by the pantomime characters terribly close to recognition of some disturbing emotions. Most of the fantasy discussed in David Mayer's study, and in this article, would be regarded by most of us as immoral, undesirable, repellent. The further we feel our sensibilities to be developed, the less acceptable such fantasy becomes. The slosh scene allows a massive emotional outbreath. It, too, is part of the elastic.

The statement it, and pantomime as a whole, makes is not so very different from that proposed by Euripides. The difference is that pantomime still speaks to a contemporary popular audience, in a language, and a tone, which is understandable and acceptable to thousands to whom the word "tragedy" has come to mean simply an unusually bad accident.

That pantomime does indeed reach the "popular" audience is not in dispute. Calculated in crude statistical terms, the numbers attending pantomimes are huge. It is a truism that pantomime underpins the budget in dozens of theatres, and that thousands attend pantomime who never go to any other form of live theatre.

One reason for this continued popular appeal is that pantomimes have maintained an aggressive anti-intellectualism, which has recently emerged as a key ingredient in some other entertainments.

One example is afforded by the runaway success in the last two years or so of the morning show *The Big Breakfast*. The chief characteristic of this programme (shared by others, such as *The Word*) is a deliberate flouting of all the accepted standards of television presentation. The presenters are raucous in tone, frequently dash out-of-shot, or seize upon studio technicians, destroy props, and generally poke fun at the medium within which they work. Regular features, such as "meet the family" are bewilderingly inane.(The most recent edition I saw featured a "rear of the year" contest!) Wide camera angles make everyone seem unattractive. Accepted standards are exuberantly debunked as the television process is vulgarised and de-mystified. The result has been massively successful.

Pantomimes are most frequently performed in a similar spirit; comics are given free rein to ad-lib, any mishap may be turned to comic advantage, and actors routinely reduce one another to uncontrollable giggles.

In the process of the pantomime performance, performance itself is ridiculed. Every feature, including the style in which scenery and props are designed and constructed, is calculated to subvert the conventions of orthodox theatricality. Highbrow intellectualism – "artiness" is lampooned by implication. For once, the theatre becomes a place in which the spectator is allowed to feel truly "comfortable".

There is also an affiliation of the audience, on the most direct level, with at least two of the performers. I have already discussed the figure I have called the "feminised man". The other, of course, is the principal comic, most usually the Dame. However one may view the Dame from an ideological standpoint, before a performer can be a successful Dame he must first be a consummate clown, in whose force of personality much of the success of the entertainment is invested. Above all else, whether the Dame, as in most pantomimes, or another character (see the examples given in my appendix), there is established a commonality with the audience. Berwick Kaler, for the past fifteen years the Dame of the pantomimes at York Theatre Royal, addresses the audience as his "babbies".There could surely be no more explicit an assertion (or example to cite in corroboration of Mayer's point[14]) of his role as "phallic mother". In this role he dominates the performance(he writes the pantomimes himself), proceeds to ridicule his fellow performers, and to govern the proceedings with a rod of iron. The spectator is made complicit throughout, is never the victim of his caprice, never made to feel uncomfortable.

This, finally, is the sum of my argument, and an explanation of the web of ambivalence and contradiction which permeates the central matrix of pantomime characters, whatever story they are enacting.

The pantomime spectator is *given permission* to experience and enjoy fantasy at the deepest level, and to remain intellectually distanced from it. The potential challenge to individually held moral and political values is continually dissipated, and need not, in consequence, be compromised by an acquiescence in enjoyment.

Appendix
In addition to the Hull *Whittington* I have referred to *Dick Whittington* at York Theatre Royal (1992/3), *Aladdin* at Hull New Theatre (1992/3) and *Cinderella* at Sheffield Crucible Theatre (1993/4). What follows is a brief, and, I acknowledge, highly selective, account of each.

Aladdin, Hull, New Theatre, 1992/3
This followed a more or less orthodox version of the Aladdin story. The focus of comic interest was the husband-and-wife double act, The Krankies. This in itself signaled a more complex sexual matrix of characters, in that the male partner took the part of Dame, Widow Twankay, while the woman played Wishee Washee in a distorted mirror-image of cross-sexual casting. Because in the course of their normal variety act it is she who is the dominant comic, this represented a shift in comic emphasis. Wishee Washee was played in her usual character of rather naughty but affecting schoolboy. She scored a great hit with her well-known "Pickin' on me" song.

Although not presented as a potential suitor to the princess (s/he was smitten by her dumb lady-in-waiting) the character fulfilled the other function of the "feminized man" in that it was s/he who most immediately engaged the audience, and acted as the intermediary.

It was s/he also, rather than her husband, the Dame, who most disrupted the performance with ad-libs, comments upon fellow cast members, and so on.

The complexity of the characters' sexuality was increased by the representation of Aladdin, as described in the main text, above.

Cinderella, **Sheffield Lyceum, 1993/4**

A close rendering of the traditional Cinderella story, this production was built around three "pairings" of characters at the centre.

In the first place, top billing was given to the double act Cannon and Ball, who played Baron Hardup and Buttons. The fact that they did not take the more obvious roles of the Ugly Sisters is probably attributable to the particularly masculine character of their humour, and the essential rapport they have with a northern working-class audience ("Have yer given up weldin'?"). Therefore another pair were the Ugly sisters, played as dames. The third pair were the Prince and Dandini, played by women in traditional(though I'm becoming chary of using the word) style.

Notable features of the costuming were the grotesque breasts sported by one Ugly Sister in an uncompromisingly mysoginistic statement, and the Principal boy costumes, most striking of which was the red satin tunic and boots described in my text.

The comic focus was firmly upon Cannon and Ball, who, inter alia, made much fun of the cross-casting, with jokes about "turning gay" for Dandini, and a generous pinch of homophobia generally "Are you a homosexual? No, but me husband is", and so on. Nevertheless, the comic talent of the pair is formidable, and they dominated most of the scenes. Here Buttons retained something of the role of soulmate to Cinderella, though his humour was much too "blue" for a posture of innocence to be credible.

There was also much subversion of the performances of other members of the cast. One other scene notable in the present context was an encounter between the Prince and Dandini and the Ugly

Sisters, in which much comic mileage was made of the quadruple cross-casting.

Notes

[1] Leopold Wagner, *The Pantomimes and All About Them* (1881).

[2] Much work has been done on the continuing significance of the fairytale, in particular by Bruno Bettelheim, Jack Zipes and, most recently, Marina Warner. None of these seminal studies, for understandable reasons, has been concerned with pantomime stories as a discrete group. This is a question being dealt with in the wider project of which this paper is a part.

[3] It is quite important at this stage to emphasise the distinction between the two. This is particularly evident in the case of Harlequinade Pantomimes, in which the same sequence of events is basic to every pantomime, irrespective of the detail of the story. See David Mayer "The Sexuality of Pantomime", *Theatre Quarterly* (1974). In contemporary Pantomime the distinction is less clear, but that it is valid is part of my present argument.

[4] Mayer, op.cit.

[5] For a critique of Mayer's analysis, of which I was not aware at the time of writing this paper, see Elaine Aston, *Out of the Doll's House* (unpublished Ph.D.Thesis, University of Warwick, 1986).

[6] A.Green, "Popular Drama and the Mummers' Play" in D.Bradby (ed.), *Performance and Politics in Popular Drama* (Cambridge, 1980)

[7] The tendency toward a male lead was strongest between about 1950 and 1970, from which time Cilla Black, Anita Harris and others re-popularised the role of the Principal Boy. The socioeconomic factors related to this remain to be investigated.

[8] See L. Senelinck, "Boys and Girls Together" in L.Ferris (ed.), *Crossing the Stage* (Routledge, 1993) p.81

[9] The phrase is, of course, Planche's

[10] The pages of *The Theatre* yield several examples. Successive volumes in 1881 carried Palgrave-Simpson's *Stage and Street Popular Types*: "Without taking matters too seriously I am still inclined to ask what spirit of brutalisation has induced our national mind to accept such a type as the Clown for a Christmas hero of [for] the jollification, enlightenment, and approbation of our rising generations, and lavish so much approbation and applause on his thieving, his gluttony, and his promiscuous cruelty?" (Aug 1881). To which Jeremiah Wiencke added in October, "The Harlequinade may be likened,

without much exaggeration, to a non-poisonous snake, and the preceding part to a viper".

As my argument shows, they and others writing in similar vein had simply lost the point that the amorality of the Clown was – and is – the basis of his psychosocial function.

[11] J.Rose, *The Case of Peter Pan, or the Impossibility of Children's Fiction* (Macmillan 1984)

[12] See Appendix

[13] See Parsons and Beales, "The Sacred Clowns of the Pueblo and Mayo-Yaqui Indians" in *American Anthropologist* 36:4 and Obeyesekere & Obeyesekere, "Comic Ritual Drama in Sri Lanka" in *Tulane Drama Review,* 1976

[14] Mayer, op. cit. Quoted supra.

Oh Yes It Is! A Practical Exploration of the Validity of the Role of Pantomime

Sarah-Jane Dickenson

In an accompanying paper to this article Robert Cheesmond attempts a re-definition of pantomime. I wish to further the debate by questioning the validity of the role of pantomime in our present cultural climate. Many definitions of pantomime attempt to validate a traditional form; however, I contend that these attempts to define the form have often resulted in an intransigent view of pantomime which consequently has made it redundant as part of a cultural theatrical context. As Peter Brook states:

> Generally speaking we can conclude that "tradition", in the sense we use the word means "frozen". It is a frozen form more or less obsolete, reproduced through automatism. [1]

The "freezing" of pantomime has removed it from any subjection to the ephemeral nature of drama and therefore it has not been allowed to develop and renew itself, consequently divorcing itself from an ever changing culture.

My exploration will take a theoretical perspective but it will also be referenced to a practical exploration: the writing and production of a pantomime, *Whittington and the Cat*, which took place in the Drama Department of Hull University with students from the single honours Drama course. Consequently, I shall also consider this issue from an educational perspective.

The multi-various debates surrounding the definition of pantomime are fuelled, in part, from the fact that most people in Britain have encountered the genre and invariably when they were very young. For many it is their first and in many cases their only theatrical experience. The combination of youthful impression combined with historical debate is a heady mixture.

Admittedly my own perceptions of pantomime are coloured by my experience of the genre in my youth. As an annual viewer of pantomime I was regularly deeply underwhelmed by the format. This used to bemuse me when young as most pantomimes were theoretically based on fairy tales for which I had an unquenchable thirst. My youthful attraction to the fairy tale is best described by Marina Warner:

> When I was young and highly robust, I still felt great hunger for fairy tales; they seemed to offer the possibility of change, far beyond the boundaries of their improbable plots or fantastically illustrated pages. The metamorphoses promised more of the same, not only in fairy land, but also in this world and this instability of appearances, these sudden swerves of destiny, created their first sustaining excitement of such stories. Like romance, to which fairy tales bear a strong affinity, they could remake the world in the image of desire. [2]

My problem with pantomime as a child was primarily with the characters, particularly the female characters. Like most children, I was at a stage of intense daydreaming and identification with all characters who were daring, brave, exciting and loveable, in that order. Consequently, I found in pantomime a distinct lack of female characters with whom to identify. Generally, I found all the representation of women, or parts played by women, confusing and alien.

With hindsight and the benefit of feminist criticism I now realise I was a "resisting reader", a term coined and best described by Julia Fetterly.[3] The American, Gayle Austin, describes her own "resisting reader" experiences when considering Eugene O'Neill in high school:

> As I read his plays I felt distanced, on the outside looking in. I was taught he was a great American playwright, but I could not find a way into his plays.[4]

As a child I could not find a way into pantomime. In order to re-evaluate whether my response to pantomime as a child is primarily justifiable or not, it is necessary to evaluate the reasons for using the pantomime format. As Peter Brook states:

The reason a play is put on is usually obscure. In justification one says, "Such a play was chosen because of our taste, our beliefs, or our cultural values demand that we put on this type of play." But for what reason? If one doesn't ask that one question then thousands of subsidiary reasons can appear: the director wants his conceptions of the play, there is an experiment in style to demonstrate, a political theory to illustrate...thousands of imaginable explanations, but secondary when compared to the underlying issue: can the theme succeed in touching the essential preoccupation or need in the audience? [5]

I would argue that traditional pantomime, as defined in the accompanying paper, accommodates the preoccupation and needs of only part of the audience. Robert Cheesmond states that:

The potential challenge to individually held moral and political values is continually dissipated and need not, in consequence, be compromised by an acquiescence in enjoyment.

I would challenge this supposition and suggest that the genre of pantomime exhibits an inequality of challenge to individually held moral and political values. If it is able to remain a true part of popular culture, pantomime needs to move on and adapt by reflecting the needs and preoccupations of both sexes. Mayer[6] argues that pantomime is fantasy, which is a mechanism for avoiding current realities and retreating to fictional realms where real problems cannot intrude. If this is the case, I would argue that is has to be fantasy for both genders whereas previously it has been primarily the domain of one gender.

My aim in attempting to experiment with the genre was to see if it could be adapted to accommodate this possibility whilst still retaining a recognisable semblance of pantomime. I wanted this pantomime to be fundamentally a children's show and to have a storyline. When considering the manipulation of the format I concentrated on characterisation. Not surprisingly my principle problem was with the female roles and the representation of women. The characters which particularly caused me problems were the role of the Dame and the Principal Boy.

The history of cross dressing on the stage can be accessed more fully in the work of Ferris, Straub, Epstein and Howe.[7] Consequently I shall briefly reiterate, but not dwell on, pertinent points. Mayer describes the two transvestite roles (The Dame and the Principal Boy) as "created by male pantomime arrangers as a means of coming to terms with women."[8] He goes on to say that some form of Dame role has been found in pantomime since its earliest origins. Always a ridiculous figure, originally the Dame was the wife or servant of the lead. However, still ridiculous, it soon changed to the role of the mother. The Dame role affords occasion for outrageous, aggressive parody of female behaviour even as it invites momentary sympathy and insight.

The Principal Boy figure is a more recent invention. Breeches parts first appeared in the Restoration with the advent of women acting on the English stage, although this role was primarily for titillation purposes. As Laurence Senelick observes:

> When the subservient sex wears the pants, such behaviour is condoned only in anodyne modes which contradict the disguise by emphasising female allure. [9]

This description was applicable to the breeches parts and is reiterated and emphasised in an extract from the diary of Samuel Pepys where he says:

> To the theatre...where women...came afterwards on the stage in men's clothes and had the best legs that I ever saw and I was very pleased by it. [10]

The tradition of breeches roles on the English stage avoided a convincing impersonation of a male and this permeated through into the pantomime genre. In more recent times, the Dame has sometimes been played by a drag queen such as Danny la Rue. However, as Jill Dolan comments:

> Women are non-existent in drag performance, but women-as-myth, as a cultural and ideological object is constructed. Male drag mirrors women's socially constructed roles.[11]

As Ferris points out, the female form in theatre has been "a site for repression and possession."[12]

I believe the above comments are particularly pertinent to present pantomime forms and considering the audiences for pantomimes comprise largely of children, I believe that the messages we are conveying through the figures of female representation are disturbing. Consequently my focus was on adapting the two main roles of Dame and Principal Boy and this would naturally have a knock on effect where other roles were concerned.

As mentioned earlier the writing of *Whittington and The Cat* took place within an educational context. To fully understand the thinking behind my writing, I feel I need to explain my theoretical perspective as an educator. As a teacher my main focus is to use drama as a learning device. I choose to pursue drama in an educational context as I believe it is the most effective and enjoyable learning medium. As Dorothy Heathcote says of the dramatic experience:

> This kind of testing behaviour can be used to create dynamic learning and cross the boundaries of subject division when it is necessary to do so. I am not suggesting that drama teaches everything. Drama teaches people by demonstrating interactive social behaviour, and encouraging critical spectatorship, because art releases the spectator/action possibility in people.[13]

Paramount to the learning process within the dramatic experience, there is the necessity for protection of the participants. This is because within any learning process, there is a level of emotional engagement. Drama can often invoke a high degree of emotional response, a response which, I believe, has been open to mismanagement in the higher educational context.

The idea of protection is not necessarily concerned with protecting participants from emotion, but rather protecting them into emotion. Unless there is some kind of emotional engagement learning is restricted. Therefore the manipulation of drama requires a careful grading of structures towards an effective equilibrium, so that self esteem, personal dignity, personal defences and group security are challenged but never over challenged. Bolton outlines three ways of protecting drama:

1. Projection in the dramatic mode
2. Indirect handling of the topic
3. Performance mode [14]

Here I shall concentrate on performance mode which is most applicable in this context. Bolton goes on to say that performance mode in:

> itself can be protective either because it is seen to be mainly a technical or intellectual task, or because the dramatic form is powerful enough to enhance whatever the participants contribution might be.[15]

For me, this combination of drama and protection which is built into the dramatic medium creates the most empowering learning situation for the participant. Groups I work with and have worked with, are generally large and the gender make up is variable. As one of my main educational aims in a practical context is to encourage ownership of the art form of drama and subsequently text in performance, I find that the more familiar and traditional texts limit the ownership that is possible in a large group context, particularly for women. Consequently the need for new texts becomes evident.

My practical work in the pantomime genre is placed alongside other work within the learning context of the art form of drama. I had just written and produced a script for the students which had been a large cast, multi-disciplinary, tense and brooding piece of theatre. So, after being tense and brooding, I decided the time was right for us to change mood and tackle pantomime.

Although time for the project was short, I began to research the present position of pantomime play text. I tended to concentrate on the most frequently performed versions, so naturally I found myself reading many of the texts of John Morley. However, when reading these I found myself re-experiencing the pantomime of my childhood, which I found unsatisfying. The most popular stories used tended to be restricted to a limited source of well known fairy tales – Dick Whittington, Mother Goose, Jack and the Beanstalk, Cinderella and Aladdin. However, the variations of each tale left me doubting my own recollection of the original.

As I have already stated, as a teacher with a focus on encouraging ownership for the students of the art form of drama and conscious of the need for protection within the art form of drama in order for optimum learning to take place, I felt that the roles of the Dame and the Principal Boy in their usual format would not be useful devices to promote for over fifty percent of the students I work with. I was aware that the main tension in the revising of the characters of the Dame and Principal Boy was that if they were drastically altered it might be considered that I had removed them altogether from the genre of pantomime. Therefore my aim when dealing with character manipulation (and with plot manipulation) was to keep the characters within a recognisable structure but to alter the content of the gender perspective. Hopefully the product would then retain enough of the recognisable characteristics of pantomime to provide familiarity and the security often associated with fantasy, but would not be biased in the disparagement of one gender. I'll now outline how I dealt with my concerns in a practical context.

The Characters
Dick
Dick's mother
The Cool Cat
King Rat
The Ratettes (4)
Honesty
Mr Makeabob
There was also a large chorus who sang throughout but only appeared on stage in the final water fight.

My main aim was to provide a duality in each character. Each character was to reflect both good and bad points in their personality. The only stereotyping of costume came with the Fairy and King Rat, and here the make-up was such as to give both an almost mask-like quality although each character still displayed an obvious duality in their characterisation. All the characters could be liked or disliked depending on the wants or needs of the audience. However, the judgement would hopefully be less to do with gender stereotyping than usual.

Dick's Mother (The Dame): The Dame was played by a woman. She was an excessive character, very much larger than life, but a feisty, misguided woman rather than a ludicrous parody. She looks to men and money to bring her happiness rather than simply sexual gratification and in this she is disappointed. She, as with most of the other characters, is cynical, particularly with regards to Dick's heroic capacities. She eventually teams up with the Fairy, is the one to hand out sweets to the audience and in the final showdown is the one to deal personally with King Rat, defending her son from him. At the same time she informs King Rat that she will marry him, as all he needs is a good woman.

Dick (The Principal Boy): Dick was played by a girl. However the role was a combination of the traditional Principal Boy and the Buttons/Wishy Washy role. Consequently, Dick is more of an adolescent youth. Enthusiastic, honest, brave, feeling, caring, a Take That fan and, in the words of several of the characters, a bit of a wally. His reason for going to London is to save Honesty, his childhood sweetheart and the daughter of Mr Makeabob. His relationship with Honesty occasionally starts to move beyond the past recollections of doctors and nurses and tying each other up but doesn't travel very far.

The Cool Cat: In this case, the Cool Cat was male but could be played by either sex. The Cool Cat is magical, extremely verbal and egotistical. He has a murky history with King Rat connections, is subversive, world weary and cynical. However, he is a close friend of the Fairy, sometimes displays a soft centre and deep down wants good to win. He is the main force which moves Dick on.

The Fairy: Played by a female. The Fairy, along with the King Rat, is the most easily recognisable fantasy figure. She usually talks in rhyme, has a magic wand and every time she appears on stage fairy dust falls on the audience. However, she is tired, fretful and obviously wearied by trying to sort out the worlds problems. She relies rather too heavily on the Cool Cat to deal with Dick, hinting that maybe she has not the power to do it herself, but is somewhat rejuvenated when she teams up with Dick's Mother.

King Rat: Androgynous, played by either sex. Three of them in the original production were American which was culturally interesting as pantomime is firmly British based. Four in number in this production, they looked quite scary but in fact are soon seen to be cowardly and incompetent. Typical sniffling sidekicks of a bully, they can hardly think for themselves and always mess up the smallest task. Under orders they continually spy on, or attempt to halt Dick's progress. However, they are always thwarted by the Cool Cat, although Dick is oblivious to them until after the event. They are involved in the physical/slapstick elements of the pantomime.

Honesty: The love interest and daughter of Makeabob. Let down by her father, she turns to Dick for help, although it is soon apparent that he is a last resort. There is a suggestion that she is more mature and worldly than is usual for a Columbine figure, and due to experience, she has a more cynical attitude towards optimism than is usual in one her age. However, she is fond of both her father and Dick and the main sentimental ballad is hers.

Mr Makeabob: A product of the eighties, Mr Makeabob is a big businessman in the slightly dodgy, but basically warm hearted, Arthur Daley mode. He left Hull and Dick's Mother to make even more money in London. He is obsessed by "that which is most precious", which is never clearly identified even when he tries to do so himself. He falls foul of his own greed and King Rat and ends up a slightly pathetic figure but still with enough dubious power to offer Dick the job of Lord Mayor, which Dick politely declines, preferring to go home to Hull.

Elements in the structure of the Pantomime: I had an amazing amount of unsolicited advice as to the structuring and content of the play, more than for any other play I've written. They ranged from the trivial such as, the fairy must come on from the right or the specific number of scenes there should be and in what order they should occur, although the order of those scenes invariably changed, as did the definitive number, depending on the speaker. Considering that throughout the history of pantomime, the format has been ever changing and malleable, I decided it was valid to use and manipulate certain elements of past forms of pantomime but to reject others.

Plot: I decided to employ a stronger storyline than is usual in present "traditional" pantomime. This was partly to move the focus of the production away from the characters and to put their behaviour in some sort of context. This was a conscious move back towards reclaiming the fairy tale element of the stories and therefore a move towards the possibility of change. I was keen to re-introduce the subversive element of pantomime primarily in the plot structure rather than merely in the characters behaviour. Ultimately I wanted the script to be fun and enjoyable for all of the audience.

Devices: My decision on the choice of devices was influence by carrying out action research with children of all ages as well as adults. The inclusion of a device was decided by its popularity. Consequently devices used in the pantomime were the use of response (Boo/Hiss, Behind you! etc.); characters talking to the audience; songs; jokes (some rude); the giving out of sweets; slapstick (including a mass water fight and the Ratettes attempting to break into a house containing the hero, but to no avail).

To evaluate the product would be to consider it on two levels. As a learning experience for the participating students it was a very valid experience. A potentially disparate group worked productively, positively and effectively, achieving a sense of perspective in the context of their learning. Moreover, each performer rapidly had confidence in and liking for their character which enhanced the production process. The slapstick and the ad-libbing were the hardest elements to elicit from the student performers mainly because they were not familiar with the format. I ended up having to write pages of ad-libs for all eventualities. Therefore, the anarchy often associated with these elements in pantomime was restricted but still in evidence.

To evaluate the product as pantomime is more difficult. On a practical level, we sought and obtained feedback from some of the schools who saw the pantomime. The feedback was very favourable from both staff and students. They made ranging observations on characterisation, the overriding factor being the considerable identification with many of the characters. The duality inherent in the character's nature was often referred to in discussion. Nevertheless, the prevailing consensus was that all had seen a "real" pantomime, a "real" Dame and a "real" Principal Boy.

On a more personal level I felt the result was a tinkering with the genre rather than a complete overhaul. Nonetheless, theoretically, the results are less clear. I was attempting to transmute certain elements of a predictable format whilst still allowing for the format to be recognisable. I have to consider whether I moved my main characters too far away from the pantomime genre, or not far enough, thus allowing them to continue to remain firmly placed in a cultural bias. I attempted to manipulate the public display of the performing body, that is, I tried to question cultural and social assumptions in order to – hopefully – bring about cultural transformation.

Robert Cheesmond's re-definition of pantomime is a re-definition of a recent form of pantomime which has moved away from the earlier, veritably political and anarchistic pantomime forms. *Whittington and the Cat* only partially adhered to this outlined re-definition. My working process, outlined above, primarily provoked the questioning of the flexibility of the definitions of the pantomime genre.

I would proffer the point that if pantomime is not flexible enough to reflect cultural transformation, not flexible enough to accept the manipulation of its own format, then it raises the question, what is the future of pantomime? There is evidence that more and more theatres are turning to the adaptation of a fairy tale or a popular children's book as their focus for the traditional Christmas children's show rather than the pantomime. If pantomime is to have long term survival, then it needs to respond to all facets of the audience. Undoubtedly, there is a place for a genre which attracts the young into the theatre and provides a therapeutic fantasy world for all:

> As long as events build to a thrilling climax with lots of interest on the way, anything is possible. [16]

Notes

[1] Peter Brook, *There Are No Secrets* (Methuen, 1993) p.50

[2] Marina Warner, *From the Beast to the Blonde* (Chatto and Windus, 1994) p. xi-xii

[3] Julia Fetterley, "The Resisting Reader", *A Feminist Approach to American Fiction* (Indiana University Press, 1978)

[4] Gayle Austin, *Feminist Theories for Dramatic Criticism* (University of Michigan Press, 1990) p.29

[5] Peter Brook (op.cit.)

[6] David Mayer, "The Sexuality of Pantomime, *Theatre Quarterly* (Spring 1974)

[7] Lesley Ferris, *Crossing the Stage* (Routledge, 1993); Epstein and Straub, *Body Guards* (Routledge, 1991); Elizabeth Howe, *The First English Actresses* (Cambridge University Press, 1992)

[8] David Mayer (op. cit.)

[9] Laurence Senelick in Lesley Ferris (op.cit.) p.80

[10] Samuel Pepys, The Diary of Samuel Pepys (New York Heritage Press, 1942) p.180

[11] Jill Dolan, "Gender Impersonating on the Stage", Women in Performance 2 (1985)

[12] Ferris (op.cit.) p.9

[13] Dorothy Heathcote, Collected Writings (Hutchinson, 1994) p.142

[14] Gavin Bolton, Drama as Education (Longman, 1984) pp.128-139

[15] Ibid.

[16] David Pickering, The Encyclopaedia of Pantomime (Gale Research International, 1993) p.x

A Draught Through the Front
Herbert Hodge, the Popular Front and the BBC

Mick Wallis

The Popular Front was by definition characterised by class collaboration. Political perspectives and practices were collapsed into one another to meet the perceived common threat of fascism. Cultural workers associated with the Communist Party of Great Britain actively sought both to mobilise popular/mass forms of entertainment and representation, in order to "popularise" the Communist perspective; and to construct a sense of the People as both the disinherited and as the one hope for the future. Thus the Popular Front in Britain simultaneously both remobilised the romantic/utopian vector available within classical Marxism, and shifted the definition of historical struggle from that between classes to that between the People and the Exploiters. I have recently demonstrated both this rhetorical shift and the twin appropriation of demotic and dominant cultural forms with reference to pageants (mass spectacles) mounted by the Party and its workers in the years 1936-39.[1]

In roughly the same period, bourgeois-liberal forces within the Talks Department at the BBC were seeking and finding working-class subjects to put on air, to realise and extend the public service ethos of its foundation and mandate. David Cardiff has both traced this development, and demonstrated contradictions between the "serious" and the "popular" inhabiting both programming policy and the uses made of different classes of speaker.[2] This chapter will explore aspects of Herbert Hodge's relationship with both the BBC and the Communist-led Unity Theatre London. An autodidact taxi-driver, Hodge was a prolific writer who aspired to combine "philosophical" discourses with his reported observations of everyday life. A declared admirer of Rabelais, he was also adept at using pastiche and the mildly scatological in order both to claim the authority of unsophistication, and to puncture pomposity and abstraction.

His two plays for Unity Theatre, *Where's That Bomb?* (co-written with Robert Buckland) and *Cannibal Carnival*, written and performed between 1936 and 1937, demonstrate an uneasy discursive negotiation between the Party/theatre and a representative of one of its most favoured constituencies.[3] I argue that *Bomb* may be seen to display rhetorical contradictions in line with those inhabiting the general project of the Front. It both disciplines its hero for self-aggrandising romantic posturing and offers a utopian model for class-collaboration; the contradiction is rhetorically masked by the use of only semi-parodic pastiche, a "popular" register associated with pantomime, variety and satire.

While this containment of rhetorical contradiction ensured the success of *Bomb* with Unity and its audiences, *Cannibal* was met with some disquiet. Here, his cartooning satirical energies not only assault the class system, imperialism and bourgeois ideology: they also turn back on the utopian discourse of the Popular Front itself. Hodge both popularises Marxism's grand narrative and subjects it to ironic scrutiny.

My concern, then, is with Hodge's "negotiation of a voice" within Unity Theatre, or more broadly within the popularisation of Marxist perspectives amongst a cross-class constituency. I also report on Hodge's negotiation of a voice with respect to the BBC. "Discovered" by producer Christopher Salmon, Hodge quickly became a well-known voice on radio. Drawing on an analysis of Hodge's correspondence with Salmon and other producers, I demonstrate a contradiction between Hodge's perception and aimed production of himself as a working-class subject, and Salmon's treatment of him as a working-class object.

Permitted Fantasy: *Where's That Bomb?*

The advent of the Popular Front in Britain was marked by changes in Communist theatrical repertoire and organisation. One way of mapping these is by the shift away from the urgent and mobile agit-prop practice of the Workers' Theatre Movement (WTM) to the work of the Unity Theatres. While some commentators have implied a regularity of Popular Front theatrical product,[4] Colin Chambers provides evidence of the variety of forms and performance situations employed by Unity. Nonetheless, a decisive move away from the hortatory style of the WTM is well established. I argue here that

Herbert Hodge and Robert Buckland (pseudonymously Roger Gullan and Buckley Roberts)'s *Where's That Bomb?* both articulates and negotiates this rhetorical shift.

Hodge was not a Communist Party member, though he was present at its formative meetings in Soho, back in 1920-21. In the interim, he had been seduced into Mosley's New Party, to the extent of standing as a Parliamentary candidate in 1931. He left when he found it too "class conscious" (i.e. snobbish) and recognised its right-wing nature (he had not been alone in mistaking its rhetoric as leftist in the first instance). Hodge also worked with the National Unemployed Workers Movement in 1920-21, and later organised an unofficial trade union for cab-drivers. He was quite an independent, even quirky, political animal, convinced of the necessity of cutting through rhetorical pretensions to get at what mattered to the common man or woman. His own account of these engagements can be found in his autobiography, *It's Draughty In Front.*[5]

In a sense, the Popular Front was draughty. Different discursive practices breezed through it. But this in itself produced the conditions for the renegotiation of values, of meanings and of rhetorical strategies. *Where's That Bomb?* and *Cannibal Carnival* can be seen to instance the (re)negotiation of form in two related particulars: shifts in political rhetorical strategies at an institutional level; and negotiations between the writer and Unity as a key institution, dominant within oppositional practice.

Where's That Bomb? is a parable about writing. It employs a pastiche of the medieval morality form in which an exemplary hero-protagonist makes a journey towards improved consciousness, which is thereby communicated to the audience. The quotedness of its form, the foregrounding of its conscious mobilisation, is signalled in the figure of Money-Power, Joe Dexter's principal antagonist. The figure appears as Satan:

> *In a lurid red glow, a satanic figure manifests itself, dressed in top hat and frock coat. It has an enormous belly, hooves in place of feet, a forked tail, and horns projecting on either side of its head. It carries a bulging money bag in its hand.*[6]

There are clear links between the basics of the medieval form and the typical form of the agit-prop sketch. Each employs a Manichean schematics, ranging Evil against Good, Damnation against Salvation, Capital against Labour. Each employs stage persons wholly determined by a social value, or stage figures whose character function consists of a moralised or politicised social typification.

This figuring of Money-Power is, then, consistent with agit-prop practice. He has the established attributes of Capital, is marked by the signifiers of class, greed and wealth. This traditional figure is itself an appropriation of contemporary and earlier popular forms, including those of burlesque and pantomime.

Here, as in many agit-prop sketches, the abstracted and personified logic, interests and practice of Capital merge with the traditional attributes of the Vice. While it might plausibly be claimed that elements of a medieval audience might read such signifiers transparently, the subsequent dominance of secular realist forms almost certainly provide the condition of opacity in the performance contract of an agit-prop sketch. The outrageousness of the agit-prop Vice as signifier – the cruelty of its abstraction – is a phatic potential, a rhetorical guarantee as much as a convenient reduction to essentials. The abstracting formulation is consciously ostended as part of the rhetoric, invites a ritual of participation in the violence of its definition.

Similar personifications can be found in the collaboratively-written *Fall of the House of Slusher*, performed at Unity in 1937, and based on a 1932 WTM script, *Love in Industry*.[7] But Hodge and Roberts do more than deploy an agit-prop figure: they *quote* it, and to the point of pastiche. This is a pantomime demon. Both *Slusher* and *Bomb*, in a general shift that Leonard Jones celebrates, untether the popular satirical energies of such characterisation from what he at least sees as the empty heroics of agit-prop.[8] A sort of political pantomime is in the making. But in the case of *Bomb*, there is an open interrogation of the very stage figures which serve the fable.

Joe Dexter at the start is a writer of revolutionary poems and stories. He makes a journey from the hortatory simplicities of agit-prop to a recognition that people make counter-analyses of their own, motivate themselves to resistance.

Dexter has been sacked from his job for his writings. While this confirms to him that his output is effective, he is now unable to pay the rent. A gentleman from the British Patriots Association declares that a Certain Personage wants to employ his skills. While successfully regulating the output of media, church and schools, the Association fears that one bastion of privacy remains to the worker – the toilet. Here, anything might be thought or done. The plan is to market toilet rolls with a story or verse on each sheet extolling patriotism, obedience and absence of thought.

Joe's forthright resistance is finally completely broken by the successive arrival of four hire purchase collectors, come to reclaim goods. He gives in. The gentleman gives the rubric: it is to be a pulp romance with a Bolshevik villain. But Joe is soon disgusted with the work: the characters are wooden dolls. He has prostituted himself. He falls asleep, and Money-Power now appears. Joe protests both that his soul is not for sale, and that *he* cannot in any case make his characters live. Money-Power counters that it is he who makes characters live and promptly summons up Joe's creations from hell for a demonstration.

The lifeless characters – a blond young working-man, his frail mother, the boss's beautiful "daughtah", and a Bolshy in Russian costume, fiercely whiskered and bomb in hand, announce themselves. The narrative Joe has written and they enact – "And Love Will Find a Way – or the Strike that Failed" – is a hilarious pastiche of reactionary romance. (A detail: Mrs Dubb hopes that her dear son Henry will escape wounding by the wicked strikers, but to her horror finds a Bolshy Party card in his overalls she sits repairing). When Joe finally calls a horrified halt to the proceedings, saying he would rather die than continue, the characters declare that they would, too.

Joe leads the characters to resist Money-Power by engaging him in sharp debate. In turn, they make cases of their own. Neither the mother nor Henry will accept meek self-sacrifice in the name of heroism or duty any longer; Miranda wants to escape her enforced idleness to work; and the "Bolshy" tears off his false whiskers to reveal a respectable trade union member who simply wants another penny an hour. Money-Power is overcome, and Miranda exits for the bomb, which explodes offstage.

The bang wakes Joe up. The commotion on the stairs turns out in fact to be made by the hire purchase collectors. The Gentleman arrives with cash for Joe's story. He tears it up. He has learned revolt from the very characters he created to bolster up capitalism. Why come to him for toilet-paper propaganda? Fleet Street has been printing the workers' toilet paper for years.

Bomb achieves a combination of effects through its intrinsic instability. While "And Love Will Find a Way" is a fine parody of reactionary romance, its characters mere stereotypes geared to crude ideological production, those same characters are then mobilised *as if real*. They come to represent interpellated individuals who come to recognise both economic exploitation and the role of ideology, and so resist. They might well, indeed, be the common addressees of Popular Front rhetoric. But the conversion is so rapid as to be a joke – and the conversion is part of a dream in any case. *Bomb* exploits the ability of stages to allow the interpenetration of multiple realities. Reactionary fictional stereotypes are presented and exploded; simultaneously, a fantasy is staged of the People's cross-class resistance to the warmongēring capitalist order and its drift into war. The fantasy is *permitted* because it is both staged as a dream and is in any case enveloped in a pantomime style – the show is full of silly songs. At the same time, the plot both depends upon the critical stereotypes of agit-prop, while suggesting that agit-prop values are redundant.

Where's That Bomb? is significant in two respects. It participates in the general shift of politics and form which characterise the practice of Unity Theatre as an institution of the Popular Front. But it is also marked by a foregrounding of this rhetorical shift, a prioritised attention to the act of formulation and argument.

It achieves a variety of ends through an active negotiation of popular forms: it reaffirms the basic binary opposition between labour and capital; it foregrounds the agency of ordinary people; it disciplines heroic fantasies about writing and representation. Its employment of a writer-protagonist and its pastiching of established forms affords it a high degree of self-referentiality.

Vulgar Spectacle: *Cannibal Carnival*

Hodge subtitled *Cannibal Carnival* "A Vulgar Spectacle in Seven Scenes" and in sampling the play for anthology, a contemporary editor dubbed it "A Theatrical Cartoon"[9]. The action takes place on the Pacific island paradise of Cana-Cary, which a shipwrecked bishop, financier and policeman decide to "civilise" through the introduction of bourgeois morals and capitalist property relations. By the end of the second scene, a state of primitive communism (French loaves and hot dogs freely available from the trees) has been supplanted by corruption, exploitation, and a cycle of unemployment and over-production. An ensuing bread-riot is quelled only by the distribution of crusts, and is followed by the pillorying and jailing of Egbert, leader of "the Reds".

As it unfolds, it becomes quite clear that the action does not refer to colonialism in particular, but rather uses colonisation in order to develop a cartooning metaphor for the processes of alienation and inversion that class society – and capitalism in particular – has brought *universally*.

The consequent model is, then, one of a primitive paradise being overturned, corrupted and debased by exploitative *interlopers*. These interlopers are *already* corrupt, arrive completely formed. A pre-existing principle of capitalist corruption intrudes in order to invert utopia. Hodge's metaphorical strategy participates – however playfully – in the Popular Front's rhetorical shift from historicised models of class conflict to models of wilful exploitation.

The overall action of the play presents: class society/capitalism as an alienating inversion of reality; the ideological and material means whereby the ruling class maintains this system of exploitation, viewed both chronologically and systematically; and finally a scenario for the overturning of the system by the oppressed.

If the opening scenes present a version of a generality, then the fourth and fifth offer events with distinctly local reverberations. A cartoon-style exposition of capitalism as an historical phenomenon is illustrated through critical satires on the immediate reality. A corollary of this is that contemporary reality is presented in a framework in which it can be analysed, understood historically, and – potentially – acted upon.

Scene 4 directly follows the jailing of Egbert. The bishop suggests that, to head off potential disaffection, the natives need to be given a little romance in their lives, in the form of a coronation. But a king must be chosen, and the short-list comprises the triplets Hoko, Moko and Boko. They are, respectively, deaf, dumb and daft. (The bishop remarks: "If only all three virtues had been united in the same man, what a perfect king he would have made.")[10] In the event, we are treated to but two of them, just as the British public were currently being treated to the quick succession of two kings – Edward VIII and George VI – in the "constitutional crisis" following George V's death in January 1936 and his son's abdication in December of that year.

At one level the scene is, then, a satire both on individuals and on their class. Boko/Edward VIII is none too bright (his main utterance is "Cockadoodledoo"), and is drawn from the throne by a dancing temptress, the Naughty Lady. Hoko/George VI's deafness signifies two things. It is a displacement of the latter's real "disability", his stutter; and it is a sign for (is supposed to be constitutive of) his unmasculinity. While the first monarch upsets the establishment by publicly pursuing Naughty Lady/Mrs Simpson with his crown tilted over one eye, "flapping and crowing",[11] the second disappoints the masses by failing to hear the Naughty Lady's sirenical signals at all ("VOICES IN THE CROWD: Boo! Baa-lamb! No-man! Give him a titty-bottle! He don't because he can't! etc. etc.")[12]

At another level, the scene is also a specific instancing of the general ploys of mystification the "vulgar spectacle" has already identified. From the beginning, Bishop Bumpus (of Belgravia) sets out to mask his and the financier Crabbe's expropriation of common wealth and property by haranguing the natives on the "wickedness of gratifying their carnal lusts". Religion and Finance join forces (are already joined as one force), with state power (policeman Joe) at their side, and rob the masses. Religion provides the gloss that blinds the masses to their being robbed. This is a common-enough staged and cartooned analysis in the decade. Accurately and nicely enough, it will be Crabbe himself who later suggest's the ultimate form of mystification: bourgeois democracy.[13]

In the meantime, however, Hodge has fun lampooning the lardings and lordlings of the ceremonial state. When Edward VIII was proclaimed in January 1936, the date for his coronation was fixed for 12 May 1937. The state could look forward to a full year of public preparations for pageantry, once sufficient pomp, sentiment and ceremony had been extracted from the bones of the incumbent. As we know and as *Cannibal Carnival* celebrates, the new king formed an unfortunate attachment to a twice-divorced woman and, by eventually abdicating, threatened to muck the whole thing up. His brother stepping into his shoes in December 1936, renewed and ostentatious preparations were then made for the show on Coronation Day, still fixed for 12 May 1937 (same show, only the cast had changed).

Performed in June 1937, *Cannibal Carnival* makes the most of this blip in dominant culture, setting its vulgar spectacle against official pageantry by inverting the latter. Bishop Bumpus declares that they need "something to worship here and now" that is not as obviously ugly as Crabbe the financier. The Coronation must have all "the usual trimmings", and will "help take their minds off the sordid affairs of every day". The monarchy will, should the need arise, provide a convenient rallying-cry in the event of war. The prospective monarch's daftness is termed an "eccentricity", a "royal prerogative". Crabbe shakes his money-satchel to attract the crowd:

> This way for the Coronation of His Majesty King Boko the First!
> See the King crowned! See the Bishop pour the Holy Oil!...

and so collects yet more money from them for his satchel:

> Coronation now commencing! Coronation now commencing!
> Only a few seats left. Any more for any more...[14]

An adult-scale infant's high-chair stands in for the throne. Crabbe then provides the (media) commentary:

> Ah! The procession is approaching. Do you hear the music? I can see them now. They're just turning the corner by Crabbe's Hot Dog repository. First come the Life Guards. Oh, what a glorious show they make! Their plumes! Their glittering breast-plates! And their chargers! Specially hired for the occasion from Crabbes the Undertakers. Here they come! Here they come![15]

Enter policeman Joe on a hobbyhorse, quickly followed by a demonstration of unemployed chanting "We want bread!". But this obtrusive utterance is quickly and violently quashed, the official commentary representing the episode as involving "an enthusiastic crowd (that) has broken through the police cordon."[16]

The king is anointed from an oil-can on a salver. Crabbes the Ironmongers have made the crown, and reap "£500,000 for the running repairs only" each year, a fact offered to the crowd for their celebration. The blessing ("In the name of Rent the Father, Interest the Son and Profit, the unholy ghost, I anoint thee king") pronounces what has already clearly been shown, and has as counterpoint the ever-enterprising Crabbe going among the natives crying "Ices! Nice Ices! Fresh roasted peanuts!"[17]

In enacting a mock ceremony of state, the scene provides an inversion of the myths of state, reveals again the material reality that gives rise to it sustaining, masking ideologies. The role of ideology in general is revealed through illustration in the specific. In the "fictional" instance of the Cana-Cary coronation, a detailed depiction of the property-interests, power relations, and manipulatory ideological maskings implicated in George VI's *and all other* coronations can be presented. A "vulgar" disregard for strict concordance with the superficials of the given liberates the satire from being tied to its immediate object (George VI).

Thus both the *structuring* and the *attitudinal tone* of *Cannibal Carnival* act together to effect this analytical inversion. Both an overall action and analysis sustained by vignette illustrations, and a cartooning vulgarity that carries the potential of arbitrary extension, enable a highly economical circulation between the specific and the general to be maintained. The desperate attempts to cover up the embarrassment of the abdication, to repair this dint in the state's ideological armour, are used to push deeper back into the construction of that ideology. Dwelling on the embarrassment helps open up the more fundamental contradictions for inspection. The abdication crisis presents a point of unravelling, an easy knot for the drama to unpick.

The play as a whole is a statement of theory in popular and accessible form. The scene I have been examining here can be seen to constitute a *ritual enactment* of critical theory as an affirmation. It gleefully and legitimately preaches to its converted. The ritual affirms both the truth of the theory (makes it patent) and its status as knowledge common to the community of spectators and actors.

Overall, the action of *Cannibal Carnival* has a comic structure: an inversion of an ideal or natural order is itself inverted, and the ideal is thus reattained. While comic realism merely *pretends* to put right what has gone wrong, remaining locked in its fictional "real", Hodge's cartooning strategies allow him to resist such closure. I would venture that it is the manner of this resistance which made the play awkward or embarrassing for some of Unity's personnel.

Cannibal Carnival is deliberately and resolutely *cheap*. It presents its vulgarity as a counter to official and dominant culture and values. It frames its oppositional view of social reality in an "oppositional" form – the traditionally counter-cultural form of popular satire and knock-about. It is deliberately outrageously ludicrous, ridiculous, bathetic, and arbitrary with regard for detail. It is even rigorously cheap about its own version of reality, let alone the dominant version. Primitive communism equals hot dogs on trees. It presents a healthy, robust cynicism, delightful improprieties, as a counter to the self-seriousness of the dominant.

Characteristically, in this "Vulgar Spectacle" the comedy is low. Thus, in the final scene:

> *The natives, led by Mrs Egbert, set fire to the court-house; then revert to their ancient customs and put Bogus and Crabbe in the cook pot (after saying grace as previously instructed by the bishop); and all ends with a savage song and dance, while Joe stirs the stew with his truncheon and leads the choruses.*[18]

The ludicrosity of the outcome, a vigorous and violent pastiche of the conclusion of a romantic comedy, complete with its poetic justice and community celebration, prevents any possibility of its being taken seriously. There is to be no wish-fulfilment, no fantasy reward to be carried from the playhouse. Yet at the same time, the ending is an integral part of a representation – mediated through Hodge's ironising lens – of the grand narrative of history which classical Marxism insists on as human possibility and proletarian project.

Hodge's vulgarity affords him the scope to produce a lantern-slide history of class struggle and a lantern lecture on bourgeois ideology. The same vulgarity invites a celebration of resistance to the dominant order – the satirical assaults constituted by cartooned characters and the wildly fantastic elaborations of the metaphorical situations have a ritual dimension to them.

His vulgarity also prevents him from falling into the trap of narrative closure: there is closure, but only in huge inverted commas, a sort of metatheatrical joke. Yet the same gesture threatens to mock the very narrative that Hodge has found the means to tell. He both bowdlerises Marxist historiography, and mocks (through insistent pastiche) the bowdlerisation. The play may appear not to take its apparent theoretical foundations seriously – or to make fun of an oversimplified version of them. While few or none in the Unity audience can have been subject to the sort of teleological utopianism that Hodge pastiches here, the implication in the playhouse can be that they might. And Popular Front rhetoric in general was demonstrating a relative *shift* in that direction, in any case.

Hodge's insistence on healthy laughter – including at oneself – and his scepticism about all totalising theories (apart from the one he planned to arrive at) combine here to make Hodge's negotiation of a voice within Unity an uneasy project.

There are two other important textual factors which add to this uneasiness. First, note that policeman Joe has switched sides by the end. Hodge has this happen in a pastiche of a Pauline conversion: Joe suddenly and quite spontaneously "comes over all class-conscious". Hodge thus resists comic realism – the provision of fantasy solutions lubricated by plausibility – but also seems to mock the very possibility of such ideological conversion as itself a crazy fantasy, a joke.[19]

Second, the "natives" as representative of the mass or "the people" are only ever given as passive beings within the narrative. They are solely acted upon, are easily swayed, gulled, interpellated. There are, of course, questions of racism to be raised here: specifically the proprieties and possible effects of even *ironically quoting* (as I think he is) racist stereotypes of the "savage native". But beyond this is the fact that Hodge lampoons the mass for their stupid docility at the very time when the Popular Front was out to characterise The People as potentially heroic and visionary.

"Oh, we working class philosophers!" Hodge and the BBC[20]

Hodge was a familiar voice on British radio for about 20 years – from his first broadcast in September 1937; throughout World War 2; and into the early 1950s, when a stroke forced his retirement.

Hodge was a cabbie. The title of his autobiography – *It's Draughty In Front* -plays on the fact that until the 1930s, London taxis had no front windscreens. Much of his broadcasting presents Hodge as the taxi-driver – the man who passes through London life, at once close to events both everyday and extraordinary, and yet also unnoticed, a part of the machinery. His is a privileged point of view.

Importantly, his is also a working-class point of view. Hodge was one – perhaps the most significant one – of a clutch of working-class broadcasters given a new sort of access to the air from the late 1930s. I want here to trace Hodge's "negotiation of a voice" to fit this new circumstance.

By the time he came on air, Hodge was already an experienced communicator. Under a variety of pseudonyms, he had been publishing short stories for a number of years in a range of magazines. What he aimed to communicate was what he would characterise as his "philosophy", his own particular angle on the world – at once popular, in the sense that it was based in common working-class experience; and special, in that it was informed by a wide range of reading and a habit of serious reflection. The Herbert Hodge who walked through the doors of Unity and offered to write them a play from a working-class perspective; and who was ushered into the BBC to provide listeners with the genuine voice of working-class Britain; was an accomplished autodidact.

There are two linked aspects to Hodge's finding utterance on the liberal airwaves of the BBC: his negotiations with the institutional apparatus and personnel, and his technical sense of relationship to the medium.

In the April of 1937, Unity producer John Allen introduced Hodge to Christopher Salmon of the BBC Talks Department. Salmon was looking for good working-class stories, with good working-class voices to match.[21]

David Cardiff associates Salmon in particular with the notion then gaining some currency at the BBC, that *social experience* as opposed to the opinions of experts could be used as a basis for exploring political or philosophical topics. Reviewing the history of BBC Talks from 1928 to 1939, he traces the evolution of a range of techniques including the straight talk, the discussion, the interview and the debate. Within each technique he discerns a hierarchy of presentational rules.

The government ban on controversial-issue broadcasts had been lifted in 1928. The repeated crises of National Government after 1931 and the radical worsening of the international situation from 1936 both prompted demands for more relevant and personable broadcasting, and gave strength to the those within the institution inclined to take their audiences seriously.

The cosily middle-class ethos of the 1920s was not entirely challenged, however, and Cardiff identifies an anxiety over the legitimation of various categories of speaker. Displacing the non-aligned intellectual chatting to his listeners as if from on high, there emerged two principal categories of single speaker. An impersonal style signalled impartiality; a more personal style invited mild diversion. Hodge was clearly expected to fall into the latter category – though his insistence on being taken seriously was to cause him some difficulty in his negotiations with Salmon.

The introduction of new, lighter, formats was designed to help popularise the medium, and escape this binary of the "serious" and the "popular" solo broadcaster. Once established as a solo broadcaster, Hodge was by 1938 acting as anchorman on his own series, *The Cinema*, for which he controlled the production of scripts. He is not only prominent among the new breed of working-class broadcasters, but also a (part-time) representative of a newly-emergent occupational group – the *professional* broadcaster.

Radio presented Hodge with both an opportunity and a model. Radio was *one* of the media through which the "public sphere" was now extended to Hodge's class as cultural producers and specialist consumers. It thus constituted part of the overall atmosphere of autodidacticism and "current affairs", helping determine that atmosphere's discursive shape. And specifically as a consumer of and potential contributor to radio, Hodge had access there to material models for the realisation of his "expression": it was somewhere to talk, a means to realise himself as an enunciator.

Correspondence between Hodge and Salmon is kept at the Written Archive Centre (WAC), Caversham. The first piece dates from May 1937, and plans meetings over proposed scripts. Their relationship seems to have got off to a good start: by June, Salmon is asking Hodge's wife Margaret to join them both at lunch.[22]

According to Hodge's autobiography, Salmon's first interest was in Hodge's *voice and personality*, but Hodge was keen to promote his *writing* and negotiated the opportunity to read one of his own stories at the audition. This soon appeared to Hodge not to have been such a good idea: practising a couple of stories, he became dismayed by the persistence of his Cockney *accent*. But dismay turned to enthusiasm when he hit upon using a first-person "Cockney sketch" he had written for a magazine's literary competition.

Hodge reports that even during the recording itself, he felt reassured that the BBC would assume he was acting, that the accent was not his own.[23] He was terrified of being let down by the very thing that Salmon was after: the *genuineness* of his accent. What for Salmon was a guarantee of social experience was for Hodge a potential betrayer of his social background. Salmon was enthusiastic about the audition:

> When I'd finished, he came in and flung out a hand towards the mike: "Well, that's your instrument" he said. "If you've got any ideas, there's an audience of millions waiting for you."[24]

Given the opportunity to name his topic, Hodge leapt at the chance to promote his philosophical opinions. He planned out a series and made a trial record of an introductory talk, based on an earlier skeleton plan for a book. Salmon suggested Margaret attend to tell him when he sounded natural. He tried impromptu talking, but this made him too long-winded. He rewrote the script several times before the final recording. Salmon was evidently disappointed. And Hodge could not understand "why the Cockney dialogue had pleased him so much, while these, in my opinion, much cleverer essays hadn't".

The BBC turned the series down, but by way of compensation offered Hodge a one-off solo broadcast on *Book Talk*, "in which a variety of different people express themselves on books of their own choosing". Hodge's disappointment turned to delight: "You couldn't have chosen a better subject for me."[26]

Hodge made his first broadcast on 16 September 1937, going out on National transmission with his book talk on "Modern Utopias". He had ten weeks in which to prepare, and to solve the taxing problem of how to obtain a naturalness of style. The answer came in a broadcast by John Hilton, in which he "betrayed" the secret of his apparently impromptu delivery: "It was absurdly obvious ... Hilton didn't write an essay, he wrote a talk."[27]:

> I saw I'd got to tackle the job like writing a play. The only difference was that my principal character was myself. All I had to do was to find out what kind of character I was, and write for him.[28]

Hodge spent time listening to himself in varying moods, and rewrote the talk for the voices he heard. The recording was a success.[29]

Hodge thereafter defined and developed his own production in relation to the style and technique of other broadcasters. Several of his letters to Salmon negotiate a critique of Talks Department product, though rarely is a producer directly implicated. Salmon evidently accepted the concentration on the speaker a sign that Hodge was eager to develop his own technique. What they both wanted was naturalness. In a covering note to one of Hodge's drafts for *Book Talk* he tells Salmon:

> I've tried to get the effect you liked so much at my first audition. Unliterary without being illiterate – using my natural Cockney idiom.[30]

Meanwhile redrafting stories for possible broadcast, he reports that "I've tried to be as colloquial as possible without destroying the original flavour" and that he plans to "scrap everything but the plot – and just tell them".[31]

While naturalness of tone and delivery was a common aim for broadcaster and producer, the respective *qualitative values* set upon this tone by Hodge and Salmon diverged. Something of this difference is apparent in the exchanges just quoted, and clearly structured the difference in expectations they brought to the first meeting. Salmon was apparently after a good voice and a strong personality. These were to be *characterised* by homespun common sense. For Hodge, his voice and personality were to be the *medium* for Hodge's ideas, perceptions, philosophy. The two men enjoyed mutual respect and indeed friendship. They like working together. But conditioning their relationship also was this early split between Hodge regarded as broadcast object (for Salmon) and as broadcasting subject (for Hodge).

Desert Island Hodge

In his first broadcast, Hodge negotiates a position for himself as an organic intellectual. He constructs this sense by speaking as if from a position of common popular experience, but in a self-reflexive manner. The reflexivity works in two ways. First, it signifies – and constitutes – an analytical attitude to an immediate social experience which Hodge shares with his target listener. Second, through a gesture of gentle self-deprecation, Hodge negotiates a display of his learning. Binding these two is an attitude of sincerity, of plain, humble and direct speaking to that "ordinary" auditor.

The talk celebrates what Hodge terms a "social satire" – Eimar O'Duffy's *The Spacious Adventures of the Man in the Street* (Macmillan) – and a "personal" one – Laurence Housman's *Trimblerigg* (Cape), both published in 1928. In Housman's novel, a minor god narrates the life of his human creation, the anti-hero Jonathan Trimblerigg. It has been dropped from the shelves of Hodge's local library. He guesses the book is too uncomfortable for many. Trimblerigg is "just an ordinary shyster", a cheat caught between "uncontainable self-worship" and deep shame, a paragon of bad faith from the age of five. Hodge reflects,

Ah well! I don't know how you feel, but I want to pat him on
the shoulder and say: "It's all right, old chap! We've all done the
same thing – at some time or another. There's no need to feel so
bad about it".[32]

Hodge then caps his refusal to take a high moral tone with a neatly
duplicitous refusal to speak with authority on literary matters. The
piece continues and ends:

I won't call either of the two books I have been talking about
great literature. I don't feel competent to judge. But I liked
them. If ever you find yourself on that island – I think you will
like them, too.[33]

Hodge has opened the talk by alluding to the "desert island"
which the "literary papers" invite the famous to imagine themselves
stranded on, able to choose just one book. Note that he proves
himself *at the outset* to be a man of letters, a regular reader of writing
about writing. He polishes off his account of O'Duffy's book by
ascribing him "a place of his own among the satirists":

He may not have the subtlety of Anatole France. Or the
incisiveness of Shaw. But he has something few other satirists
or social critics seem to possess: an appreciation of the human
animal.
He isn't horrified like Swift at Celia's digestive system. Or
scornful like Shaw at the thought of "those two greasy
commonplaces – flesh and blood..."[34]

And so on via Voltaire and Wells, finally suggesting that O'Duffy
combines "the spirit of Swift with the substance of Smollett, suffusing
the one's intellectual vision with the other's physical zest". Clearly,
Hodge is very competent indeed to judge, if the ability to map out such
a literary terrain is a measure of competence. He uses a well-worn ruse
to considerable effect – the false apology for being just an ordinary
bloke, which in fact claims *authority* for the speaker. He implies that
his is an unsophisticated point of view, unspoiled by pretence. He

meanwhile demonstrates a high degree of literary discrimination. What he thereby does is to bracket off the mappings of high culture, and put down a marker for a demotic, unheroic humanism – his *own* "appreciation of the human animal". Hodge presents himself as an object of critical scrutiny in the construction of such a discourse. His sense of his own limitations, and his ability to think and imagine beyond them, is something to be shared with the interlocutor he constructs.

He ends his talk by recommending the two books to anyone who finds themselves on the same island as him. This is not the desert island of the literary reviews: he has opened by playing that metaphor into new meanings. The ability definitively to say that one book exceeds all others in value is in fact to be living on a *mental* desert island – to be imaginatively stranded. Hodge, by contrast, want to be stranded *next to a public library*. He marks himself out as one who singularly delights in a breadth of knowledge and experience – one with a direct and sensual, voracious appetite for literature. From this position of strength, he can admit a weakness, in order to share it:

> But there's one particular island that has wrecked me much too often lately, especially when I've been reading too much about what the papers call "the world situation". Have you ever wished all the world – all humanity – had only one body, so you could grip it by the shoulders and shake some sense into it? And then suddenly realised how powerless you are? One man – one little man – in the whole stampeding herd? Well, that's my desert island. And I don't think I'm alone there, not nowadays.[35]

It is this sense of political anomie coupled with an active frustration that leads Hodge to celebrate and share the two books. They are the means whereby to share a structure of feeling:

> When I'm there I want something to help me laugh at it all. The world *and* myself. Something to lift me up, and give me a god's eye view, a god who tolerates us because we are such ridiculous little devils...[36]

As for O'Duffy's book, "its very roughness makes it feel all the more genuine, like a bit of unplaned oak". In the course of the book, the hero finds himself in a place of perpetual night. The race that works there never sees light: the race that does not work lives in constant artificial summer. Encouraged by the familiarity of this class-divided culture, the hero tries to dominate the planet – but fails. In desperation, he demands of the gods a purpose in life, a philosophy. In Hodge's words, "he challenges them all with the simple searching questions of the puzzled plain man".

The answers O'Duffy provides, Hodge admits are limited. He only eventually generates "a few well-worn platitudes, like Life's what we make it, and that sort of thing". But Hodge turns the notion of platitude into that of "an article of faith" that has become "fossilised":

> As H.G. Wells says, these things need restatement in every generation. And that is what O'Duffy's tried to do here: re-state, in terms of this generation, Man's faith in himself.[37]

Hodge's first twenty minutes on air declare his double probity as a man of letters who is also a man from the people. He also constructs an attitude for himself and for the listener which insists on the absence of hope and perspective in the immediate circumstances, yet simultaneously believes in the ability of the collective (and note male) human subject to see a way through. The implication of his style is that such sightedness will depend on a discriminating and cultured intelligence. And he directly contends that it will depend on a collective, self-critical laughter.

Hodge and the Art of Radio

As Hodge was making arrangements for his first broadcast, *Cannibal Carnival* was nearing the end of its first run. Dissatisfied with the production and his own achievement, Hodge asked Salmon not to be too distressed about missing it. Hodge appears at first to have been constructing Salmon as a mentor: he writes with self-conscious intimacy, as to a confessor. About *Cannibal* he writes:

I feel as if I've seen through a glass all too darkly. One of these days, I may see the vision clear. It'll only come once. And if it does come, I must let it do what it will with me, untrammelled, and then drop my pen down the nearest drain.[38]

Hodge is also being pretentious – pretending to the status of artist-philosopher as medium. I take this to be part of his negotiation of a role within the dominant apparatus. As medium rather than as initiator, Hodge can enter the ranks of those bred and educated to control communications and academy without offence. The same mantle serves to define his role in relation to his own class: he is no different, except in his activity as seer.

Quite soon, Hodge's passivity was to be paired with an actively critical attitude to Salmon and Talks. Soon after the success of his first broadcast, and disagreements I shall go on to describe, Hodge wrote to Salmon:

And have you ever considered a series treating working class life as natural – instead of quaint? ... Battersea Bridge Road is being repaired and as I write, everybody's dashing out with baths and boxes and perambulators to get wood for their winter fires. There's nothing extraordinary about it. It's the thing to do. But the middle class commentator either denounces it as a crime; or weeps over the wrongs of the noble proletariat compelled to get their living this way; or treats it as a quaint custom of the Battersea aborigine.[39]

The disagreements were over the specific content of talks scripted by Hodge for his first series, Night Taxi. Reflections from a London Rank. It was intended to be "a peg for [Hodge] to hang reflections on." Salmon wrote, "what would you like to talk about?"[40] Hodge celebrated Salmon's ability to "bring out the philosopher" in him.[41]

But Salmon returned Hodge's first script, detailing amendments. The philosopher that Salmon "brought out" in Hodge was suppressed, with Hodge's embarrassed acquiescence. He wrote back, "The meditation goes out with pleasure..."[42] But if the "philosophical" was a domain in which Salmon could be authoritative, the experience he wanted to extract was not. Hodge continues:

... but I'm sorry about the rest. Perhaps I can amplify it in another talk. There's half a lifetime of experience behind the sentences you find unbelievable and sounding "a trifle insincere". What a pity we can't change places for six months![43]

Hodge and Salmon were out to construct different "Herbert Hodges". Hodge's *expression* was ultimately being produced according to criteria different from his own: bourgeois liberal criteria as opposed to working-class populist criteria. Hodge was in pursuit of a "voice" that would allow him to talk to a working-class audience with familiarity. Talks were at least as interested in producing a working-class persona as *object*. If cynicism and irony suited the first purpose, they contradicted the proprieties of the second.

Hodge worked on his differences with Salmon on two fronts: of *technique* and of *content*. On the first front he presents himself as a creative artist struggling towards a new form and in need of help to realise his vision; on the second he insists on the authenticity of his experience, and of the need for this to be communicated pure. Together they constitute Hodge's negotiation of a rhetorical means, within the section of the dominant apparatus made available to him.

There are two broadly distinguishable, but complementary, attitudes that Hodge took to radio technique. He took a *scientific* attitude, regarding himself as an object of his own study, always conscious that he was *constructing* "Herbert Hodge" the broadcaster from the means at his disposal. He regularly listened to recordings of his own voice. At the same time, he was deeply aware of himself as a *creative artist* in need of a channel of communication. He wrote to Salmon, "I yearn for that mike as a musician for his harp."[44] A musician's attention to pace, rhythm and tone is geared to a project to make the scripted broadcast sound spontaneous, to make "Herbert Hodge" the broadcast signal and Herbert Hodge the sincere individual coincide. Hodge was developing an autobiographical naturalism for radio.[45]

A Ripping Yarn

There is much more to be said about Hodge's relationship with the BBC. But for present purposes, it seems apt to end with a short account of Hodge's broadcast on BBC London Region about Unity Theatre. The 15-minute talk, which went out on 1 June 1939, was produced by Joanna Quigley. In May, she wrote that there were "one or two pitfalls in the subject that we may have to be careful about, for instance the political angle."[46] She was accordingly gratified that Hodge had suggested he take a *personal* angle. Quite so, respond ed Hodge, "I'll concentrate on the theatrical and personal aspects – the adventure of starting an amateur theatre from zero..."[47]

Hodge begins with mild self-deprecation:

> I've called this talk MYSELF and UNITY – but, as a matter of fact, I don't come into it much. I'm one of the thousands of Unity Club members who've helped to build it. (By rights, I ought to be anonymous. We're most of us anonymous at Unity. Even the actors. The whole thing's a co-operative job.)[48]

At some considerable stretch, this might just pass for subtle socialist propaganda. But it is soon rendered into sentiment, by Hodge's account of London Unity's origins:

> Like most things it started as an idea. An idea in the mind of an East End tailor ... he wanted plays about people who did matter. Real people. The kind of people he knew. So he started a theatre of his own. A rather special kind of amateur theatre where he and his friends could act plays about the kind of life they lived. /// These friends were none of em theatrical people. There was a carpenter – and a painter – a shop-assistant – a clerk – a typist. And two younger girls.[49]

Unity's origins are rendered into a petit-bourgeois romance of individualism and innovation; the account drips with sentiment. Whatever position one takes on the politics of Unity, this account leaves much to be desired. While there was no contradiction between the BBC's gentle demands and what Hodge deemed appropriate to say in the circumstances, there was a glaring contradiction between what was broadcast and the real Unity. The painstakingly playful artist here retreats into what was to become an all-too habitual homeliness when he offers:

> For most of us – I think – Unity just meant the sheer delight of letting ourselves rip.[50]

The Conservative Mayor and the Parlour Bolshevik

In his 1937 autobiography, Hodge recalls a 1920 campaign to get a council hall in Paddington for meetings of the unemployed. They fight a resistant council bureaucracy and win. "The [Conservative] Mayor was inclined to treat the whole thing as a lark. And as I had seen it as a lark – justified as a demand for "rights" – we understood each other."[51] Hodge at this time identified himself as a communist. In the same account, he reports that "the misery I saw ... in the houses of the unemployed made me forget ultimate aims in immediate objects".[52] Happy to be charged therefore with being "a reformer – a bolsterer-up of capitalism", he describes himself in those years as "as much a means-to-an-ender as the most superior parlour-bolshevik"[53] The autobiography as a whole is a sardonically fond looking back, a gentle admonition, as well as celebration, of this younger more vigorous self.

Hodge was no radical. As *Draughty* testifies, his philosophy was one of ultimate optimism, predicated on the notion of "sympathetic imagination": the serious hope that folk will manage, if only they try, to understand one another and so get along – but a hope perpetually deferred. His broadcasting career was largely dedicated to promoting that sensibility.

Neither individuals, nor organised politics, were to take themselves too seriously, get too bound up in themselves. If I have Hodge right, the fantasy of cross-class resistance to tyranny dream-staged in *Bomb* is not merely a permitted fantasy, but also a sad joke. It *will happen*, he suggests, but not here and not by these means.

The draughtiness of the Front stirred up discourses deviating very strongly from the Marxist. Hodge was one of its typical breezes.

Notes

[1] Mick Wallis, "Pageantry and the Popular Front: Ideological Production in the 'Thirties", *New Theatre Quarterly* 38 (1994) pp.132-156 and "The Popular Front Pageant: Its Emergence and Decline", *New Theatre Quarterly* 41 (1995) pp.17-32

[2] David Cardiff, "The Serious and the Popular: Aspects of the Evolution of Style in the Radio Talk 1928-1939" in Richard Collins et al (eds.), *Media, Culture and Society: A Critical Reader* (Sage, 1986) pp.228-246

[3] Colin Chambers, *The Story of Unity Theatre* (Lawrence and Wishart, 1989), Chapter 2, demonstrates how Hodge and Buckland met London Unity's need for home-grown working-class dramatic material: Unity's dependence on US scripts such as Odets' *Waiting for Lefty* had come to constitute a crisis of repertoire. *Where's That Bomb* opened on 13 November 1936 and *Cannibal Carnival* on 5 June 1937. While Lawrence & Wishart published *Bomb* in 1937, *Cannibal* was not published in its entirety, and no complete script has been located. Citations here are from typescripts in the Unity Theatre papers deposited by Herbert Marshall at the Morris Library, University of Southern Illinois, Carbondale; and for parts of *Cannibal* from the fragment reprinted in a 1938 anthology. See Chambers for full bibliographies, production details and plot synopses.

[4] See, for example, Raphael Samuel, "Introduction" in Raphael Samuel, Ewan MacColl and Stuart Cosgrove, *Theatres of the Left, 1880-1935* (Routledge, 1985)

[5] Herbert Hodge, *It's Draughty in Front* (Michael Joseph, 1937)

[6] Roger Gullan & Buckley Roberts [Herbert Hodge and Robert Buckley], *Where's That Bomb? A Comedy in two Acts* (Typescript, Morris Library, University of Southern Illinois, accession no. 29-4-1, 1936) p.21

[7] Colin Chambers (op. cit.) pp.79-80

[8] See Leonard Jones, "The Workers' Theatre Movement in the Twenties", *Zeitschrift fur Anglistik und Amerikanistik* XIV (1966) p.259-281 & "The Workers' Theatre in the Thirties", *Marxism Today* XVIII (1974) pp.300-310.

[9] Herbert Hodge, *Cannibal Carnival. A Vulgar Spectacle in Seven Scenes* (Scenes 4 & 5, typescript, Morris Library, University of Southern Illinois, accession no. 29-4-5) & "*Cannibal Carnival*. A Theatrical Cartoon" in E.Allen Osborne (ed.), *In Letters of Red* (Michael Joseph, 1938), which together comprise scenes 4 and 5 only, plus a synopsis of the whole play.

[10] Ibid. p.5

[11] Ibid. p.9

[12] Ibid. p.120

[13] Scene 5 principally comprises a staged election, in which Crabbe and Bumpus pretend to compete for power from opposing platforms, while in fact they have an identical interest – the exploitation of the masses. It mocks both the nature of bourgeois democracy in general, and the immediate fact of the National Government.

[14] Herbert Hodge, *Cannibal Carnival* (op.cit.) p.4

[15] Ibid. p.6

[16] Ibid. p.7

[17] Ibid. p.8

[18] Herbert Hodge in E.Allen Osborne (op.cit.) p.125

[19] Joe is about to execute Egbert as a Marxist and a Jew, but Egbert keeps shouting "Up the Workers!" Joe cannot bring down his axe while he repeatedly hears "up", and finally gives in. A case of phatic repetition! See Herbert Hodge in E.Allen Osborne (op. cit.) p.124

[20] The phrase occurs in a letter to Salmon in which Hodge reports on meetings with working-class author George Thomas, whom Salmon was considering for broadcast. Hodge is more keen than Salmon, and Hodge writes with evident self-consciousness based on their class difference. He is both defensive and mildly aggressive. CVS to HH 11/8/38; HH to CVS 26/3/38; HH to CVS 26/3/38, 30/3/38. References are to items in Hodge's correspondence files held at BBC Written Archive Centre, Caversham. CVS = Christopher V. Salmon; HH = Herbert Hodge; JQ = Joanna Quigley; NGL = Norman G. Luker.

[21] Herbert Hodge, *It's Draughty* (op.cit.) p.265

[22] CVS to HH ?/5/37, ?/6/37

[23] Herbert Hodge, *It's Draughty* (op.cit.) p.266-267

[24] Ibid. p.268

[25] Ibid. p.269

[26] NGL to CVS ?/6/37; CVS to HH 19/6/37; HH to CVS 19/6/37

[27] Herbert Hodge, *It's Draughty* (op.cit.) p.270

[28] Ibid. p.271

[29] Significantly, David Cardiff (op.cit.) notes that while Hilton set out in 1933 as a serious broadcaster on industrial relations, he had by 1939 so perfected the fireside technique that he was almost solely used for "a kind of agony column of the air, championing the cause of the little man." (p.231)

[30] HH to CVS 7/8/37

[31] HH to CVS 25/6/37, 7/8/37

[32] Herbert Hodge, "Two Modern Satirists", The Listener XVIII p686-7. Since no script survives, quotations are taken from this redaction.

[33] Ibid.

[34] Ibid.

[35] Ibid.

[36] Ibid.

[37] Ibid.

[38] HH to CVS 19/6/37

[39] HH to CVS 28/9/37

[40] CVS to HH 26/8/37

[41] HH to CVS 27/8/37

[42] HH to CVS 12/9/37

[43] Ibid.

[44] HH to CVS 26/8/37

[45] Quite soon Hodge is underlining and capitalising stress-words, and inserting leader dots, short and long dashes, double and triple bars (//, ///), to indicate the position and value of pauses. By the summer of 1938 he was inserting marginal words and pauses to indicate mood and shifts in rhetorical posture: "SMILE; SLOW; FAST; LIGHTLY: FAST; SMILE; SLOW; THOUGHTFUL; SUDDEN PLAIN..." (script for The Fortnight's Films, 31 July 1938)

[46] JQ to HH 5/5/39

[47] HH to JQ 6/5/39

[48] Herbert Hodge, "Myself and Unity" (typescript of BBC London Region Broadcast, 1st June 1939 in "The Theatre" series, BBC Written Archive Centre, Caversham. Transmitted nationally 17 July 1939)

[49] Ibid.

[50] Ibid.

[51] Herbert Hodge, It's Draughty (op.cit.) p.83

[52] Ibid. p.77

[53] Ibid.

Practices of the Adelphi Players 1941-44. Richard Ward's "Theatre of Persons": the Ideology and Working

Peter Billingham

In this seminar I intend to discuss the nature of Richard Ward's theories relating to theatre as expressed principally in his manifesto article "Theatre of Persons", published in *The Adelphi* magazine in 1941. In doing so, I also intend to look briefly at the extent to which he endeavoured to apply some of those ideas in practice in forming The Adelphi Players, a touring theatre company that was in existence, with some changes in personnel, from 1941 to 1951.

Before proceeding to examine Ward's article in any detail, it is essential to consider the broader social, cultural and ideological background against which Ward's views and aims need to be understood. In 1938, in a speech delivered in Paris under the title "The Future of English Poetic Drama", W.H. Auden asserted that:

> The dramatist today must show man in relation to nature ... He must show the reaction in private and public life upon the ... individual and upon society ... and this struggle is taking place in the political field. Now I do not mean that, for that reason, one must throw characterisation overboard ... It is no use calling [characters] "Striving" or "Rabble" or something ... What will happen to the stage I do not know, but I know this: that the search for a dramatic form is very closely bound up with something much wider and much more important, which is the search for a society which is both free and unified.

This quotation from Auden's speech just twelve months before the outbreak of war refers to issues that were of predominant concern to a number of artists, writers and intelligentsia on the broad left, such as Auden and Ward, throughout the nineteen thirties. In that context, it is appropriate to quote Richard Ward, in broadly similar mode, from his manifesto article of 1941 "Theatre of Persons":

Theatre of Persons is a theatre which offers its audience experience, the experience first and foremost of seeing themselves face to face. The real function of theatre is one of illumination, the casting of light upon the familiar, so that it is seen fully and for what it is ... in a word, the theatre must be seen in terms of people; the transformed theatre must be a theatre of human beings, run by human beings for the sake of other human beings

Both Auden and Ward were clearly striving for a theatre that would be transformed in a way which would have wider social, cultural and political implications. I don't wish to stretch comparisons between the two and in a broader sense, it is arguable that Auden's notion of the term "political" would have been narrower and more formalised than that employed by Ward. Auden's identification with Communism and Ward's involvement with the Independent Labour Party – and more particularly, the Peace Pledge Union – offer helpful reference points both to their own creative output and also to an understanding of "The Pink Thirties" as Ronald Blythe refers to the period in his collection of essays about that decade: *The Age of Illusion*. In his account of The Group Theatres of the Nineteen Thirties, *Dances of Death*, Michael Sidnell observes that:

Confusingly, political and religious drama often had much in common in motive and techniques. Hence Auden's equivocally Marxist *The Dance of Death* and Eliot's unequivocally Christian *The Rock* were bracketed together as products of a new school of playwrights.

Sidnell's identification of both the diversity of ideological motivation and the commonality of form and style, characterises much of the theatrical experimentation of the period. Throughout the nineteen thirties there was a rich inter-play of artistic experimentation across the arts. Whilst the Adelphis were never conspicuously a "political" theatre company in the conventional sense of the term, it is my contention that, in their broader ideological and artistic concerns, they did embody significant preoccupations and initiatives from that pre-

war period. In one important respect, this included their contribution –
in the broader movement within the non-commercial theatre of that
time towards a more progressive, artistically accountable, democratic
and, in an important sense, popular theatre. This movement, discussed
so cogently in Rowell and Jackson's *The Repertory Movement*, had its
roots in the reforms sought by Shaw, Granville-Barker, Archer and
others at the turn of the century. As Rowell and Jackson assert:

> Already at the turn of the century, the idea of repertory – as a
> form of theatre opposed in every way to the dominant
> commercial theatre of the time – had become an integral part
> of the developing concern with the future of theatre in Britain.
> It had become inseparably linked to other such central issues as
> the need to establish a state-subsidised national theatre
> organised on repertory principles, the need to encourage new
> British playwrights, and the need to raise the general standards
> of production. At the same time, awareness was growing of the
> theatre's potency as an educative as well as artistic or
> entertainment medium, and therefore of its importance in the
> cultural life of the country as a whole.

In an important sense, many of these concerns identified by
Rowell and Jackson in the emerging repertory movement were central
to much of the thinking and practice of practitioners such as Richard
Ward. The clamour for artistic and structural reform within British
theatre came against the continuing backdrop of a sterile commercial
theatre that seemed deliberately immune from both its detractors
within the wider profession, and also against the political and social
turmoil of the pre-war period. Richard Ward spoke of this theatrical
establishment as "a garish and showy facade, reared upon the shifting
sands of fashion". Amongst others who attempted to challenge this
complacent theatrical orthodoxy were those such as Terence Gray at
the Cambridge Festival Theatre, Peter Godfrey and later Norman
Marshall at The Gate, Barry Jackson's Birmingham Rep and, perhaps
most memorably, Lilian Baylis at the Old Vic. In addition, there were
also of course, Rupert Doone and The Group Theatre, Ashley Dukes
and his Mercury Theatre, and the politically inspired Unity and Left

theatre companies. One important principle that was shared by these companies, including Ward's Adelphi Players, was a commitment to perform plays in repertoire that were of artistic value, but which would not find a platform within the commercial theatre of the West End. In their programme/prospectus circulated by the Adelphis in 1943, they expressed this sentiment formally:

> It is becoming increasingly evident that the people of Britain feel the need and the value of their cultural heritage in the darkness of the present. Where the theatre is concerned, there is clear and growing demand, not only for plays which will provide entertainment ... but more especially for plays which are essentially re-creative in the sense of building up the human mind and spirit.

The choice of plays which the Adelphis then proceeded to play in their repertoire did not always, however, meet with unanimous approval, as the following reviewer from the *Doncaster Gazette* made clear in 1943:

> ..the Adelphi Players [put] on plays in the spirit of giving the public what the Adelphi Players think is good for them, whether the public like it or not. One does not blame the average family of home-holiday makers for avoiding *The Duchess of Malfi*, an Elizabethan tragedy that might possibly interest the keen student of drama but would certainly pass over the heads of ordinary people.

One of the significant contributions to the creation of the broad left Popular Front in the nineteen thirties was the campaigning work of Victor Gollancz. Through his formation of The Left Book Club with its accompanying magazine, *Left News*, Gollancz and his enterprise not only created the opportunity for a broad range of leftist literature to be published, distributed and read, but also stimulated the emergence of a network of discussion groups around the country who engaged in debate about social and political issues of the day. In addition to Left News, there were many other literary journals with socio/political agendas in circulation during this period. These included *New Atlantis*, Claud Cockburn's *The Week* and John Middleton Murry's *The Adelphi* – from which Ward drew inspiration in naming his theatre company. In this same period, the Communist Party of Great Britain, which in 1930 had 1,376 members, had passed 15,500 members by the close of the thirties. Meanwhile at Oxford, the Reverend Dick Shepherd was establishing the Peace Pledge Union, an increasingly active and eloquent platform for the expression of broadly leftist, anti-militaristic and pacifist thinking. Shepherd's formation of the PPU in 1936 represented the significant embodiment of an ideological and ethical movement which had its origins in the inter-active debate between oppositional Christian theology and socialism from the turn of the century. Ward was a close friend and personal assistant to Shepherd and was very active in the early weeks and months of the movement. He also wrote several articles for their weekly newspaper *Peace News*. In one such article, "What is Non-Violent Technique?", Ward asserted that:

> War is not a disease which breaks out here and there in history, but the symptom of a disease which is the actual condition of the present social order, other symptoms of which, capitalism and imperialism, are as inseparable from it and from one another as war is inseparable from it. It is in effect against this unholy trinity: capitalism, imperialism and war, that the pacifist finds himself under the necessity of struggling

When Ward formed the Adelphi Players in May 1941, the male actors within the company – including of course, Ward himself – were all Conscientious Objectors. The company's initial base was at The Adelphi Centre, owned and founded by John Middleton Murry. The Adelphi Centre was a pacifist/socialist community run by Max Plowman, at that time editor of *The Adelphi* magazine, and a close friend and mentor to Ward and his company. The two men had met through their mutual involvement in the PPU earlier in 1936. *The Adelphi* was a magazine started in 1923 as a monthly literary journal under the editorship of Middleton Murry, intended as a platform in particular for the writings of D H Lawrence. The journal ran until

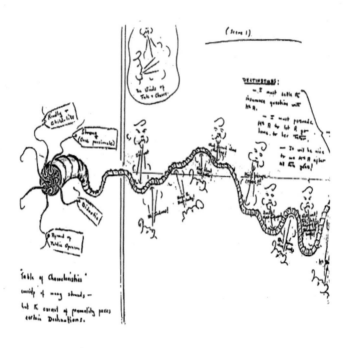

Fig 1 Sketch by Jack Boyd Brent used to analyse Pastor Manders character

1955 with contributors during that period ranging from Ward through Yeats, Auden, Eliot, and Day-Lewis to Orwell. Murry intended that the Adelphi Centre should be non-sectarian and welcomed Socialists who were sympathetic to its basic ethos. He envisaged that the community living at the Centre would revolve around a relatively permanent nucleus of twelve persons, half of whom would be middle-class with some form of economic security, and the other half working class-unemployed. It was at the invitation of Max Plowman that Ward and his company were invited to use the Adelphi Centre, also known as The Oaks, for their rehearsal and touring base.

In January 1941, an article by Richard Ward entitled "The Theatre of Persons" appeared in *The Adelphi* magazine in which he outlined his theoretical principles concerning the nature and function of theatre:

> The Theatre of Persons is a theatre which offers its audiences experience, the experience first and foremost of seeing themselves face to face. The real function of the theatre is one of illumination, the casting of light upon the familiar, so that it is seen fully and for what it is. And the familiar, where the common man is concerned, is the whole range of his inward and outward life ... the theatre, by presenting them with the vision and the wholeness which belong to art and the artist, can make them intelligible.

Ward proceeds further to define theatre in terms of a catalyst for stimulating the awareness and raising the consciousness of the audience in terms of their understanding of themselves. Theatre is perceived as a means of illuminating, through the depiction and exploration of fictive characters, the existential condition of the audience. Within this conceptual model, there are clearly echoes of Aristotle's concept of catharsis and, to a lesser extent, Stanislavski's concept of the empathetic relationship that he argued should exist between the actor and audience. Later in the same article, Ward proceeds to discuss and define theatre in terms of allegory as a means of opening human consciousness:

For the theatre is an allegory, and must be so treated by those who work in it ... by its vividness – and even its sensationalism – it brings to the human mind, even by shock methods, comprehension of things so ordinary, so deeply rooted in nature and history, that we pass them by as too familiar ... so the great plays: *Faust*, *Hamlet* and *Oedipus* are the stories of ourselves, revealing us for our own understanding.

At the risk of oversimplification, it is arguable that this concept of theatre has received considerable attention and provoked debate throughout the post-war period. It is a perspective developed, for example, by Peter Brook in his notion of "The Holy Theatre", where he draws upon the example and work of Artaud and Grotowski. In the opening passages of his influential book *The Empty Space*, Brook defines the essential prerequisites for theatre to take place: "I can take any empty space and call it a bare stage. A man walks across this empty space whilst someone else is watching him, and that is all that is needed for an act of theatre to be engaged". Ward shares some similar ground with Brook as the following extract from "Theatre of Persons", indicates:

Shakespeare's audiences, when told that they were looking at another part of the wood, believed it and were left free by a nearly naked stage to watch the play. Lately, it has not been possible to see the play for the trees [!] ... If the theatre is to speak directly of the realities of human life ... it must be allowed, both by actors and producers, to say [it] in terms of sincerity and simplicity ... the theatre is illusion ... and this illusion is the instrument by which the human consciousness is opened to a fuller understanding of the realities that permeate and underlie nature.

Ward's thinking concerning the production of Shakespeare owes much to Poel and other innovators such as Nugent Monck at the Maddermarket Theatre in Norwich who made such a significant contribution to the re-evaluation of Shakespeare in performance.

In broader terms, Ward's view of theatre was as much philosophical and ethical as artistic. When he argues for "a transformed theatre ... of human beings, run by human beings and for the sake of other human beings", he is drawing upon his interest in Hegelian ethics and advocating the same humanistic concern for the centrality and integrity of the individual that he discusses in his article "The Human Factor", published in *Peace News* in 1939: "The world is what we make it, and when we refuse to be human beings, to be persons and treat others as persons, we make it hell". However, it was not only human individuals who sought or needed transformation in Ward's view but also, as a direct consequence, the political and cultural institutions that they created, as he states again in "The Theatre of Persons":

> The theatre has been insecure for a long time, a showy and garish facade, reared upon the shifting sands of fashion and money ... Whatever emerges from this war (and the commercial theatre, the racket we have made believe the theatre, will not) must emerge transformed. There was something rotten in the status quo and that manifestation of the theatre's life is dead for good ... a new theatre will arise ...

Whilst Ward's aims, ideals and convictions have been far from realised in the post-war period, with large scale technologically based musicals such as *Cats* and many others continuing to dominate the West End, and the RSC engaging in commercially-abortive dramatisations of Stephen King's "pulp-horror" *Carrie*, this reflects more Ward's failure to accurately analyse the broader financial power-base underlying the commercial theatre establishment. Furthermore, it is fair to say that the kind of radical idealism informing Ward's thinking was a common characteristic of much broad left thinking at this time, especially in the context of the ideology of the anti-Fascist front. Also, of course, a new theatre, did arise, and has grown in the post-war period, following on from the initial breakthrough, in 1956, of the English Stage Company with Osborne's *Look Back in Anger* and the emergence of fringe and alternative theatre in the nineteen sixties and seventies.

Not all of the company necessarily shared Ward's more precise ideological and theoretical motivations. Nevertheless, as I have already mentioned, the male actors were all Conscientious Objectors, though not all on the basis of direct Pacifist convictions. Their involvement with the company was recognised by the Tribunals as "War Work", the equivalent for many CO's of land labour, ambulance work etc. The combination of persons with diversely motivated anti-war convictions, along with the unique venture of taking theatre to new venues and audiences, understandably helped to define the progressive outlook of the company. In their insistence upon equal salaries for all company members and the central function of the regular democratic company meetings, the Adelphis prefigured some of the significant developments that were to emerge through the theatre co-operatives and experimental companies of the later post-war period. Each company member received £2 a week when the company was in performance, whilst there were equal billeting privileges, firstly at The Adelphi Centre and then, when the company began to tour more extensively, board and lodging would rely upon the hospitality of hosts at various venues. The company were in fact "capitalised" by two well-wishers, one of whom lent the small van by which they made their early tours, whilst the other provided an interest-free loan of £50. In order to help sustain this fragile financial basis, the company requested a minimum guarantee from most venues of about £5. By working on that basis, any small profits that did arise from their work was used to subsidise their performances in venues such as prisons and air raid shelters where there was clearly no possibility of their guarantee being paid.

In the minutes of a company meeting dated 18 January 1942, Richard Ward is quoted as follows regarding the issue of artistic policy for the company and the subsequent criteria for repertoire:

> The time is coming when our own age must evolve, out of its own soul, its own theatre – and by theatre, I mean its own plays, its own methods of acting and presentation. So far as I can see, our day has no theatrical heart; the Old Vic is essentially a survival; the plays of Auden and Isherwood seem to have been abortive; the Unity has died of propaganda ...

Working on a very limited budget and performing almost exclusively in non-theatre venues including open-air locations, it is remarkable that the Adelphis managed to achieve the commendable standards of performance which they undoubtedly did. Some of this credit must go in part to those productions which benefited from the designs of Osborne Robinson who had arrived as resident designer at the Northampton Repertory Theatre in 1928. The production photograph of his designs for the Adelphi production (opened May 1942) of *Comus* by John Milton show Robinson's celebrated expertise in producing excellent artistic results from minimal material resources, indicated by his use of stylised, geometric black and white costumes. They are distinctive, a visually aesthetic as well as financially effective economy of style. A critic reviewing this production remarked that:

> The [company] delighted those who saw this play by their splendid verse speaking and by the subtle pattern of movement and colour they gave to it ... The costumes, designed by Osborne Robinson ... made a fascinating pattern of black, white and gold and reflected accurately the seventeenth Century Puritanism and Renaissance Paganism within the play.

Their production of *Comus* was specifically designed and produced for an open air production. The difficulties presented by locations not intended for theatrical performance is well illustrated by the following newspaper review from January 1942:

> Autumn touring took the company to East Anglia, where they played for both Army and civilian audiences, and to Hampshire, where they played in an evacuee's camp, their theatre a marquee surrounded by a sea of mud, the stage tilted by the slope of a hill and their footlights two hurricane lamps.

Ward was working primarily with inexperienced male actors and therefore the degree of attention that could be given to actor training and so on was limited. Another obvious factor in this respect was the fact that the company was almost always constantly on the

289

road with therefore little opportunity to develop detailed or analytical rehearsal practices. Nevertheless, a unique insight into one company member's approach to his part is afforded by the diagram and accompanying jotted notes which seem to confirm Ward's familiarity and interest in the Stanislavskian approach. The diagram seems to indicate some inner through line of action, the Stanislavskian term for the motivating inner impulse, of a character's psychological objective or dramatic purpose. The diagram is labelled "Table of Characteristics made up of many strands – the current of personality passes ... Destinations." The character has been divided up into four principal characteristics: Kindly and Child-like, Strong(once passionate), Didactic and Afraid of Public Opinion. The actor has also identified "The Winds of Chance and Fate" which exert external influence upon the character's actions and thoughts (rather as in Stanislavski's Given Circumstances) and also "Destinations", (or Objectives to employ Stanislavskian terminology once more) These "Destinations" are identified as follows:

- I must settle the insurance question with Mrs A

- I must persuade Mr A to let R go home to her Father

- It will be nice to see Mrs A after all these years!

Pastor Manders – Ghosts – Mrs Alving – Oswald Alving

So much has happened in British theatre over the last fifty years, much of it encouraging in its ideological and cultural diversity. It is true that the commercial theatre, still essentially London based, can seem as depressingly reactionary and complacent as its nineteen thirties counterpart. Ward and others like him believed that it could not survive the war but, despite pressure from the cinema and the television, it has proved enduring if not endearing.

In his conclusion to his *Other Theatres*, Andrew Davies questions whether theatre has ever truly been a part of popular culture. Having recognised the cultural and ideological diversity of many developments in the last thirty years or so – for example the Fringe movement and the emergence of Gay, Lesbian and Black theatre – he nevertheless defines:

> ...the limited role that theatre plays in most people's everyday lives. Not since the early sixteenth – century has more than a fraction of the country ever attended live theatre...Alternative theatre in Britain has never dented this state of affairs...The labour movement has been of little or no help, and the attempt to introduce theatre into schools is being undermined by a lack of funds.

In the context of Richard Ward's understanding of theatre as something which was of inherent value to persons and communities, he and the Adelphis embodied a faith in theatre, and its broad relationship towards progressive social change, which seems both historically and ideologically remote from the perspective of British society in the mid-1990's. In their breaking of new ground in terms of the venues and the audiences that they played to, I would argue that they helped to create the social and cultural conditions which facilitated the growth of regional and community theatre in the post-war period.

In conclusion let me close by quoting from Ward, writing in retrospect about the Adelphi Players:

> The Adelphi Players were never a specifically "pacifist" company... and propaganda was certainly never part of their purpose... It may be asked what we felt to be behind the work? ... No doubt we had ideals of a kind; but I think we were a good deal more aware of certain practical facts...the difficulty of putting on a good performance in an air raid shelter and so forth. We wanted to be of use to the society in which we found ourselves by taking, to ordinary men and women anywhere, plays and performances of the highest quality that we could achieve.

Popular Theatres?